Tax and Financial Planning for Tax-Exempt Organizations

Tax and Financial Planning for Tax-Exempt Organizations: Forms, Checklists, Procedures

1992 Cumulative Supplement

Jody Blazek

John Wiley & Sons, Inc.

New York • Chichester • Brisbane • Toronto • Singapore

ISBN 0-471-51279-6
ISBN 0-471-54947-9 (Supplement)
Printed in the United States of America
10 9 8 7 6 5 4 3 2 1

Preface

The best news for tax-exempt organizations (EOs) this year was the Treasury Department's decision not to recommend changes in the unrelated business income (UBI) tax rules. The Assistant Secretary for Tax Policy, Kenneth Gideon, informed the House Ways & Means Committee in a May 23, 1991, letter that the Treasury Department had decided that the task force proposals would not "significantly improve tax administration with respect to UBI" nor "command a broad base of support."

Meanwhile the Internal Revenue Service (IRS) is gathering statistical information about UBI with the data submitted on the new page 5 of Form 990 and expects by 1993 to issue a comprehensive report to enable all interested persons to evaluate the need for changes in the rules. Strategies for coping with the codes for the "analysis of income-producing activities" part of Form 990 are explained in § 3.3.

The Exempt Organization Charitable Solicitations Compliance Improvement Program, started in 1988, continues and is still spooking contributors and board members. Keep in mind that the tax deduction for a gift to charity must be reduced by the value of any goods and services received by the donor in connection with the donation. The format of the program was to first examine the charities to find fund-raising programs in which premiums, free admissions, dinners, raffles, and other benefits were used to entice donors. Once the list of such events was compiled from the charity's records, the IRS would examine the donors to find out whether the tax deduction was overstated. The results were poor and the checksheet designed for the program is still being used to examine EOs. The outcome for individuals won't be known until the exams are finished sometime late in 1992. The rules are discussed in detail in § 3.4A.

The IRS fund-raising scrutiny is part of several "Special Emphasis Programs" initiated in response to Congress' directive that the IRS improve the quality of its exempt organization audit programs. The Director of the IRS EO Technical Division, Marcus Owens, has announced continuation of these programs in 1992 with fewer but more extensive exams under a "large case initiative." These exams will focus on conglomerate EOs with subsidiaries and for-profit/nonprofit related entities. Each key district has been directed to examine two major hospitals and one large university in fiscal year 1992. As reported in § 1.10, the team examinations will pool income tax agents, lawyers, and other specialists with the EO technicians. The IRS is also hiring additional tax law specialists and upgrading their positions to attract and retain the most qualified persons.

While the target issues for the examinations were not revealed precisely, it is apparent UBI in general, and in particular bowl game sponsorships, joint ventures with private investors, and tax-exempt bonds are top priority. Trade associations can also expect increased scrutiny as the IRS reviews the responses to Part VII, Information Regarding Transfers, Transactions, and Relationships with Other Organizations, according to Owens.

For hospitals, the exams will also evaluate the relationship between the charity care being provided and tax benefits received in the health care industry. Two different legislative proposals to codify new definitions for hospitals qualifying for tax exemption are outlined in § 1.10.

The publicity surrounding Stanford University's allocation of expenses to federal grants has also focused the EO examiners on the issue of deductible expenses for UBI purposes. Owens says the IRS will look to see if the "creative" accounting methods of universities conducting scientific research carries over to tax matters. New guidelines for expense allocations can be expected.

The UBI court cases seesawed between IRS and taxpayer victory this year. Although the IRS has announced strong disagreement with the decision, the National College Athletic Association successfully fought to exclude its tournament program advertising from UBI as irregular activity. On the other hand, the Disabled American Veterans lost their second fight to avoid income tax by classifying the revenue from their extensive mailing list sales as royalties. The Portland Golf Club and a host of other country clubs lost their battle to deduct non-member losses in 1990. In recognition of its importance, § 3.8 on UBI has been totally revised and expanded for this supplement.

The lack of clear guidance in the Internal Revenue Code and the number of conflicting decisions behoove organizations and their advisors to continually seek up-to-date information and pay attention for potential new legislation on the subject of UBI.

Combinations of organizations, reorganizations, spin-offs, and joint ventures with business organizations are being considered and implemented by organizations as astute survival methods in today's economic climate. A new section on relationships, § 3.8A, covers this very important subject that faces many tax-exempts as they seek enhanced efficiency and economies of scale at the same time, as discussed above, the IRS is planning to give such arrangements scrutiny this year.

Prior to 1988, IRS exempt organization examiners did not review payroll tax matters. The results of their examinations during the past two years caused concern as they found too many employees classified as independent contractors. EOs under examination face the possibilities of payroll tax assessments for such workers. New § 3.1A, on employment taxes has been added to outline the applicable rules.

Bankruptcy is uncommon and certainly undesirable for a tax-exempt organization. Nevertheless the unthinkable happens and a new § 3.11B on the tax consequences and filing requirements during a bankruptcy proceeding has been added this year.

The IRS in March, 1991, released proposed regulations on the calculation of the foreign tax credit that would be disastrous to charities conducting activities outside the United States. Donations by multinational corporations to such charities may be curtailed under the proposed regulations to Section 861. The regulation would require that donations be allocated between U.S.- or foreign-source income based upon respective amounts of foreign and domestic gross income. Typically, most corporations with foreign income incur foreign taxes at a rate greater than the U.S. tax on the same income. Thus the allocation of contribution deductions to foreign income reduces the amount of credit available to offset U.S. tax and effectively removes some or all of the tax benefit from the donation. During August, 1991, hearings, representatives of charities emphasized that the human needs are global and it is a bad time in our history to discourage the continuation of worldwide philanthropy.

On a positive note, an extension until June, 1992, has been passed by the Congress for the full tax deductibility of gifts of tangible personal property to charities using such property in their exempt activities, such as art works given to museums. The alternative minimum tax was slapped on such donations in 1986 in the heat of tax reform. This provision that taxes the unrealized and untaxed appreciation inherent in art gifts was lifted for 1991 and now also for the first six months of 1992. Charities seeking such gifts will want to lobby for another extension and expansion of this valuable exclusion and also to take advantage of this window of opportunity to encourage such donations.

Although there was very little change from the third set of proposed regulations issued in 1988, the Section 501(h) lobbying election regulations were at last issued in final form in August, 1990, and are reviewed in § 3.9.

My personal favorite addition to the book is a checklist on Endowments and Restricted Funds in Chapter 5. Lack of attention to this subject can wreak financial havoc for a nonprofit organization.

A chart of checklists and exhibits has been provided to make them more readily accessible.

The updated Form 1023 is included. To accompany Form 1023, a chart correlating the new forms to the original descriptions has been prepared, along with references tying the form to the portion of the book where the relevant material is discussed. This chart should prove invaluable for anyone trying to ascertain why the IRS is asking particular questions.

In these supplements, I have addressed current developments and added to some of the materials in the original text. The response to the book has been very positive and encouraging, and I welcome the opportunity to add more materials and to consider many issues in more depth. Readers with technical inclinations will be glad tax citations are provided in this supplement and will be added to the entire text in the second edition.

JODY BLAZEK

Houston, Texas
January 1992

Supplement Contents

Note to the Reader: Materials new to *this* supplement are indicated by an asterisk (*) in the left margin of the contents listed below and throughout the supplement. Sections not in the main text are indicated by a (New) after the title.

SUPPLEMENT CONTENTS

SUPPLEMENT CONTENTS

SUPPLEMENT CONTENTS

SUPPLEMENT CONTENTS

SUPPLEMENT CONTENTS

TABLE OF CHECKLISTS AND EXHIBITS

*Page numbers refer to main text unless it is a new exhibit or checklist. In this case the page number will be in parentheses.

SUPPLEMENT CONTENTS

TABLE OF CHECKLISTS AND EXHIBITS (continued)

TABLE OF CHECKLISTS AND EXHIBITS (continued)

CHAPTER ONE

Before You Establish a Nonprofit Organization

§ 1.10 QUALIFYING UNDER SECTION 501(c)(3)

p. 25. *Add to item 5:*
(See § 3.8A for more discussion of transactions and associations between one exempt organization and another or between an exempt organization and private individuals or businesses.)

p. 25. *Add after item 5:*
In determining whether the organization can satisfy the prohibition against use of its assets or income for the benefit of its directors or other private individuals, ask whether the organization will serve a charitable class. Will the product of its exempt activity (teaching, health care, and so on) be made available to a broad enough group of beneficiaries on a nondiscriminatory basis? Within each of the charitable purposes described in this section (pp. 27–37), you will find a variety of specific criteria applied by the IRS in answering this question.

The answer is sometimes difficult and confusing because the results are not always logical. For example, why would a neighborhood youth sports organization qualify for exemption when an adult health club may not? How can the advancement of a particular ethnic culture, such as Italians or Asians, be considered charitable when a genealogical society to trace family roots is not?

A campaign management school organized to train individuals for professional careers in political race administration was denied exemption because it provided "private benefit" to the Republican Party. Most of the school graduates were associated with candidates and committees supporting Republican candidates. In its application for exemption, the American Campaign Academy revealed it was an outgrowth of a National Republican Congressional Committee project—its funding solely provided by the National Republican Congressional Trust.

The Academy argued, nevertheless, that it met all the definitions of a school and did not discriminate on the basis of political preference, race, color, or national or ethnic origins in its admission policies. The Court agreed with the IRS that the facts—actual curriculum and admission applications—evidenced narrow partisan interests. The Court found that the size of the class, number of Republican party members, will not per se transform the benefited class into a charitable class.[1]

* Nonpartisan voter registration drives do not constitute prohibited political activity if they are truly nonpartisan. An organization ostensibly formed to engage in nonpartisan analysis, study, and research and to conduct educational programs for voters had its exemption revoked by the IRS because of its overt partisan activity.[2]

p. 26. *Add after first paragraph:*
The IRS policy is to require the dissolution, inurement, purpose, and political action clauses of a proposed (c)(3) exempt to contain the literal words, "501(c)(3) purposes." Descriptive language limiting the activity solely to charitable purposes (without mentioning 501(c)(3)) may be acceptable, but other language, such as for educational purposes, is not, as discussed under Organizational Test. The IRS routinely requires revision of deficient articles prior to issuance of a positive determination of 501(c)(3) exempt status.

The Tax Court disagreed with this policy in the *Colorado State Chiropractic Society v. Commissioner.*[3] A charitable organization, in the Court's opinion, need not satisfy the organizational test solely by language in its corporate articles. Other factual evidence in addition

[1] *American Campaign Academy v. Commissioner,* 92 T.C. 66 (1989).
[2] Priv. Ltr. Rul. 9117001, April, 1991.
[3] *Colorado State Chiropractic Society v. Commissioner,* 93 T.C. 39 (1989).

to the charter, such as the by-laws, can be considered in determining passage of the test.

As of October, 1991, the Dallas EO Technical staff has not changed its policy in the face of the Chiropractic case. They will continue to require that literal language specifically limit the purposes to charitable ones and preferably use the words, "501(c)(3)."

* **p. 26.** *Add at end of Operational Test:*

Amount of Charitable Expenditures

There is no rule requiring a specific amount of annual expenditures by a public charity. Presumably the contributors and supporters of an organization expect and require that their money be spent for worthy causes and monitor the manner in which funds are expended. A private foundation, however, is without such public monitoring and is required to make charitable grants and programs equaling at least 5 percent of the average annual value of its investment assets (see Chapter 4).

Income Accumulations

One criteria for measuring whether an EO operates "exclusively" for charitable purposes is the portion of its revenues actually expended on charitable projects. Is the EO saving its income instead of spending it for charitable purposes? If the organization is squirreling away funds, why? Some profits, or excess of revenues over expenditures, can be accumulated. The purposes for which funds can be accumulated must, as a general rule, be to better advance the charitable interests of the EO over a period of time. Acceptable reasons why funds might be saved include:

- To maintain sufficient working capital to assure ongoing, continuous provision of charitable services. Working capital can be saved to protect against years when income declines due to loss of grants, lower donations, reduced investment income, and other uncontrollable outside forces. The standards concerning for-profit corporation earnings accumulations can be applied. A minimum of one year's operating budget should be a minimum reasonable amount for a working capital fund.

- To acquire a new building, replace obsolete equipment, or other capital assets dedicated to charitable purposes. The savings is prudent because the EO does not want to incur excessive indebtedness.

- To establish new programs or expand services for charitable constituents when the funds required exceed current available resources.

Commensurate Test

Another criteria applied by the IRS is called the "commensurate test." Are the expenditures commensurate in scope to the financial resources of the EO? The theory was first espoused in 1964 in looking at what portion of the EO's assets could be invested in unrelated business activities.[4] In addition to operating exclusively for charitable purposes, a charity's primary purpose must also be charitable.[5] The distinction between the two tests is minimal. It is sufficient to say both should be satisfied to assure maintenance of exempt status.

Revenue agents are specifically directed to measure whether fund-raising organizations could meet the test in its special emphasis checklist found in Exhibit 3–4A. This test is being used to determine whether professional fund raisers receive an excessive portion of the funds they raise for charity. State charitable regulators are also concerned and, in some cases, have specific limitations on such payments.

The commensurate test was used to revoke the exempt status of United Cancer Council, Inc. (UCC), a bogus charity conducting mail solicitations. Out of over $7 million raised during 1986, UCC spent less than $300,000 on patient services and research and paid the balance to its fund-raising counsel, Watson & Hughey. Needless to say, the commensurate test was failed. Bingo operations paying

---

[4] Rev. Rul. 64-182, 1964 (Part I) C.B. 186.
[5] Treas. Reg. 1.501(c)(3)-1(e).

excessive operating costs and salaries with little or no profits left for charity also fail the test.[6]

* **p. 27.** *Add at end of second paragraph:*

The IRS fourteen-point test for qualifying as a church was applied and judicially sanctioned by the Eighth Circuit.[7] The "church" in question was founded for the stated purpose of spreading "God's love and hope throughout the world." It conducted bimonthly programs with prayers and gospel music in an amphitheater. It built a small chapel for unsupervised meditational activities and individual prayer but did not conduct religious services in the chapel.

Although the society argued that the test discriminated against new, rural, and poor religious organizations, the court agreed that the IRS's higher standards for qualification as a church were appropriate. The failure to meet three particular criteria influenced the court:

1. The society did not have a regular congregation and its attendees did not consider it their church.

2. It did not ordain ministers but held services conducted by guest ministers.

3. It did not conduct school for religious instruction of the young.

* **p. 28.** *Replace last paragraph of Religious Purposes section:*

The IRS has limited information and power to review the tax exempt status of a church. As discussed in Chapters 2 and 3, churches are not required to file Form 1023 or Form 990. A church may only be audited by the IRS if an appropriate high-level Treasury official (the principal internal revenue officer for the IRS region in which the church is located or the Secretary of the Treasury) reasonably believes on the basis of written facts and circumstances that the church is not exempted or may be carrying on an unrelated trade or business.[8]

---

[6] Priv. Ltr. Rul. 9132005, May 3, 1991. For a good history of the commensurate issue, read G.C.M. 32689 published in 1963, G.C.M. 34682 in 1971, and G.C.M. 38742 in 1981.

[7] *Spiritual Outreach Society v. Commissioner,* 91-1 USTC § 50,111, No. 90-1501 (8th Cir. 1991).

[8] Section 7611(a).

The Church of Scientology and some of its branches are waging battles with the IRS in the courts about the application of the rules that may influence the manner in which the IRS considers exemption of religious organizations and examinations of churches. The church won a judicial test of the IRS's right to request information under the Section 7611(b)(1)(A) summons provisions when the court provided that the records were not necessary to determine the church's tax liability.[9] The Supreme Court refused to review an employment tax matter for want of jurisdiction. The church in Los Angeles sued the IRS under the freedom of information act for details of a "tax shelter litigation project" designating the church and its parishioners.

Religious Orders

The IRS has provided a list of criteria for qualifying as a "religious order." The characteristics below will be considered by the IRS.[10] Other than the first one, all factors must not necessarily be present:

- The order is an organization otherwise qualifying for exemption under Section 501(c)(3).

- The order is, directly or indirectly, under the control and supervision of a church or convention or association of churches.

- The members of the order vow to live under set rules of moral and spiritual self-sacrifice of their material well-being and to dedicate themselves to the goals of the organization.

- Members make a long-term commitment, normally more than two years, to the organization after successful completion of the training and probationary period.

- The organization's members ordinarily live together in a community and are held to a significantly stricter level of moral and religious discipline than that required of lay church members.

[9] *U.S. v. Church of Scientology of Boston, Inc.,* 90-2 USTC § 50,349 (D.C. Mass).
[10] Rev. Proc. 91-20, 1991-10 I.R.B. 26.

- Members work or serve full-time on behalf of the religious, educational, or charitable goals of the organization.

- Members regularly participate in public or private prayer, religious study, teaching, care of the aging, missionary work, or church reform or renewal.

Status as a religious order is significant for group whose members wish to claim exemption from participation in the social security system under Section 1402(c)(4). (See Form 4361, Exhibit § 3–1C.)

p. 29. *Add before last paragraph:*

A testamentary charitable trust created to benefit "worthy and deserving white persons" over the age of 60 years who cannot support themselves is not qualified for exemption according to G.C.M. 39792 (June, 1990). Denying trust benefits to members of the charitable class that have historically been the subject of race discrimination violates public policy, further expanding this concept traditionally applied to educational institutions (see comments for p. 35).

* **p. 31.** *Add at end of first sentence:*

Whether or not an organization lessens the burdens of government is more difficult to prove than other categories of charitable exemption. During 1991, applications for exemption under this category were "national office" cases, meaning that they could be approved only by the Washington office, not by the key district offices. The import of the policy is that it is up to the government to decide whether their burdens need relieving, not the proposed organization. Absent written delegation of such responsibility or enabling legislation providing the framework, such exemptions are difficult to obtain.

The regulations provide a two-part test that form the guidelines for qualification:[11]

1. Are the activities the EO engages in ones which a governmental unit considers to be its burden and recognizes that the EO as acting on its behalf?

---

[11] Reg. 1.501(c)(3)-1(d)(2).

2. Does the EO's performance of the activities actually lessen the burden of government?

The strictness with which the EO determination branch applies this test caused *Prison Industries* to fail in its attempts to achieve exempt status. While the federal and some state statutes encourage productivity of prisoners and programs providing their rehabilitation, the rules specifically prohibit sales to the public in competition with private enterprise—the program Prison Industries planned. Thus, exempt status was denied.[12]

Proving that the EO will lessen the burden of government requires also that there be agreement on what those burdens are and whether or not it is the responsibility of the government to relieve them—sometimes a political philosophy question. Particularly when the government is not shouldering its burden, it may be difficult to prove qualification for exemption. In the case of a business consulting service, the "mere fact that (the EO's) activities might improve the general economic well-being of the nation or a state or reduce any adverse impact from the failure of government to carry out such activities is not enough" to prove an EO is relieving the burden of government.[13] In other words, the fact that the government is not conducting the program may prove in the IRS' or a court's mind that it is not the burden of government.

* **p. 31.** *Add at the end of Advancement of Religion listing:*
For reasons of its "commerciality" (a doctrine being espoused by the IRS on a number of fronts), a religious organization was denied exemption although conducting programs with clear religious purpose and relationship.

A Seventh-Day Adventist Church affiliate was denied exemption as a religious organization for its vegetarian restaurant and food store operation that provided food stuffs in accordance with church

---

[12] *Prison Industries, Inc. v. Commissioner,* T.C. M. Dec. 47,104(M), January 8, 1991.
[13] *B.S.W. Group, Inc. v. Commissioner,* 70 T.C. 352, 359 (1978) and *Columbia Park & Recreation Assn. v. Commissioner,* 838 F.2d 465 (4th Cir. 1988), aff'g 88 T.C. 1, 21 (1987).

doctrines. Although not so stated, perhaps the fatal flaw was the fact that the stores were open to the general public evidencing a commercial purpose beyond that of ministering to the spiritual needs of the church members.[14]

p. 32.   *Add at the end of Charity Care listing:*

The House Select Committee on Aging held hearings in June, 1990, on hospital clientele and tax-exempt status. The focus of the testimony was charity care: Do tax-exempt hospitals provide enough care for those that cannot pay and how much should they provide? A GAO Study entitled "Nonprofit Hospitals: Better Standards Needed for Tax Exemption" was released. The study quantified the relationship between charity care and the value of federal and state exemptions. In 57 percent of the hospitals studied, the value of the charity care (not counting bad debt) was less than the tax benefits received by the organization and the GAO concluded a disproportionate share of charity care is provided by the major urban teaching hospitals. GAO recommended the criteria for tax exemption be revised to require certain levels of care to Medicaid patients, free care to the poor, or emphasis on improving the health of underserved portions of the community in which the hospital is located.

The IRS Assistant Chief Counsel for Employee Benefits and Exempt Organizations, James McGovern, reviewed the history of the tax law of health care organizations for the hearing. He commented that the IRS would continue to follow its existing "community benefit" standard (outlined on p. 32), which contains no specific numerical levels of charity care. Minimally, he said, the IRS would expect all hospitals to meet the Medicare standards that require emergency facilities to be open to all regardless of ability to pay. He announced the IRS will conduct joint audits with the Department of Health and Human Services using teams of experts including exempt specialists, income tax agents, lawyers, and computer auditors, all with expertise in the healthcare field.

Congressman Edward R. Roybal, chairman of the House Select Committee on Aging, on the other hand, has specific proposals which

---

[14] *Living Faith, Inc. v. Commissioner,* T.C. M. Dec. 46,860(m), 60 T.C.M. 710, 1990-484.

he calls the "Charity Care Act." The drafted legislation contains two specific requirements:

1. An exempt hospital would be required to serve a reasonable number, proportionate to its size, of Medicaid patients in a nondiscriminatory manner and provide documentation to that effect, and

2. Provide charity health care in a nondiscriminatory manner that at least equals the value of the hospital's tax benefits (calculated on a value of charges basis) unless the hospital can demonstrate financial inability.

Preparers of applications for exemptions for healthcare organizations and those representing existing institutions must consider whether to voluntarily comply with these evolving standards of accountability for the public service.

Hospital exemption standards remain unchanged (as of December, 1991), but Representative Donnelly introduced House Bill 1374 to add another set of legislative proposals to House Bill 790 introduced in 1990 by Representative Roybal. The provisions of H.B. 1374 would be effective immediately so hospitals must be vigilant in monitoring the bill's progress through the Congress.

Under the Donnelly bill, a tax-exempt hospital would have to meet one of the following criteria:

1. The hospital is a sole community hospital for Medicare purposes (meaning a hospital located more than 35 miles from any other hospital).

2. The hospital serves a disproportionate share of low-income individuals and receives additional Medicare or Medicaid payments for such patients.

3. The hospital's percentage of indigent patients is within one standard deviation of the mean of all hospitals within a geographic area used to calculate Medicare wage adjustments.

4. Five percent or more of the hospital's gross revenue is devoted to the provision of charity care (not including bad debts).

5. At least 10 percent of the hospital's gross revenues are used to provide "qualified services and benefits" in its community, including a community health center located in a medically underserved area offering primary health care, a drug addiction or substance abuse clinic, or other services to be outlined in the regulations.

In its 1990 *Audit Guide for Providers of Health Care Services,* the AICPA requires financial statement disclosure of charity care policies and the dollar amount of the hospital's charity care. The standards for charitable exemption of hospitals continue to evolve. The definition of "sufficient qualified charity care" is being redefined and those involved with maintaining tax-exempt status for a hospital should keep close watch for legislative developments or new IRS regulations.

The loss of tax-exempt status for hospitals can be a many pronged sword. The expected consequence of loss of deductibility for donors and liability for income tax on any profits would be accompanied by a loss of state and local property tax exemptions and an inability to issue private activity bonds. Thus the hospital would be deprived of its normal source of low-cost building capital presumably more available only if its bonds are tax-exempt to the purchasers.

p. 33. *Add at the end of HMOs:*

HMOs providing "commercial-type" insurance as a substantial part of their activities are not tax exempt under Section 501(m) passed as a part of the Tax Reform Act of 1986. Insubstantial insurance activity which does not prevent exemption is subject to unrelated business income tax. See G.C.M.s 39828, 39829, and 39830, issued in September, 1990, for discussion of the insurance issue and the technicalities of an HMO losing its exemption under these new rules.

p. 33. *Add at the end of Medical Centers:*

Operation of a health and fitness center that provides access to handicapped persons and offers reduced daily rates for persons of limited financial means serves a health care organization's exempt purposes.[15] As a part of a new medical complex, a sports and physical

---

[15] Priv. Ltr. Rul. 8935061.

medicine facility is designed to serve patients referred by the center's hospitals and physicians, as well as the general public. What distinguishes the center as a charitable facility is primarily its provision of services to patients and employees of the medical center. Its availability to the general public is provided in a noncommercial manner and contributes to the center's exempt purpose of providing health care to the community in which it is located.

* *Medical Clinics.*

A clinic providing private medical care to individuals is normally owned by the doctors and operated for their profit-making purposes and cannot qualify for tax exemption even though it operates for the exempt purpose of promoting health. However, where a clinic has no private ownership, provides a reasonable level of free or reduced charge care to members of a charitable class, and otherwise distinguishes itself as a charitable organization, exemption can be sought.

Clinics operated in conjunction with charity hospitals and medical schools, so called "faculty practice plans," have traditionally been granted exemption but there are no clear precedents in the area. In one case approving exemption for such a clinic, the physicians were staff members of a teaching hospital and full-time medical school faculty members.[16] About 25 percent of the patients were indigent or students and medical research was conducted evidencing a significant element of charitable purpose in addition to the promotion of health.

p. 35. *Add after second paragraph under Educational Purposes:*

A private school, which adopted a nondiscrimination policy in connection with seeking application for recognition of its exemption as an educational organization, was denied exemption when the facts revealed that it failed the "good faith" test. The Tax Court denied tax exemption for Calhoun Academy[17] because the "clear and convincing evidence" indicated the school operated in a discriminatory fashion. The case noted that the school was established concurrently with court-ordered desegregation plans, the community was 50 percent

---

[16] *University of Maryland Physicians, P.A. v. Commissioner,* 41 T.C.M. 732 (1981).
[17] *Calhoun Academy v. Commissioner,* 94 T.C. 17 (1990).

black, no black student had ever been admitted (school argued unsuccessfully that none had applied). Although the school had been in existence for 15 years, the nondiscrimination policy was only implemented in connection with the exemption application. The Court noted that a school could qualify for tax-exempt status without establishing that it took the specific affirmative acts provided in the IRS procedures, if in fact it operates in a racially nondiscriminatory manner.

p. 35. *Add after third paragraph of Educational Purposes:*
Art galleries that sell the works of art they exhibit must overcome a presumption that they are operating a business, rather than serving a purely educational purposes and therefore entitled to exemption. The question is whether taking home the objects enhances the educational experience and thereby produces "related" income. The answer to the question is answered differently dependent upon whether the object is an original work of craft, an original work of fine art, a reproduction or replica of an object, or a handicraft item. An organization whose unrelated business activity is more than insubstantial (commonly thought to equal 15 percent) may not qualify for exemption. (See pp. 277–278 for more details about art sales.)

p. 37. *Add at the end of page:*
See § 3.5A for detailed definition of various categories of public charities and requirements for obtaining public status.

* **p. 38.** *Replace paragraph at top of page:*
An exempt organization that receives unrelated business income has the burden of proving that operation of the business is not its primary purpose. While all of the facts and circumstances are considered in evaluating the scope of the activity, the customary measure of "primariness" is the portion of the EO's overall budget produced by the business. The regulations provide no specific numerical percentage, but court cases over the years indicate a safe level of unrelated income would be under 20 to 25 percent of the EO's overall revenues.[18]

[18] *Manning Association v. Commissioner,* 93 T.C.M. 596, 603–604 (1989).

Proving that a business is related, rather than unrelated, is often necessary for an organization to achieve or maintain exempt status. In evaluating the relatedness of a business enterprise, the purpose toward which the activity is directed, rather than the nature of the activity itself, determines whether the activity serves an exempt purpose.[19] In other words, if a resale shop run with handicapped workers provides a livelihood for the workers not otherwise able to support themselves, the fact that the shop is in business competing with commercial resale shops does not prevent relatedness. (See § 3.8 for more discussion of unrelated business income.)

§ 1.11 QUALIFYING AS A CIVIC LEAGUE OR LOCAL ASSOCIATION OF EMPLOYEES: SECTION 501(c)(4)

p. 39. *Add at the end of Similarities to 501(c)(3):*

Classification of a (c)(3) as a (c)(4) Organization (New)

It is possible that an organization can qualify for both categories of exemption—(c)(3) and (c)(4). As outlined under "Differences from 501(c)(3)," a (c)(4) can engage in extensive lobbying. In the case of an organization planning such activity, a (c)(4), not (c)(3), qualification will be sought. However, an organization that loses its exemption as a (c)(3) because it engages in excessive lobbying cannot then covert to the (c)(4) class, but instead loses exempt status and becomes a taxable entity.

Conversion to (c)(3) (New)

To explore the issues involved in converting a 501(c)(4) organization to a 501(c)(3) consider two examples:

Example 1: Representing the population of a planned community of 100,000 residents in Columbia, Maryland, qualifies for (c)(4),

---

[19] *Junaluska Assembly Housing, Inc. v. Commissioner,* 86 T.C.M. 1114, 1121 (1986).

not (c)(3), status in the opinion of the Tax Court.[20] Columbia Park and Recreation Association, Inc. (CPRA) is a not-for-profit organization formed to build and operate the "facilities and services for the common good and social welfare of the people" of Columbia, Maryland; to represent the property owners and residents with respect to owner assessment and collection of fees for such service; and to enforce property covenants.

CPRA builds the public utility and transportation systems, parks, pools, neighborhood and community centers, and recreational facilities such as tennis courts, golf courses, zoo, ice rink, boat docks, and athletic clubs for the community. CPRA essentially functions like a municipality, but is not a political subdivision of the county in which it is located. CPRA was formed by the private developers of Columbia. Columbia has "villages" that have formed separate civic associations.

For the first 12 years of CPRA's existence, it was classified as a 501(c)(4) organization. To qualify for tax-favored bond financing, CPRA sought reclassification as a (c)(3) organization in 1982. The IRS denied the (c)(3) exemption based upon failure of both the operational and organizational test, as follows:

- *Private benefit and control.* Regardless of the size of the group benefited (there was no argument that Columbia resembles a city that would qualify), CRPA is owned and controlled by the homeowners and residents and serves their private interests. Every property owner possesses an ownership right in CPRA's facilities and services. The facilities open to the public represented less than 2 percent of the total and, out of 110,000 families, only 190 received reduced fees.

- *Funding source.* Another factor distinguishing it from a (c)(3) was its source of funds; no voluntary contributions were solicited from the public and the sole source of financing was property owner fees (nondeductible for Section 170 purposes).

- *No charitable purpose.* CRPA did not lessen the burdens of government. There was no proof that the State of Maryland or

[20] *Columbia Park and Recreation Association, Inc. v. Commissioner*, 88 T.C. 1 (1987).

Howard County accepted such responsibility and, based upon documents regarding the public transportation system, Columbia was expected to bear the cost.

- *Dissolution clause.* There are three possible recipients of CRPA's assets upon dissolution: Howard County, an agency or instrumentality of the county, or one of the village associations. The first two qualify as (c)(3) recipients, but the last doesn't because they are (c)(4) organizations. Thus the assets are not dedicated permanently to (c)(3) purposes.

Example 2: A civic welfare organization[21] "operated to meet the financial and emotional needs of individuals employed in an industry worldwide" was allowed to merge itself into its subsidiary (c)(3) organization since it possessed the requisite charitable characteristics, as follows:

- *Contributions.* Over one-third of the organization's support is received from contributions from the general public (non-industry members).

- *Charitable services.* Gerontology, social services (legal and emotional counseling), job placement for unemployed, and scholarships were considered charitable services.

- *Charitable class.* Because of its size (over 10,000 members), its dedication to members of a particular industry was ruled not to negate its charitable purposes.

In both of the examples, note that the organizational activities benefit a limited class of individuals. What distinguishes the two is (1) the character of the activities and (2) the sources of support. Relieving suffering in distress situations is generally considered charitable, as is promotion of health and education. Recreation, preservation of property values, and commuting to work are not generally classified as charitable activities.

Section 3.8A on relationships between (c)(3) and (c)(4) organizations.

[21] Priv. Ltr. Rul. 9019046.

§ 1.12 QUALIFYING AS A LABOR UNION OR AGRICULTURAL OR HORTICULTURAL ORGANIZATION: SECTION 501(c)(5)

p. 41. *Add at end of page:*

Membership made up of both employees and non-employees can, however, raise additional questions. Do the revenues received from different categories of membership have varying tax characteristics? Do fees related to member services create related income for employee members and unrelated income for associate members?

Two recent cases provide excellent insight into the answers. At issue was unrelated business income tax on profits realized from the union's group health insurance plans. Both cases involved insurance plans administered by the Office of Personnel Management through the Federal Employee Health Benefits Act (FEHBA).

The first case involved the American Postal Workers Union (APWU).[22] The IRS proposed a portion of the associate (nonpostal worker) member dues was attributable to the group health insurance plan and thereby produced unrelated business income, essentially saying that associate member concerns were unrelated to the basic purpose of serving postal worker members. Thus, the IRS assessed unrelated business income tax on the profits from the associate member group insurance.

After reviewing the charter and bylaws of the union, the Court found the APWU was organized to serve not only postal workers but any classified federal employee, and not limited to those employed by the U.S. Postal Service. This broad scope of coverage of all federal employees is permissible under Section 501(c)(5) regulations pertaining to labor unions which says, "a labor union is a voluntary association of workers which is organized to pursue common economic and social interests." Any particular union is free to define its constituents.

Further, the Court found that there were "no requirements in the Internal Revenue Code that a union member receive any particular quantum of benefit in order to be considered a bona fide member." Likewise, the Court found that the IRS's position that members had to have the right to vote was wholly without authority.

[22] *American Postal Workers Union, AFL-CIO v. United States,* 91-1 U.S.T.C. § 50,096 (D.C. C. 1991), rvg. 90-1 U.S.T.C. § 50013 (D.D.C. 1990).

The Court decided that the APWU's sponsorship of a group insurance plan therefore served an exempt purpose as a mutual benefit organization. The Court also decided that the insurance program was not undertaken to make a profit and "providing economic benefits to members in return for dues is not a trade or business," citing the 1921 Congressional record.

* The Circuit Court, however, disagreed and stipulated that the provision of insurance to nonpostal workers was not related to the union's stated focus on the interests of postal employees. The judge admitted the case was difficult because nothing in the regulations or any other authoritative source defines the exempt purposes of a labor union. However, based upon a review of the organization's constitution, the court found privileges of membership were granted only to active members and provision of insurance benefits to nonmembers could not be substantially related to the union's exempt purpose. The court was also swayed by the substantial profit generated by nonmember fees.

The Court of Claims also decided the National Association of Postal Supervisors (NAPS)[23] was taxable on its health insurance activity because it was an unrelated trade or business operated to produce a profit and was in competition with taxable insurance providers.

The NAPS case facts were distinguishable from APWU in one important respect: The court decided their associate members were not members. The nonpostal employee members were called "limited members." Their dues were calculated to produce a profit, they did not participate in other union programs, and their memberships were dropped if they failed to continue coverage in the health plan. Although not stated, perhaps the deciding factor in the case was the fact that within five years of starting the insurance program, the limited benefit members made up 71 percent of the total members in the plan. Thus, the facts supported the IRS's position that the insurance program's purpose was primarily to produce profit not to serve members.

p. 42. *Add "In" to last item in bulleted list to read:*
In other circumstances . . . .

[23] *National Association of Postal Supervisors v. United States,* 90-2 U.S.T.C. § 50,445 (Ct.Cl. 1990).

§ 1.13   QUALIFYING AS A BUSINESS LEAGUE: SECTION 501(c)(6)

p. 46. *Add after third full paragraph:*

The "line of business" argument continues as another trade association that limits its membership to users of IBM mainframe computers is denied exemption.[24] *Guide's* stated purposes are to promote sound professional practices and disseminate information with respect to data processing systems. Its main activity is a one-week conference held three times a year at which IBM makes presentations and provides equipment. The Court decided that the organization operates to benefit IBM, which represents a particular segment of the computer business, not the required line of business.

Based upon the cases, a working definition of a "line of business" is a trade or occupation the entry into which is not restricted by a patent, trademark, or similar device that would allow private parties to restrict the right to engage in the business.

p. 46. *Add before last paragraph:*

An organization conducting professional certification programs provides information to protect and benefit the general public, as well as its particular profession, and may arguably qualify as both a 501(c)(3) and 501(c)(6) organization. Many business leagues possess characteristics of educational and charitable exempts. In G.C.M. 39721, the IRS unequivocally took the position that certification programs are "directed in whole or in part to the support and promotion of the economic interests" of the members, not the public, and therefore could not qualify the organization for (c)(3) status.

* **p. 47.** *Add at end of second paragraph:*

Different classes of members are permitted as long as the purpose is to advance the interests of the profession and all members share the same, common business interest. Junior, senior, retired, associate, student, and many other types of categories are common—either in recognition of age or stature or active versus peripheral involvement in the business. Varying level of dues can also be charged to different

---

[24] *Guide International Corp.,* 91-2 U.S.T.C. § 50,573 (7th Cir. 1991)

types of members presumably based upon their ability to pay or their involvement in league activities. Those members required to have continuing education might pay more than those inactive or student members not required to participate in classes, for example.

The charging of substantially greater dues to associate members may, however, evidence private inurement benefiting the active members. The IRS agrees that higher dues are permissible where the revenues benefit the entire industry by allowing more extensive programs.[25] The excess payments likewise did not constitute UBI because the administration of associate members under a graduated dues structure is not the performance of a service or sale of a good.

p. 48. *Add after first full paragraph:*

Often a business, trade, or professional association described in Section 501(c)(6) forms a Section 501(c)(3) organization to pursue educational, cultural, scientific, health care-related, orother charitable interests. The motivation is usually fund raising—to solicit funds from supporters entitled to charitable deductions for their payments.

The charitable organization cannot, of course, operate to benefit the business league and care must be taken to insure any interlocking personnel or other sharing arrangements do not result in such benefit. See § 3.8A for discussion of such relationships.

§ 1.14 QUALIFYING AS A SOCIAL CLUB: SECTION 501(c)(7)

p. 49. *Add at the end of Discrimination:*

On the discrimination front, Princeton's last two "male only" social clubs were ordered to admit women by the Supreme Court of New Jersey in July, 1990. The Massachusetts Commission Against Discrimination in March, 1990, on the other hand, refused to rule, saying it did not have jurisdiction, to require the Harvard Fly Club to admit women.

The decisions are interesting in view of the basic statutory requirement of IRC Section 501(i), added to the code in 1976, that

---

[25] Priv. Ltr. Rul. 9128002, August 17, 1990.

prohibits discrimination for all types of exempt 501 organizations. A social club's charter, bylaws, or other governing instrument, or other written policy statement, may not contain provisions that provides for discrimination against any persons on the basis of race, color, or religion. Note the code does not contain the word "sex." The IRS has allowed continued tax exemption of the many clubs that do in fact discriminate against women and minorities, but under the broader Civil Rights legislation, their exemption is being challenged.

p. 51.   *Delete second paragraph of Unrelated Business Income and add:*

Social clubs are significantly different from other tax-exempt entities in one important respect: the definition of their unrelated business income subject to regular income tax. Section 512(a)(3)(A) proscribes a special definition of social club (and VEBAs, group legal services plans, and supplemental unemployment funds) taxable income to include all gross income except exempt function, rather than only gross income from unrelated trade or business. What this accomplishes is to subject social club investment income to income tax and only exclude from tax revenues dues, fees, charges, or similar amounts paid by members of the organization as consideration for providing such members or their dependents or guests goods, facilities, or services constituting the club's basis for exemption.

Rationale for Different UBI Treatment (New)

In extending the unrelated business income tax to social clubs in 1969, the Congress reiterated its intention to allow individuals to join together to provide recreational or social facilities or other benefits on a mutual basis without tax consequences. However, it made clear that tax exemption only operated properly when the sources of income of the organization are limited to receipts from the membership. When the club receives income from sources outside the membership, such as interest income on its savings or charges to outsiders for use of its facilities, it is taxed. Exempting such income from tax would allow club members to use tax-free dollars to pay for recreational and pleasure pursuits.

Classification of Nonmember Losses (New)

For a number of years, the IRS and social clubs have been fighting in the courts about an issue that isn't very clear: the offset of losses from nonmember activities against investment income. The battle has been fought from two different angles: how to calculate the loss (what portion of the club's fixed, or indirect, expenses are deductible) and the deductibility of the loss itself.

Section 512(a)(3)(A) allows deductions that are directly connected with the production of the gross income otherwise allowed by the Code (meaning ordinary and necessary business expenses allowed to for-profit businesses under Section 162). However, since 1981, the IRS has taken the position that a profit motive must be present for the expenses to qualify as allowable trade or business expenses.[26] Also the IRS argued different activities were not to be aggregated. The Tax Court in a 1985 memo decision, *The Brook, Inc.,*[27] took the narrower position that nonmember activity expenses were not "connected with the production of" income at all. The Second Circuit Court of Appeals in 1986 overruled the Brook decision and deemed all ordinary and necessary expenses of producing nonmember income, including investment income, were deductions only so long as they were incurred for the purpose of producing a profit. For a thorough history, read the *North Ridge Country Club*[28] case (Ninth Circuit ruled against the club) and the *Cleveland Athletic Club*[29] (Sixth Circuit allowed losses).

Direct and Indirect Costs (New)

The issue of deductible expenses is additionally complicated because there are two types of expenses involved in calculating the profit or loss from any activity of the club:

1. Fixed or indirect (club facility costs, such as insurance, mortgage interest, depreciation, utilities, managers, and other

---

[26] Rev. Rul 81-69, 1981-1 C.B. 351.
[27] *The Brook, Inc.,* 86-2 U.S.T.C. § 9646 (2d Cir. 1986).
[28] *North Ridge Country Club,* 89-1 U.S.T.C. § 9363 (9th Cir. 1989).
[29] *Cleveland Athletic Club,* 86-1 U.S.T.C. § 9116 (6th Cir. 1986).

overhead that the club incurs to serve its basic membership and sustains whether or not nonmembers are served, "but for expenses"); and

2. Variable or direct (food, waiters, golf caddies, and other expenses incurred in direct relationship to number of persons served: members and nonmembers).

The confusion starts when the terms normally used in cost accounting texts—fixed and variable, direct and indirect—are absent from the code. The regulations only add a stipulation that the expenses have a proximate and primary relationship to the income and provides for allocable of expenses attributable to both related and unrelated income.

In *Portland Golf Club v. Commissioner,*[30] in June, 1990, the U.S. Supreme Court unanimously decided that Portland's nonmember activity losses were not deductible against investment income because the activity was neither profitable nor profit motivated and to calculate the loss for both purposes direct and indirect costs had to be taken into account.

The Supreme Court agreed in this case with the IRS's longstanding position that the fixed and indirect expenses that the club incurs whether or not it serves nonmembers are not deductible to the extent they exceed nonmember income. Essentially, a social club cannot deduct an allocable portion of its basic member fixed expenses against its investment income unless the nonmember activity is profit motivated. The Court looked to the hobby loss standards of IRC Section 183 to test the profit motivation, particularly because Portland incurred losses in every year from 1975 through 1984.

How to Measure Profit Motive

A secondary, but important, aspect of the case was an argument about how to measure profit motive. Are both direct and indirect taken into account? Or does the fact that the nonmember direct

---

[30] *Portland Golf Club v. Commissioner* 90-1 USTC § 50,332 (S.C. 1990).

income covers nonmember direct expenses (without any reduction for allocable indirect expense) sufficient evidence of profit motive? Portland argued that since its nonmember income exceeded its nonmember direct expenses, it had a profit motive. The Court disagreed; and unless the Congress acts to change the tax code, profit motive for this purpose is calculated by deducting both direct and indirect costs associated with nonmember income.

The last issue to consider is whether one cost allocation method can be used to measure profit motive and another to calculate taxable income. This issue was not settled by the case although the answer by most of the judges was: Only one method can be used for both purposes. The question then becomes which method to use. Any method reasonably calculated to arrive at a fair allocation and consistently applied can be used. The regulations under Section 512 provide allocations must be made on a reasonable basis. The two basic methods used in the social club field are:

1. *Gross-to-gross method.* Actual gross revenues from members and nonmembers are used to allocate the costs.

2. *Actual use method.* Square footage occupied and hours of actual use are tabulated to calculate fixed cost allocations. Here the numerator of the equation is important. The IRS and taxpayers have argued in the case of a football stadium whether the proper divisor was the total number of hours in the year or the total number of hours the stadium was used. (See p. 273 for further discussion of cost allocations.)

* Charitable Set-Aside (New)

A charitable deduction is allowed to a social club for any income paid directly for charitable purposes or as a grant to a charitable organization. Funds that are earmarked or set aside for future charitable purposes may be deductible. Set asides must meet the requirements of Section 170(c)(4) that the contribution or gift be used only for specified charitable purposes. The IRS was confirmed by the courts in ruling that the *Phi Delta Theta* fraternity magazine was not educational but rather served the recreational purposes of the members.[31] Endowment income used to support the publication did not qualify for the charitable set aside donation.

Amended Returns (New)

The IRS has announced it is reopening cases held in suspense pending the Supreme Court's decision in *Portland*. Field offices have also been instructed to monitor "filing patterns" of social clubs to see that amended Forms 990-T are filed to reflect the decision.[32]

[31] *Phi Delta Theta Fraternity v. Commissioner*, 887 F.2d 1302 (6th Circ. 1989) aff'g 90 T.C.M. 1033 (1988).
[32] IRS Announcement 90-138, IRB 1990-51, November 29, 1990.

Obtaining IRS Recognition of 501(c) Exempt Status

§ 2.2 PREPARING SECTION 501(c)(3) APPLICATIONS FOR EXEMPTION: FORM 1023

* **p. 60.** *Add reference to end of first paragraph:*
The IRS has ruled that the date of organization is the date the organization comes into existence under applicable state law.[1]

* **p. 60.** *Add after second paragraph on page:*
   The effect of withdrawing an application was outlined by the IRS under three different scenarios. As a general rule, the withdrawal cancels previous notice and the time period prior to withdrawal is lost and a resubmitted application is treated as a new filing, with exemption effective prospectively from the date of resubmission.[2]
   Scenario 1. Form 1023 seeking 501(c)(3) status is timely filed but withdrawn. Two years later, application is resubmitted asserting that the organization had operated as exempt from day one and therefore exemption should be allowed from the original date of filing.
   Scenario 2. Same facts except upon withdrawal of the original application, the organization requested treatment a 501(c)(4) organization.

---

[1] Rev. Rul. 75-290, 1975-29, 17.
[2] Rev. Rul. 90-100, 1990-49, I.R.B. 6.

Scenario 3. Subordinate member of group exemption withdraws from the group and within fifteen months of withdrawal submits an independent application.

In the first two scenarios, exemption is effective only from the date of resubmission. In the third, exemption is effective from original inclusion in a group continuing on with new timely filing when such notice was required.

p. 60. *Add at the end of Expeditious Handling:*

Absent approval for special handling, careful preparation of the application can save considerable time in obtaining approval. In June, 1990, a helpful General Accounting Office (GAO) study of the process was released. The GAO report is entitled *"Tax Administration: IRS Can Improve Its Process for Recognizing Tax-Exempt Organizations"* (GAO/ GGD-90-55). Several issues are addressed: the determination process, advanced ruling followups and case closing procedures. Of primary importance is a discussion of the IRS's "expedited determination process." Beginning in 1987, the Key District Offices have been authorized to "dispose of cases quickly." The process allows experienced personnel to make a final decision on qualification for exemption without referring the file to specialists. Certain types of organizations that typically cause controversy during the determination process because of their complexity, such as schools and churches, are not eligible for expedited determination (although the GAO criticizes the IRS for failure to develop a list of exemption categories that could qualify).

The GAO found that the use of the process varies from Key District Offices with the highest district reporting a 17 percent usage rate to the lowest using the process for only 2 percent of its cases. Lack of guidance from the National IRS Office to the field was pinpointed by the GAO for low, sporadic, and inconsistent usage of the abbreviated processing system. The GAO encourages use of the system and made two recommendations: (1) evaluation of the usage with a goal to establish clear guidance on when the process is used and (2) assess the possibility of increasing the expedited determination process and freeing IRS funds to examination. The GAO by reference creates an opportunity for Form 1023 preparers.

A complete and clearly prepared application has the possibility of immediate approval, a consistently desired result. Contributors and volunteers are often waiting in the wings to move into action upon receipt of the IRS determination.

* **p. 60.**   *Add new comment for Expeditious Handling:*
Another name for expeditious handling is "speedy determination."
The specific steps to take in requesting such handling include:

- Enclose a money order or cashier's check in payment of the filing fee to eliminate check clearing delays. Application processing awaits the clearing of the check in payment of the fee, a process the Dallas determination group reports takes up to two weeks.

- A covering letter requesting special handling and describing the reason the speed is necessary. Examples of good reasons include the emergency nature of the project, such as disaster relief or the possibility that a grant will not be received if approval is delayed.

- If possible, include independent documentation of reasons, such as letter from funder denying funds if there is a delay.

* **p. 64.**   *Add at end of § 2.2:*

Filing Fee

The filing fee for group exemption application is $500. Otherwise, the procedures outlined in the book as provided by the IRS in 1980[3] are still followed.

Withdrawal from Group

For a variety of reasons, a subordinate organization covered by a group exemption may wish to withdraw from the group and operate independently. The question that arises is how such an organization can assure its qualification as a tax exempt organization is ongoing and uninterrupted.

A new Form 1023 for the withdrawing member is due to be filed within fifteen months of the date of withdrawal. Such filing satisfies the notice requirements of Section 508 according to a 1982 IRS memo recently released.[4] The regulations make no mention of the issue.[5]

[3] Rev. Proc. 80-27, 1980-1 C.B. 677.
[4] G. C. M. 39833, released Dec. 10, 1990.
[5] Treas. Reg. § 1.508-1(a)(2)(i).

Exhibit 2–1A

Form **1023**	**Application for Recognition of Exemption**	OMB No. 1545-0056
(Rev. December 1989) Department of the Treasury Internal Revenue Service	**Under Section 501(c)(3) of the Internal Revenue Code**	If exempt status is approved, this application will be open for public inspection.

Read the instructions for each Part carefully.
A User Fee must be attached to this application.

If the required information and appropriate documents are not submitted along with Form 8718 (with payment of the appropriate user fee), the application may be returned to you.

Part I   Identification of Applicant

1a Full name of organization (as shown in organizing document) CAMPAIGN TO CLEAN UP AMERICA	**2** Employer identification number **(If none, see instructions.)** 44 : 4444444
1b c/o Name (if applicable)	**3** Name and telephone number of person to be contacted if additional information is needed Jody Blazek, CPA
1c Address (number and street) 1111 ANY STREET	(707) 444-4444
1d City or town, state, and ZIP code HOMETOWN, TX 7777	**4** Month the annual accounting period ends June

5 Date incorporated or formed June 14, 1990	**6** Activity codes (See instructions.) 354 125 402	**7** Check here if applying under section: **a**☐ 501(e) **b**☐ 501(f) **c**☐ 501(k)

8 Did the organization previously apply for recognition of exemption under this Code section or under any other section of the Code? . . . . ☐ Yes ☒ No
If "Yes," attach an explanation.

9 Has the organization filed Federal income tax returns or exempt organization information returns? . . . . . ☒ Yes ☐ No
If "Yes," state the form number(s), years filed, and Internal Revenue office where filed.

    Form 990EZ for fiscal year ending June 30, 1990   Austin, Texas

10 Check the box for your type of organization. BE SURE TO ATTACH A COMPLETE COPY OF THE CORRESPONDING DOCUMENTS TO THE APPLICATION BEFORE MAILING.

a ☒ Corporation— Attach a copy of your Articles of Incorporation, (including amendments and restatements) showing approval by the appropriate state official; also include a copy of your bylaws.

b ☐ Trust— Attach a copy of your Trust Indenture or Agreement, including all appropriate signatures and dates.

c ☐ Association— Attach a copy of your Articles of Association, Constitution, or other creating document, with a declaration (see instructions) or other evidence the organization was formed by adoption of the document by more than one person; also include a copy of your bylaws.

If you are a corporation or an unincorporated association that has not yet adopted bylaws, check here . . . . ▶ ☐

I declare under the penalties of perjury that I am authorized to sign this application on behalf of the above organization and that I have examined this application, including the accompanying schedules and attachments, and to the best of my knowledge it is true, correct, and complete.

**Please
Sign
Here** ▶ _____   President   April 7, 1991
          (Signature)   (Title or authority of signer)   (Date)

For Paperwork Reduction Act Notice, see page 1 of the Instructions.

Complete the Procedural Checklist (page 7 of the Instructions) prior to filing.

Exhibit 2–1A *(continued)*

CAMPAIGN TO CLEAN UP AMERICA   44-4444444

Form 1023 (Rev. 12-89)   Page **2**

Part II   **Activities and Operational Information**

· 1 Provide a detailed narrative description of all the activities of the organization—past, present, and planned. **Do not merely refer to or repeat the language in your organizational document.** Describe each activity separately in the order of importance. Each description should include, as a minimum, the following: (a) a detailed description of the activity including its purpose; (b) when the activity was or will be initiated; and (c) where and by whom the activity will be conducted.

Attachment 3

2 What are or will be the organization's sources of financial support? List in order of size.

Contributions/disqualified persons	5	%
Contributions/general public	52	
Grants/corporations and private foundations	37	
Exempt function revenues	5	
Investment income	1	= 100%

3 Describe the organization's fundraising program, both actual and planned, and explain to what extent it has been put into effect. (Include details of fundraising activities such as selective mailings, formation of fundraising committees, use of volunteers or professional fundraisers, etc.) Attach representative copies of solicitations for financial support.

The fundraising program will commence with selective mailings and other attempts to reach the general public with brochures, flyers, and news notices. The Campaign will seek gifts of money and property, including charitable bequests; a capital fund drive is anticipated, but not yet formalized. A professional fundraising consultant will be hired, but no agreements have been reached (budgeted at $15,000/20000). A copy of a sample fundraising letter is attached at Exhibit C.

■ **31** ■

Exhibit 2–1A *(continued)*

Part II	**Activities and Operational Information** *(Continued)*

4 Give the following information about the organization's governing body:

a Names, addresses, and titles of officers, directors, trustees, etc.	**b** Annual Compensation
John J. Environmentalist, President 333 First Street, Hometown, TX 77777	none
Jane D. Environmentalist, Secretary/Treasurer 333 First Street, Hometown, TX 77777	none
James F. Friend, Vice President 444 Second Street, Hometown, TX 77777	none

c Do any of the above persons serve as members of the governing body by reason of being public officials or being appointed by public officials? . . . . ☐ Yes ☒ No
If "Yes," name those persons and explain the basis of their selection or appointment.

d Are any members of the organization's governing body "disqualified persons" with respect to the organization (other than by reason of being a member of the governing body) or do any of the members have either a business or family relationship with "disqualified persons"? (See the Specific Instructions for line 4d.) . . . . ☐ Yes ☒ No
If "Yes," explain.

5 Does the organization control or is it controlled by any other organization? . . . . ☐ Yes ☒ No
Is the organization the outgrowth of (or successor to) another organization, or does it have a special relationship to another organization by reason of interlocking directorates or other factors? . . . . ☐ Yes ☒ No
If either of these questions is answered "Yes," explain.

6 Does or will the organization directly or indirectly engage in any of the following transactions with any political organization or other exempt organization (other than 501(c)(3) organizations): (a) grants; (b) purchases or sales of assets; (c) rental of facilities or equipment; (d) loans or loan guarantees; (e) reimbursement arrangements; (f) performance of services, membership, or fundraising solicitations; or (g) sharing of facilities, equipment, mailing lists or other assets, or paid employees? . . . . ☐ Yes ☒ No
If "Yes," explain fully and identify the other organization(s) involved.

7 Is the organization financially accountable to any other organization? . . . . ☐ Yes ☒ No
If "Yes," explain and identify the other organization. Include details concerning accountability or attach copies of reports if any have been submitted.

Exhibit 2–1A *(continued)*

Form 1023 (Rev. 12-89)   CAMPAIGN TO CLEAN UP AMERICA   44-4444444   Page **4**

Part II	**Activities and Operational Information** *(Continued)*

8 What assets does the organization have that are used in the performance of its exempt function? (Do not include property producing investment income.) If any assets are not fully operational, explain their status, what additional steps remain to be completed, and when such final steps will be taken. If "None," indicate "N/A." The Campaign will acquire computers, desks, office furniture, trash cleaning tools, and other assets to carry out its exempt activities.

9a Will any of the organization's facilities or operations be managed by another organization or individual under a contractual agreement? . . . ☐ Yes ☒ No

b Is the organization a party to any leases? . . . ☒ Yes ☐ No

If either of these questions is answered "Yes," attach a copy of each such contract and explain the relationship between the applicant and each of the other parties. The Campaign will initially sublease office space in its President's office (building owned by unrelated party). A proportionate part of the current rent based upon space actually used by the Campaign will be paid. There is no written lease; the sublease is month-to-month; as funds are available new space will be sought. Considerable cost savings to the Campaign will be gained by this sublease.

10 Is the organization a membership organization? . . . ☐ Yes ☒ No
If "Yes," complete the following:

a Describe the organization's membership requirements and attach a schedule of membership fees and dues.

b Describe your present and proposed efforts to attract members and attach a copy of any descriptive literature or promotional material used for this purpose.

c What benefits do (or will) your members receive in exchange for their payment of dues?

11a If the organization provides benefits, services or products, are the recipients required, or will they be required, to pay for them? . . . ☐ N/A ☒ Yes & ☒ No
If "Yes," explain; show how the charges are determined; and attach a copy of your current fee schedule.
Most of the Campaign's educational materials will be distributed free of charge. A minimal charge designed to defray costs will be made for seminars and publications.

b Does or will the organization limit its benefits, services or products to specific individuals or classes of individuals? . . . ☐ N/A ☐ Yes ☒ No
If "Yes," explain how the recipients or beneficiaries are or will be selected.

12 Does or will the organization attempt to influence legislation? . . . ☒ Yes ☐ No
If "Yes," explain. Also, give an estimate of the percentage of the organization's time and funds which it devotes or plans to devote to this activity. The Campaign may spend up to five percent of its annual budget on legislative activity. See also response to Part II, item 1. (III,3).

13 Does or will the organization intervene in any way in political campaigns, including the publication or distribution of statements? . . . ☐ Yes ☒ No
If "Yes," explain fully.

Exhibit 2–1A *(continued)*

Form 1023 (Rev. 12-89)   CAMPAIGN TO CLEAN UP AMERICA   44–4444444   Page **5**

| Part III | Technical Requirements |

1 Are you filing Form 1023 within 15 months from the end of the month in which you were created or formed? . ☒ **Yes**   ☐ **No**
If you answer "Yes," do not answer questions 2 through 6.

2 If one of the exceptions to the 15-month filing requirement shown below applies, check the appropriate box and proceed to question 7.
Exceptions—You are not required to file an exemption application within 15 months if the organization:

☐ **(a)** Is a church, interchurch organization, local unit of a church, a convention or association of churches, or an integrated auxiliary of a church;

☐ **(b)** Is not a private foundation and normally has gross receipts of not more than $5,000 in each tax year; or,

☐ **(c)** Is a subordinate organization covered by a group exemption letter, but only if the parent or supervisory organization timely submitted a notice covering the subordinate.

3 If you do not meet any of the exceptions in question 2, do you wish to request relief from the 15-month filing requirement? . . . . ☐ **Yes**   ☐ **No**

4 If you answer "Yes" to question 3, please give your reasons for not filing this application within 15 months from the end of the month in which your organization was created or formed.

5 If you answer "No" to both questions 1 and 3 and do not meet any of the exceptions in question 2, your qualification as a section 501(c)(3) organization can be recognized only from the date this application is filed with your key District Director. Therefore, do you want us to consider your application as a request for recognition of exemption as a section 501(c)(3) organization from the date the application is received and not retroactively to the date you were formed? . . . . ☐ **Yes**   ☐ **No**

6 If you answer "Yes" to question 5 above and wish to request recognition of section 501(c)(4) status for the period beginning with the date you were formed and ending with the date your Form 1023 application was received (the effective date of your section 501(c)(3) status), check here ▶ ☐ and attach a completed page 1 of Form 1024 to this application.

■ 34 ■

Exhibit 2–1A *(continued)*

Part III **Technical Requirements** *(Continued)*

---

7 Is the organization a private foundation?
☐ **Yes**   (Answer question 8.)
☒ **No**   (Answer question 9 and proceed as instructed.)

---

8 If you answer "Yes" to question 7, do you claim to be a private operating foundation?
☐ **Yes**   (Complete Schedule E)
☐ **No**

After answering this question, go to Part IV.

---

9 If you answer "No" to question 7, indicate the public charity classification you are requesting by checking the box below that most appropriately applies:

THE ORGANIZATION IS NOT A PRIVATE FOUNDATION BECAUSE IT QUALIFIES:

(a) ☐ As a church or a convention or association of churches (MUST COMPLETE SCHEDULE A.)		Sections 509(a)(1) and 170(b)(1)(A)(i)
(b) ☐ As a school (MUST COMPLETE SCHEDULE B).		Sections 509(a)(1) and 170(b)(1)(A)(ii)
(c) ☐ As a hospital or a cooperative hospital service organization, or a medical research organization operated in conjunction with a hospital (MUST COMPLETE SCHEDULE C).		Sections 509(a)(1) and 170(b)(1)(A)(iii)
(d) ☐ As a governmental unit described in section 170(c)(1).		Sections 509(a)(1) and 170(b)(1)(A)(v)
(e) ☐ As being operated solely for the benefit of, or in connection with, one or more of the organizations described in (a) through (d), (g), (h), or (i) (MUST COMPLETE SCHEDULE D).		Section 509(a)(3)
(f) ☐ As being organized and operated exclusively for testing for public safety.		Section 509(a)(4)
(g) ☐ As being operated for the benefit of a college or university that is owned or operated by a governmental unit.		Sections 509(a)(1) and 170(b)(1)(A)(iv)
(h) ☒ As receiving a substantial part of its support in the form of contributions from publicly supported organizations, from a governmental unit, or from the general public.		Sections 509(a)(1) and 170(b)(1)(A)(vi)
(i) ☐ As normally receiving not more than one-third of its support from gross investment income and more than one-third of its support from contributions, membership fees, and gross receipts from activities related to its exempt functions (subject to certain exceptions).		Section 509(a)(2)
(j) ☐ We are a publicly supported organization but are not sure whether we meet the public support test of block (h) or block (i). We would like the Internal Revenue Service to decide the proper classification.		Sections 509(a)(1) and 170(b)(1)(A)(vi) or Section 509(a)(2)

If you checked one of the boxes (a) through (f) in question 9, go to question 14.
If you checked box (g) in question 9, go to questions 11 and 12.
If you checked box (h), (i), or (j), go to question 10.

Exhibit 2–1A *(continued)*

Part III **Technical Requirements** *(Continued)*

10 If you checked box (h), (i), or (j) in question 9, have you completed a tax year of at least 8 months?

☐ No—You must request an advance ruling by completing and signing 2 Forms 872-C and attaching them to your application.

☐ Yes—Indicate whether you are requesting:

   ☐ A definitive ruling (Answer question 11 through and including question 14.)

   ☒ An advance ruling (Answer questions 11 and 14 and attach 2 Forms 872-C completed and signed.)

11 If the organization received any unusual grants during any of the tax years shown in Part IV-A, attach a list for each year showing the name of the contributor; the date and the amount of the grant; and a brief description of the nature of each such grant.

12 If you are requesting a definitive ruling under section 170(b)(1)(A)(iv) or (vi), check here ▶ ☐ and:

  a Enter 2% of line 8, column (e) of Part IV-A _____

  b Attach a list showing the name and amount contributed by each person (other than a governmental unit or "publicly supported" organization) whose total gifts, grants, contributions, etc., were more than the amount you entered on line **12a** above.

13 If you are requesting a definitive ruling under section 509(a)(2), check here ▶ ☐ and:

  a For each of the years included on lines 1, 2, and 9 of Part IV-A, attach a list showing the name of and amount received from each person who is a "disqualified person."

  b For each of the years included on line 9 of Part IV-A, attach a list showing the name of and amount received from each payer (other than a "disqualified person") whose payments to the organization were more than $5,000. For this purpose, "payer" includes, but is not limited to, any organization described in sections 170(b)(1)(A)(i) through (vi) and any governmental agency or bureau.

14 Indicate if your organization is one of the following, and if so, complete the required schedule. (Submit only those schedules, if any, that apply to your organization. **Do not submit blank schedules.**)

	Yes	No	If "Yes," complete schedule:
Is the organization a church?		x	A
Is the organization, or any part of it, a school?		x	B
Is the organization, or any part of it, a hospital or medical research organization?		x	C
Is the organization a section 509(a)(3) supporting organization?		x	D
Is the organization an operating foundation?		x	E
Is the organization, or any part of it, a home for the aged or handicapped?		x	F
Is the organization, or any part of it, a child care organization?		x	G
Does the organization provide or administer any scholarship benefits, student aid, etc.?		x	H
Has the organization taken over, or will it take over, the facilities of a "for profit" institution?		x	I

Exhibit 2–1A (continued)

Part IV   Financial Data

Complete the financial statements for the current year and for each of the 3 years immediately before it. If in existence less than 4 years, complete the statements for each year in existence. If in existence less than 1 year, also provide proposed budgets for the 2 years following the current year.

A.—Statement of Revenue and Expenses

		Current tax year	3 prior tax years or proposed budget for 2 years			
		(a) From 6/90 to 3/91	**(b)** 19 90/91	**(c)** 19 91/92	**(d)** 19 92/93	**(e) TOTAL**
	1 Gifts, grants, and contributions received (not including unusual grants—see instructions)	10,000	60,000	260,000	910,000	1,240,000
	2 Membership fees received					
	3 Gross investment income (see instructions for definition)	0	500	1,000	10,000	11,500
	4 Net income from organization's unrelated business activities not included on line 3					
	5 Tax revenues levied for and either paid to or spent on behalf of the organization					
	6 Value of services or facilities furnished by a governmental unit to the organization without charge (not including the value of services or facilities generally furnished the public without charge)					
Revenue	**7** Other income (not including gain or loss from sale of capital assets) (attach schedule)					
	8 **Total** of lines 1 through 7	10,000	60,500	261,000	920,000	1,251,500
	9 Gross receipts from admissions, sales of merchandise or services, or furnishing of facilities in any activity that is not an unrelated business within the meaning of section 513		1,000	10,000	40,000	51,000
	10 **Total** of lines 8 and 9	10,000	61,500	271,000	960,000	1,302,500
	11 Gain or loss from sale of capital assets (attach schedule)					
	12 Unusual grants					
	13 **Total** revenue (add lines 10 through 12)	10,000	61,500	271,000	960,000	1,302,500
	14 Fundraising expenses	1,000	10,000	25,000	50,000	
	15 Contributions, gifts, grants, and similar amounts paid (attach schedule)					
	16 Disbursements to or for benefit of members (attach schedule)					
	17 Compensation of officers, directors, and trustees (attach schedule)					
Expenses	**18** Other salaries and wages	2,000	10,000	113,000	410,000	
	19 Interest					
	20 Occupancy (rent, utilities, etc.)	1,000	2,000	45,000	110,000	
	21 Depreciation and depletion			2,000	5,000	
	22 Other (attach schedule)	1,000	5,000	41,000	185,000	
	23 **Total expenses**	5,000	27,000	226,000	760,000	
	24 Excess of revenue over expenses (line 13 minus line 23)	5,000	34,500	45,000	200,000	

■ **37** ■

Exhibit 2–1A *(continued)*

Part IV	Financial Data *(Continued)*

B.—Balance Sheet (at the end of the period shown)		Current tax year Date March 31, 1991
Assets		
1 Cash	1	5,000
2 Accounts receivable, net	2	
3 Inventories	3	
4 Bonds and notes receivable (attach schedule)	4	
5 Corporate stocks (attach schedule)	5	
6 Mortgage loans (attach schedule)	6	
7 Other investments (attach schedule)	7	
8 Depreciable and depletable assets (attach schedule)	8	
9 Land	9	
10 Other assets (attach schedule)	10	
11 Total assets	11	5,000
Liabilities		
12 Accounts payable	12	
13 Contributions, gifts, grants, etc., payable	13	
14 Mortgages and notes payable (attach schedule)	14	
15 Other liabilities (attach schedule)	15	
16 Total liabilities	16	–0–
Fund Balances or Net Assets		
17 Total fund balances or net assets	17	5,000
18 Total liabilities and fund balances or net assets (add line 16 and line 17)	18	5,000

If there has been any substantial change in any aspect of your financial activities since the end of the period shown above, check the box and attach a detailed explanation . . . . ▶ ☐

Exhibit 2-1A (continued)

Schedule A.—Churches
N/A

1 Provide a brief history of the development of the organization, including the reasons for its formation.

2 Does the organization have a written creed or statement of faith? . . . . ☐ **Yes** ☐ **No**

If "Yes," attach a copy.

3 Does the organization require prospective members to renounce other religious beliefs or their membership in other churches or religious orders to become members? . . . . ☐ **Yes** ☐ **No**

4 Does the organization have a formal code of doctrine and discipline for its members? . . . . ☐ **Yes** ☐ **No**

If "Yes," describe.

5 Describe your form of worship and attach a schedule of your worship services.

6 Are your services open to the public? . . . . ☐ **Yes** ☐ **No**

If "Yes," describe how you publicize your services and explain your criteria for admittance.

7 Explain how you attract new members.

8 (a) How many active members are currently enrolled in your church?

(b) What is the average attendance at your worship services?

9 In addition to your worship services, what other religious services (such as baptisms, weddings, funerals, etc.) do you conduct?

Exhibit 2–1A *(continued)*

Schedule A.—Churches *(Continued)*

10 Does the organization have a school for the religious instruction of the young?   ☐ **Yes**   ☐ **No**

11 Were your current deacons, minister, and pastor formally ordained after a prescribed course of study? . . . .   ☐ **Yes**   ☐ **No**

12 Describe your religious hierarchy or ecclesiastical government.

13 Does your organization have an established place of worship? . . . .   ☐ **Yes**   ☐ **No**

If "Yes," provide the name and address of the owner or lessor of the property and the address and a description of the facility.

If you have no regular place of worship, state where your services are held and how the site is selected.

14 Does (or will) the organization license or otherwise ordain ministers (or their equivalent) or issue church charters? . . . .   ☐ **Yes**   ☐ **No**

If "Yes," describe in detail the requirements and qualifications needed to be so licensed, ordained, or chartered.

15 Did the organization pay a fee for a church charter? . . . .   ☐ **Yes**   ☐ **No**

If "Yes," state the name and address of the organization to which the fee was paid, attach a copy of the charter, and describe the circumstances surrounding the chartering.

16 Show how many hours a week your minister/pastor and officers each devote to church work and the amount of compensation paid each of them. If your minister or pastor is otherwise employed, indicate by whom employed, the nature of the employment, and the hours devoted to that employment.

Exhibit 2–1A *(continued)*

Schedule A.—Churches *(Continued)*

17 Will any funds or property of your organization be used by any officer, director, employee, minister, or pastor for his or her personal needs or convenience? . . . . ☐ **Yes**   ☐ **No**

If "Yes," describe the nature and circumstances of such use.

18 List any officers, directors, or trustees related by blood or marriage.

19 Give the name of anyone who has assigned income to you or made substantial contributions of money or other property. Specify the amounts involved.

Instructions

Although a church, its integrated auxiliaries, or a convention or association of churches is not required to file Form 1023 to be exempt from Federal income tax or to receive tax deductible contributions, such an organization may find it advantageous to obtain recognition of exemption. In this event, you should submit information showing that your organization is a church, synagogue, association or convention of churches, religious order or religious organization that is an integral part of a church, and that it is carrying out the functions of a church.

In determining whether an admittedly religious organization is also a church, the Internal Revenue Service does not accept any and every assertion that such an organization is a church. Because beliefs and practices vary so widely, there is no single definition of the word "church" for tax purposes. The Internal Revenue Service considers the facts and circumstances of each organization applying for church status.

The Internal Revenue Service maintains two basic guidelines in determining that an organization meets the religious purposes test:

(a) that the particular religious beliefs of the organization are truly and sincerely held, and

(b) that the practices and rituals associated with the organization's religious beliefs or creed are not illegal or contrary to clearly defined public policy.

In order for the Internal Revenue Service to properly evaluate your organization's activities and religious purposes, it is important that all questions in this Schedule are answered accurately.

The information submitted with this Schedule will be a determining factor in granting the "church" status requested by your organization. In completing the Schedule, the following points should be considered:

(a) The organization's activities in furtherance of its beliefs must be exclusively religious,

(b) An organization will not qualify for exemption if it has a substantial nonexempt purpose of serving the private interests of its founder or the founder's family.

Exhibit 2-1A (continued)

Schedule B.—Schools, Colleges, and Universities   N/A

1 Does, or will, the organization normally have: (a) a regularly scheduled curriculum, (b) a regular faculty of qualified teachers, (c) a regularly enrolled body of students, and (d) facilities where its educational activities are regularly carried on? . . . . ☐ **Yes**   ☐ **No**

If "No," do not complete the rest of this Schedule.

2 Is the organization an instrumentality of a State or political subdivision of a State? . . . . ☐ **Yes**   ☐ **No**

If "Yes," document this in Part II and do not complete items 3 through 10 of this Schedule. (See instructions for Schedule B.)

3 Does or will the organization (or any department or division within it) discriminate in any way on the basis of race with respect to:

a Admissions? . . . . ☐ **Yes**   ☐ **No**
b Use of facilities or exercise of student privileges? . . . . ☐ **Yes**   ☐ **No**
c Faculty or administrative staff? . . . . ☐ **Yes**   ☐ **No**
d Scholarship or loan programs? . . . . ☐ **Yes**   ☐ **No**

If "Yes," for any of the above, explain.

4 Does the organization include a statement in its charter, bylaws, or other governing instrument, or in a resolution of its governing body, that it has a racially nondiscriminatory policy as to students? . . . . . . ☐ **Yes**   ☐ **No**

Attach whatever corporate resolutions or other official statements the organization has made on this subject.

5a Has the organization made its racially nondiscriminatory policies known in a manner that brings the policies to the attention of all segments of the general community that it serves? . . . . ☐ **Yes**   ☐ **No**

If "Yes," describe how these policies have been publicized and how often relevant notices or announcements have been made. If no newspaper or broadcast media notices have been used, explain.

b If applicable, attach clippings of any relevant newspaper notices or advertising, or copies of tapes or scripts used for media broadcasts. Also attach copies of brochures and catalogues dealing with student admissions, programs, and scholarships, as well as representative copies of all written advertising used as a means of informing prospective students of your programs.

6 Attach a numerical schedule showing the racial composition, as of the current academic year, and projected as far as may be feasible for the next academic year, of: (a) the student body, and (b) the faculty and administrative staff.

7 Attach a list showing the amount of any scholarship and loan funds awarded to students enrolled and the racial composition of the students who have received the awards.

8a Attach a list of the organization's incorporators, founders, board members, and donors of land or buildings, whether individuals or organizations.

b State whether any of the organizations listed in **8a** have as an objective the maintenance of segregated public or private school education, and, if so, whether any of the individuals listed in **8a** are officers or active members of such organizations.

9a Indicate the public school district and county in which the organization is located.

b Was the organization formed or substantially expanded at the time of public school desegregation in the above district or county? . . . . ☐ **Yes**   ☐ **No**

10 Has the organization ever been determined by a State or Federal administrative agency or judicial body to be racially discriminatory? . . . . ☐ **Yes**   ☐ **No**

If "Yes," attach a detailed explanation identifying the parties to the suit, the forum in which the case was heard, the cause of action, the holding in the case, and the citations (if any) for the case. Also describe in detail what changes in your operation, if any, have occurred since then.

For more information, see back of Schedule.

Exhibit 2-1A (continued)

A "school" is an organization that has the primary function of presenting formal instruction, normally maintains a regular faculty and curriculum, normally has a regularly enrolled body of students, and has a place where its educational activities are carried on. The term generally corresponds to the definition of an "educational organization" in section 170(b)(1)(A)(ii). Thus, the term includes primary, secondary, preparatory and high schools, and colleges and universities. The term does not include organizations engaged in both educational and non-educational activities unless the latter are merely incidental to the educational activities. A school for handicapped children would be included within the term, but an organization merely providing handicapped children with custodial care would not.

For purposes of this Schedule, "Sunday schools" that are conducted by a church would not be included in the term "schools," but separately organized schools (such as parochial schools, universities, and similar institutions) would be included in the term.

A private school that otherwise meets the requirements of section 501(c)(3) as an educational institution will not qualify for exemption under section 501(a) unless it has a racially nondiscriminatory policy as to students. This policy means that the school admits students of any race to all the rights, privileges, programs, and activities generally accorded or made available to students at that school, and that the school does not discriminate on the basis of race in the administration of its educational policies, admissions policies, scholarship and loan programs, and athletic, or other school-administered programs. The Internal Revenue Service considers discrimination on the basis of race to include discrimination on the basis of color and national or ethnic origin. A policy of a school that favors racial minority groups in admissions, facilities, programs, and financial assistance will not constitute discrimination on the basis of race when the purpose and effect is to promote the establishment and maintenance of that school's racially nondiscriminatory policy as to students. See Rev. Proc. 75-50, 1975-2 C.B. 587, for guidelines and recordkeeping requirements for determining whether private schools that are applying for recognition of exemption have racially nondiscriminatory policies as to students.

Line 2. An instrumentality of a State or political subdivision of a State may qualify under section 501(c)(3) if it is organized as a separate entity from the governmental unit that created it and if it otherwise meets the organizational and operational tests of section 501(c)(3). (See Rev. Rul. 60-384, 1960-2 C.B. 172.) Any such organization that is a school is not a private school and, therefore, is not subject to the provisions of Rev. Proc. 75-50.

Schools that incorrectly answer "Yes" to line 2 will be contacted to furnish the information called for by lines 3 through 10 in order to establish that they meet the requirements for exemption. To prevent delay in the processing of your application, be sure to answer line 2 correctly and complete lines 3 through 10 if applicable.

Exhibit 2–1A *(continued)*

Schedule C.—Hospitals and Medical Research Organizations   N/A

☐ Check here if you are claiming to be a hospital; complete the questions in Section I of this Schedule; and write "N/A" in Section II.
☐ Check here if you are claiming to be a medical research organization operated in conjunction with a hospital; complete the questions in Section II of this Schedule; and write "N/A" in Section I.

| Section I | **Hospitals** |

1a How many doctors are on the hospital's courtesy staff? . . . . |

b Are all the doctors in the community eligible for staff privileges? . . . . ☐ **Yes**   ☐ **No**
If "No," give the reasons why and explain how the courtesy staff is selected.

2a Does the hospital maintain a full-time emergency room? . . . . ☐ **Yes**   ☐ **No**
b What is the hospital's policy on administering emergency services to persons without apparent means to pay?

c Does the hospital have any arrangements with police, fire, and voluntary ambulance services for the delivery or admission of emergency cases? . . . . ☐ **Yes**   ☐ **No**
Explain.

3a Does or will the hospital require a deposit from persons covered by Medicare or Medicaid in its admission practices? . . . . ☐ **Yes**   ☐ **No**
If "Yes," explain.

b Does the same deposit requirement apply to all other patients? . . . . ☐ **Yes**   ☐ **No**
If "No," explain.

4 Does or will the hospital provide for a portion of its services and facilities to be used for charity patients? . . . ☐ **Yes**   ☐ **No**
Explain your policy regarding charity cases. Include data on the hospital's past experience in admitting charity patients and arrangements it may have with municipal or government agencies for absorbing the cost of such care.

5 Does or will the hospital carry on a formal program of medical training and research? . . . . ☐ **Yes**   ☐ **No**
If "Yes," describe.

6 Does the hospital provide office space to physicians carrying on a medical practice? . . . . ☐ **Yes**   ☐ **No**
If "Yes," attach a list setting forth the name of each physician, the amount of space provided, the annual rent (if any), the expiration date of the current lease and whether the terms of the lease represent fair market value.

| Section II | **Medical Research Organizations** |

1 Name the hospital(s) with which you have a relationship and describe the relationship(s).

2 Attach a schedule describing your present and proposed (indicate which) medical research activities; show the nature of the activities, and the amount of money that has been or will be spent in carrying them out. (Making grants to other organizations is not direct conduct of medical research.)

3 Attach a statement of assets showing the fair market value of your assets and the portion of the assets directly devoted to medical research.

For more information, see back of Schedule.

Exhibit 2–1A *(continued)*

Cooperative hospital service organizations (section 501(e)) should not complete Schedule C.

In order to be entitled to status as a "hospital," an organization must have, as its principal purpose or function, the providing of medical or hospital care or medical education or research. "Medical care" includes the treatment of any physical or mental disability or condition, the cost of which may be taken as a deduction under section 213, whether the treatment is performed on an inpatient or outpatient basis. Thus, a rehabilitation institution, outpatient clinic, or community mental health or drug treatment center may be a hospital if its principal function is providing the above described services. On the other hand, a convalescent home or a home for children or the aged would not be a hospital. Similarly, an institution whose principal purpose or function is to train handicapped individuals to pursue some vocation would not be a hospital. Moreover, a medical education or medical research institution is not a hospital, unless it is also actively engaged in providing medical or hospital care to patients on its premises or in its facilities on an inpatient or outpatient basis.

To qualify as a medical research organization, the principal function of the organization must be the direct, continuous and active conduct of medical research in conjunction with a hospital which is described in section 501(c)(3), a Federal hospital, or an instrumentality of a governmental unit referred to in section 170(c)(1). For purposes of section 170(b)(1)(A)(iii) only, the organization must be set up to use the funds it receives in the active conduct of medical research by January 1 of the fifth calendar year after receipt. The arrangement it has with donors to assure use of the funds within the five-year period must be legally enforceable. As used here, "medical research" means investigations, experiments and studies to discover, develop, or verify knowledge relating to the causes, diagnosis, treatment, prevention, or control of the physical or mental diseases and impairments of man. For further information, see Regulations section 1.170A-9(c)(2).

Exhibit 2–1A *(continued)*

Schedule D.—Section 509(a)(3) Supporting Organization   N/A

1a Organizations supported by the applicant organization: Name and address of supported organization	**b** Has the supported organization received a ruling or determination letter that it is not a private foundation by reason of section 509(a)(1) or (2)?	
....	☐ Yes	☐ No
....	☐ Yes	☐ No
....	☐ Yes	☐ No
....	☐ Yes	☐ No
....	☐ Yes	☐ No

c If "No" for any of the organizations listed in 1a, explain.

2 Does the organization you support have tax-exempt status under section 501(c)(4), 501(c)(5), or 501(c)(6)? ☐ Yes ☐ No
If "Yes," attach: (a) a copy of its ruling or determination letter, and (b) an analysis of its revenue for the current year and the preceding three years. (Provide the financial data using the formats in Part IV-A (lines 1–13) and Part III (questions 11, 12, and 13).)

3 Does your governing document indicate that the majority of your governing board is elected or appointed by the supported organization(s)? ☐ Yes ☐ No
If "Yes," skip to question 9.
If "No," you must answer questions 4 through 9.

4 Does your governing document indicate the common supervision or control that you and the supported organization(s) share? ☐ Yes ☐ No
If "Yes," give the article and paragraph numbers. If "No," explain.

5 To what extent does (do) the supported organization(s) have a significant voice in your investment policies, the making and timing of grants, and in otherwise directing the use of your income or assets?

6 Does the mentioning of the supported organization(s) in your governing instrument make you a trust that the supported organization(s) can enforce under state law and compel to make an accounting? ☐ Yes ☐ No
If "Yes," explain.

7a What percentage of your income do you pay to each supported organization?

b What is the total annual income of each supported organization?

c How much do you contribute annually to each supported organization?

For more information, see back of Schedule.

■ **46** ■

Exhibit 2–1A *(continued)*

Schedule D.—Section 509(a)(3) Supporting Organization *(Continued)*

8 To what extent do you conduct activities that would otherwise be carried on by the supported organization(s)? Explain why these activities would otherwise be carried on by the supported organization(s).

9 Is the applicant organization controlled directly or indirectly by one or more "disqualified persons" (other than one who is a disqualified person solely because he or she is a manager) or by an organization which is not described in section 509(a)(1) or (2)?   . . . .   ☐ **Yes**   ☐ **No**

If "Yes," explain.

For an explanation of the types of organizations defined in section 509(a)(3) as being excluded from the definition of a private foundation, see Publication 557, Chapter 3.

Line 1.—List each organization that is supported by your organization and indicate in item 1b if the supported organization has received a letter recognizing exempt status as a section 501(c)(3) public charity as defined in section 509(a)(1) or 509(a)(2).

If you answer "No" in 1b to any of the listed organizations, please explain in 1c.

Line 3.—Your governing document may be articles of incorporation, articles of association, constitution, trust indenture, or trust agreement.

Line 9.—For a definition of a "disqualified person," see specific instructions for Part II, line 4d, on page 3 of the application's instructions.

Exhibit 2-1A *(continued)*

Schedule E.—Private Operating Foundation   N/A

	Income Test		Most recent tax year
1a	Adjusted net income, as defined in Regulations section 53.4942(a)-2(d)	1a	
b	Minimum investment return, as defined in Regulations section 53.4942(a)-2(c)	1b	
2	Qualifying distributions:		
a	Amounts (including administrative expenses) paid directly for the active conduct of the activities for which organized and operated under section 501(c)(3) (attach schedule)	2a	
b	Amounts paid to acquire assets to be used (or held for use) directly in carrying out purposes described in section 170(c)(1) or 170(c)(2)(B) (attach schedule)	2b	
c	Amounts set aside for specific projects that are for purposes described in section 170(c)(1) or 170(c)(2)(B) (attach schedule)	2c	
d	**Total** qualifying distributions (add lines 2a, b, and c)	2d	
3	Percentages:		
a	Percentage of qualifying distributions to adjusted net income (divide line 2d by line 1a)	3a	%
b	Percentage of qualifying distributions to minimum investment return (divide line 2d by line 1b) . . . . . (Percentage must be at least 85% for 3a or 3b)	3b	%

	Assets Test		
4	Value of organization's assets used in activities that directly carry out the exempt purposes. Do not include assets held merely for investment or production of income (attach schedule)	4	
5	Value of any stock of a corporation that is controlled by applicant organization and carries out its exempt purposes (attach statement describing corporation)	5	
6	Value of all qualifying assets (add lines 4 and 5)	6	
7	Value of applicant organization's total assets	7	
8	Percentage of qualifying assets to total assets (divide line 6 by line 7—percentage must exceed 65%) . . .	8	%

	Endowment Test		
9	Value of assets not used (or held for use) directly in carrying out exempt purposes:		
a	Monthly average of investment securities at fair market value	9a	
b	Monthly average of cash balances	9b	
c	Fair market value of all other investment property (attach schedule)	9c	
d	**Total** (add lines 9a, b, and c)	9d	
10	Acquisition indebtedness related to line 9 items (attach schedule)	10	
11	Balance (subtract line 10 from line 9d)	11	
12	Multiply line 11 by 3⅓% (⅔ of the percentage for the minimum investment return computation under section 4942(e)). Line 2d above must equal or exceed the result of this computation	12	

	Support Test		
13	Applicant organization's support as defined in section 509(d)	13	
14	Gross investment income as defined in section 509(e)	14	
15	Support for purposes of section 4942(j)(3)(B)(iii) (subtract line 14 from line 13)	15	
16	Support received from the general public, 5 or more exempt organizations, or a combination of these sources (attach schedule)	16	
17	For persons (other than exempt organizations) contributing more than 1% of line 15, enter the total amounts that are more than 1% of line 15	17	
18	Subtract line 17 from line 16	18	
19	Percentage of total support (divide line 18 by line 15—must be at least 85%)	19	%
20	Does line 16 include support from an exempt organization that is more than 25% of the amount of line 15? .	☐ Yes	☐ No

21 Newly created organizations with less than one year's experience: Attach a statement explaining how the organization is planning to satisfy the requirements of section 4942(j)(3) for the income test and one of the supplemental tests during its first year's operation. Include a description of plans and arrangements, press clippings, public announcements, solicitations for funds, etc.

22 Does the amount entered on line 2a include any grants that you made? . . . . ☐ Yes ☐ No
If "Yes," attach a statement explaining how those grants satisfy the criteria for "significant involvement" grants described in section 53.4942(b)-1(b)(2) of the regulations.

For more information, see back of Schedule.

Exhibit 2–1A *(continued)*

If the organization claims to be an operating foundation described in section 4942(j)(3) and—

(a) bases its claim to private operating foundation status on normal and regular operations over a period of years; or

(b) is newly created, set up as a private operating foundation, and has at least one year's experience;

provide the information under the income test and under one of the three supplemental tests (assets, endowment, or support). If the organization does not have at least one year's experience, provide the information called for by line 21. If the organization's private operating foundation status depends on its normal and regular operations as described in (a) above, attach a schedule similar to the one shown on the front of this schedule showing the data in tabular form for the three years preceding the most recent tax year. (See Regulations section 53.4942(b)-1 for additional information before completing the "Income Test" section of this schedule.) Organizations claiming section 4942(j)(5) status must satisfy the income test and the endowment test.

A "private operating foundation" described in section 4942(j)(3) is a private foundation that spends substantially all of the lesser of its adjusted net income (as defined below) or its minimum investment return directly for the active conduct of the activities constituting the purpose or function for which it is organized and operated. The foundation must satisfy the income test under section 4942(j)(3)(A), as modified by Regulations section 53.4942(b)-1, and one of the three supplemental tests: (a) the assets test under section 4942(j)(3)(B)(i); (b) the endowment test under section 4942(j)(3)(B)(ii); or (c) the support test under section 4942(j)(3)(B)(iii).

Certain long-term care facilities described in section 4942(j)(5) are treated as private operating foundations for purposes of section 4942 only.

"Adjusted net income" is the excess of gross income for the tax year over the sum of deductions determined with the modifications described below. Items of gross income from any unrelated trade or business and the deductions directly connected with the unrelated trade or business will be taken into account in computing the organization's adjusted net income:

Income modifications (adjustments to gross income).—

(1) Section 103 (relating to interest on certain governmental obligations) does not apply. Thus, interest that otherwise would have been excluded should be included in gross income.

(2) Except as provided in (3) below, capital gains and losses are taken into account only to the extent of the net short-term gain. Long-term gains and losses will be disregarded.

(3) The gross amount received from the sale or disposition of certain property should be included in gross income to the extent that the acquisition of the property constituted a qualifying distribution under section 4942(g)(1)(B).

(4) Repayments of prior qualifying distributions (as defined in section 4942(g)(1)(A)) will constitute items of gross income.

(5) Any amount set aside under section 4942(g)(2) that has been determined to be "not necessary for the purposes for which it was set aside" will constitute an item of gross income.

Deduction modifications (adjustments to deductions).—

(1) Expenses for the general operation of the organization according to its charitable purposes (as contrasted with expenses for the production or collection of income and management, conservation, or maintenance of income producing property) should not be taken as deductions. If only a portion of the property is used for production of income subject to section 4942 and the remainder is used for general charitable purposes, the expenses connected with that property should be divided according to those purposes and only expenses related to the income producing portion will be allowed as a deduction.

(2) Charitable contributions, deductible under section 170 or 642(c), should not be taken into account as deductions for adjusted net income.

(3) The net operating loss deduction prescribed under section 172 should not be taken into account as a deduction for adjusted net income.

(4) The special deductions for corporations (such as the dividends-received deduction) allowed under sections 241 through 250 should not be taken into account as deductions for adjusted net income.

(5) Depreciation and depletion should be determined in the same manner as under section 4940(c)(3)(B).

Section 265 (relating to the expenses and interest connected with tax-exempt interest) should not be taken into account.

You may find it easier to figure adjusted net income by completing Column (c), Part 1, Form 990-PF, according to the instructions for that form.

An organization that has been held to be a private operating foundation will continue to be such an organization only if it meets the income test and either the assets, endowment, or support test in later years. See Regulations section 53.4942(b) for additional information. No additional request for ruling will be necessary or appropriate for an organization to maintain its status as a private operating foundation. However, data related to the above tests must be submitted with the organization's annual information return, Form 990-PF.

Exhibit 2–1A *(continued)*

Schedule F.—Homes for the Aged or Handicapped   N/A

1   What are the requirements for admission to residency? Explain fully and attach promotional literature and application forms.

2   Does or will the home charge an entrance or founder's fee? . . . . ☐ **Yes**   ☐ **No**
    If "Yes," explain and specify the amount charged.

3   What periodic fees or maintenance charges are or will be required of its residents?

4a What established policy does the home have concerning residents who become unable to pay their regular charges?

 b What arrangements does the home have or will it make with local and Federal welfare units, sponsoring organizations, or others to absorb all or part of the cost of maintaining those residents?

5   What arrangements does or will the home have to provide for the health needs of its residents?

6   In what way are the home's residential facilities designed to meet some combination of the physical, emotional, recreational, social, religious, and similar needs of the aged or handicapped?

7   Provide a description of the home's facilities and specify both the residential capacity of the home and the current number of residents.

8   Attach a sample copy of the contract or agreement the organization makes with or requires of its residents.

For more information, see back of Schedule.

Exhibit 2–1A *(continued)*

Line 1.— Provide the criteria for admission to the home and submit brochures, pamphlets, or other printed material used to inform the public about the home's admissions policy.

Line 2.— Indicate whether the fee charged is an entrance fee or a monthly charge, etc. Also, if the fee is an entrance fee, is it payable in a lump sum or on an installment basis? If no fee, indicate "N/A."

Line 4.— Indicate the organization's policy regarding residents who are unable to pay. Also, indicate whether the organization is subsidized for all or part of the cost of maintaining those residents who are unable to pay.

Line 5.— Indicate whether the organization provides health care to the residents, either directly or indirectly through some continuing arrangement with other organizations, facilities, or health personnel. If no health care is provided, indicate "N/A."

Exhibit 2–1A   *(continued)*

Schedule G.—Child Care Organizations   N/A

1 Is the organization's primary activity the providing of care for children away from their homes? . . . . □ **Yes**   □ **No**

2 How many children is the organization authorized to care for by the state (or local governmental unit) and what was the average attendance during the past 6 months, or the number of months the organization has been in existence if less than 6 months?

3 How many children are currently cared for by the organization?

4 Is substantially all (at least 85%) of the care provided for the purpose of enabling parent(s) to be gainfully employed or to seek employment? . . . . . . □ **Yes**   □ **No**

5 Are the services provided available to the general public? . . . . □ **Yes**   □ **No**
If "No," explain.

6 Indicate the category, or categories, of parents whose children are eligible for your child-care services (check as many as apply):

□   low income parents

□   any working parents (or parents looking for work)

□   anyone with the ability to pay

□   other (explain)

7 Do you operate a school? . . . . □ **Yes**   □ **No**
If "Yes," complete Schedule B.

Instructions

Line 5.— If your services are not available to the general public, indicate the particular group or groups that may utilize your services.

Line 7.— Providing for the care of children away from their homes is an exempt purpose (educational) as described in section 501(c)(3) of the Internal Revenue Code. However, a child care organization is not a school unless it: (1) has the primary function of presenting formal instruction; (2) normally maintains a regular faculty and curriculum; (3) normally has a regular enrolled body of students; and (4) has a place where educational activities are carried on.

Note: There is no page 26.

Exhibit 2-1A *(continued)*

Schedule H.—Organizations Providing Scholarship Benefits, Student Aid, etc., to Individuals   N/A

1a Describe the nature of the scholarship benefit, student aid, etc., including the terms and conditions governing its use, whether a gift, or a loan, and the amount, and how the availability of the scholarship is publicized. If the organization has established or will establish several categories of scholarship benefits, identify each kind of benefit and explain how the organization determines the recipients for each category. Attach a sample copy of any application the organization requires or will require of individuals to be considered for scholarship grants, loans, or similar benefits. (Private foundations that make grants for travel, study, or other similar purposes are required to obtain advance approval of scholarship procedures. See Regulations sections 53.4945-4(c) and (d)).

b If you want this application considered as a request for approval of grant procedures in the event we determine that you are a private foundation, check here . . . . ▶ ☐

c If you checked the box in 1b above, indicate the section(s) that you wish to be considered.

☐ 4945(g)(1)   ☐ 4945(g)(2)   ☐ 4945(g)(3)

2 What limitations or restrictions are there on the class of individuals who are eligible recipients? Specifically explain whether there are, or will be, any restrictions or limitations in the selection procedures based upon race and whether there are, or will be, restrictions or limitations in selection procedures based on the employment status of the prospective recipient or any relative of the prospective recipient. Also indicate the approximate number of eligible individuals.

3 Indicate the number of grants you anticipate making annually . . . . ▶

4 If you base your selections in any way on the employment status of the applicant or any relative of the applicant, indicate whether there is or has been any direct or indirect relationship between the members of the selection committee and the employer. Also indicate whether relatives of the members of the selection committee are possible recipients or have been recipients.

5 Describe any procedures you have for supervising grants (such as obtaining reports or transcripts) that you award, and any procedures you have for taking action if the terms of the grant are violated.

For more information, see back of Schedule.

■ 53 ■

Exhibit 2–1A *(continued)*

Private foundations that make grants for travel, study, or other similar purposes are required to obtain advance approval of their grant scholarship procedures from the Internal Revenue Service. Such grants that are awarded under selection procedures that have not been approved by the Internal Revenue Service are subject to a 10% excise tax under section 4945. (See Regulations sections 53.4945-4(c) and (d).)

If you are requesting advance approval of your grant procedures, the following sections apply to line 1c:

4945(g)(1)— The grant constitutes a scholarship or fellowship grant that meets the provisions of section 117(a) prior to its amendment by the Tax Reform Act of 1986 and is to be used for study at an educational organization (school) described in section 170(b)(1)(A)(ii).

4945(g)(2)— The grant constitutes a prize or award that is subject to the provisions of section 74(b), if the recipient of such a prize or award is selected from the general public.

4945(g)(3)— The purpose of the grant is to achieve a specific objective, produce a report or other similar product, or improve or enhance a literary, artistic, musical, scientific, teaching, or other similar capacity, skill, or talent of the grantee.

Exhibit 2–1A *(continued)*

Form 1023 (Rev. 12-89)   CAMPAIGN TO CLEAN UP AMERICA   44-4444444   Page **29**

Schedule I.—Successors to "For Profit" Institutions   N/A

1 What was the name of the predecessor organization and the nature of its activities?

2 Who were the owners or principal stockholders of the predecessor organization? (If more space is needed, attach schedule.)

Name and address	Share or interest

3 Describe the business or family relationship between the owners or principal stockholders and principal employees of the predecessor organization and the officers, directors, and principal employees of the applicant organization.

4a Attach a copy of the agreement of sale or other contract that sets forth the terms and conditions of sale of the predecessor organization or of its assets to the applicant organization.

  b Attach an appraisal by an independent qualified expert showing the fair market value at the time of sale of the facilities or property interest sold.

5 Has any property or equipment formerly used by the predecessor organization been rented to the applicant organization or will any such property be rented? . . . . □ **Yes**   □ **No**
If "Yes," explain and attach copies of all leases and contracts.

6 Is the organization leasing or will it lease or otherwise make available any space or equipment to the owners, principal stockholders, or principal employees of the predecessor organization? . . . . □ **Yes**   □ **No**
If "Yes," explain and attach a list of these tenants and a copy of the lease for each such tenant.

7 Were any new operating policies initiated as a result of the transfer of assets from a profit-making organization to a nonprofit organization? . . . . □ **Yes**   □ **No**
If "Yes," explain.

Additional Information

A "for profit" institution for purposes of this Schedule includes any organization in which a person may have a proprietary or partnership interest, hold corporate stock, or otherwise exercise an ownership interest. The institution need not have operated for the purpose of making a profit.

Exhibit 2–1A *(continued)*

Form **872-C** (Rev. 12-89)	Department of the Treasury—Internal Revenue Service **Consent Fixing Period of Limitation Upon Assessment of Tax Under Section 4940 of the Internal Revenue Code** (See instructions on reverse side.)	OMB No. 1545-0056 **To be used with Form 1023. Submit in duplicate.**

Under section 6501(c)(4) of the Internal Revenue Code, and as part of a request filed with Form 1023 that the organization named below be treated as a publicly supported organization under section 170(b)(1)(A)(vi) or section 509(a)(2) during an advance ruling period,

CAMPAIGN TO CLEAN UP AMERICA

(Exact legal name of organization as shown in organizing document)
1111 ANY STREET

HOMETOWN, TX 77777

(Number, street, city or town, state, and ZIP code)

} and the

District Director of
Internal Revenue, or
Assistant Commissioner
(Employee Plans and
Exempt Organizations)

Consent and agree that the period for assessing tax (imposed under section 4940 of the Code) for any of the 5 tax years in the advance ruling period will extend 8 years, 4 months, and 15 days beyond the end of the first tax year.

However, if a notice of deficiency in tax for any of these years is sent to the organization before the period expires, the time for making an assessment will be further extended by the number of days the assessment is prohibited, plus 60 days.

Ending date of first tax year ....June 30, 1990..............
(Month, day, and year)

Name of organization (as shown in organizing document) CAMPAIGN TO CLEAN UP AMERICA	Date April 7, 1991

Officer or trustee having authority to sign

Signature ▶

For IRS use only

District Director or Assistant Commissioner (Employee Plans and Exempt Organizations)	Date

By ▶

For Paperwork Reduction Act Notice, see page 1 of the Form 1023 Instructions.

Exhibit 2–1A (*continued*)

You must complete this form and attach it to your application if you checked box (h), (i), or (j) of Part III, question 9, and you have not completed a tax year of at least 8 months.

> For example: If you incorporated May 15 and your year ends December 31, you have completed a tax year of only 7½ months. Therefore, Form 872-C must be completed.

(a) Insert the name of the organization. This must be entered exactly as it is written in the organizing document. Do not use abbreviations unless the organizing document does.

(b) Enter the proper address.

(c) Enter ending date of first tax year.

> For example:
>
> (a) If you were formed on June 15 and you have chosen December 31, as your year end, enter December 31, 19 ....
>
> (b) If you were formed June 15 and have chosen June 30 as your year end, enter June 30, 19 .... In this example your first tax year consists of only 15 days.

(d) The form must be signed by an authorized officer or trustee, generally the President or Treasurer.

(e) Enter the date that the form was signed.

DO NOT MAKE ANY OTHER ENTRIES.

■ 57 ■

Exhibit 2–1A *(continued)*

Activity Code Numbers of Exempt Organizations (select up to three codes which best describe or most accurately identify your purposes, activities, operations or type of organization and enter in block 6, page 1, of the application. Enter first the code which most accurately identifies you.)

Code

Religious Activities
001 Church, synagogue, etc.
002 Association or convention of churches
003 Religious order
004 Church auxiliary
005 Mission
006 Missionary activities
007 Evangelism
008 Religious publishing activities
.... Bookstore (use 918)
.... Genealogical activities (use 094)
029 Other religious activities

Schools, Colleges and Related Activities
030 School, college, trade school, etc.
031 Special school for the blind, handicapped, etc.
032 Nursery school
.... Day care center (use 574)
033 Faculty group
034 Alumni association or group
035 Parent or parent-teachers association
036 Fraternity or sorority
.... Key club (use 323)
037 Other student society or group
038 School or college athletic association
039 Scholarships for children of employees
040 Scholarships (other)
041 Student loans
042 Student housing activities
043 Other student aid
044 Student exchange with foreign country
045 Student operated business
.... Financial support of schools, colleges, etc. (use 602)
.... Achievement prizes or awards (use 914)
.... Student bookstore (use 918)
.... Student travel (use 299)
.... Scientific research (see Scientific Research Activities)
046 Private school
059 Other school related activities

Cultural, Historical or Other Educational Activities
060 Musuem, zoo, planetarium, etc.
061 Library
062 Historical site, records or reenactment
063 Monument
064 Commemorative event (centennial, festival, pageant, etc.)
065 Fair
088 Community theatrical group
089 Singing society or group
090 Cultural performances
091 Art exhibit
092 Literary activities
093 Cultural exchanges with foreign country
094 Genealogical activities
.... Achievement prizes or awards (use 914)
.... Gifts or grants to individuals (use 561)
.... Financial support of cultural organizations (use 602)
119 Other cultural or historical activities

Other Instruction and Training Activities
120 Publishing activities
121 Radio or television broadcasting
122 Producing films
123 Discussion groups, forums, panels, lectures, etc.
124 Study and research (non-scientific)
125 Giving information or opinion (see also Advocacy)
126 Apprentice training
.... Travel tours (use 299)
149 Other instruction and training

Health Services and Related Activities
150 Hospital
151 Hospital auxiliary
152 Nursing or convalescent home
153 Care and housing for the aged (see also 382)
154 Health clinic
155 Rural medical facility
156 Blood bank
157 Cooperative hospital service organization
158 Rescue and emergency service
159 Nurses register or bureau
160 Aid to the handicapped (see also 031)
161 Scientific research (diseases)
162 Other medical research
163 Health insurance (medical, dental, optical, etc.)
164 Prepared group health plan
165 Community health planning
166 Mental health care
167 Group medical practice association
168 In-faculty group practice association
169 Hospital pharmacy, parking facility, food services, etc.
179 Other health services

Scientific Research Activities
180 Contract or sponsored scientific research for industry
181 Scientific research for government
.... Scientific research (diseases) (use 161)
199 Other scientific research activities

Business and Professional Organizations
200 Business promotion (chamber of commerce, business league, etc.)
201 Real estate association
202 Board of trade
203 Regulating business
204 Better Business Bureau
205 Professional association
206 Professional association auxiliary
207 Industry trade shows
208 Convention displays
.... Testing products for public safety (use 905)
209 Research, development and testing
210 Professional athletic league
.... Attracting new industry (use 403)
.... Publishing activities (use 120)
.... Insurance or other benefits for members (see Employee or Membership Benefit Organizations)
211 Underwriting municipal insurance
212 Assigned risk insurance activities
213 Tourist bureau
229 Other business or professional group

Farming and Related Activities
230 Farming
231 Farm bureau
232 Agricultural group
233 Horticultural group
234 Farmers cooperative marketing or purchasing
235 Financing crop operations
.... FFA, FHA, 4-H club, etc. (use 322)
.... Fair (use 065)
236 Dairy herd improvement association
237 Breeders association
249 Other farming and related activities

Mutual Organizations
250 Mutual ditch, irrigation, telephone, electric company or like organization
251 Credit union
252 Reserve funds or insurance for domestic building and loan association, cooperative bank, or mutual savings bank
253 Mutual insurance company
254 Corporation organized under an Act of Congress (see also 904)
.... Farmers cooperative marketing or purchasing (use 234)
.... Cooperative hospital service organization (use 157)
259 Other mutual organization

Employee or Membership Benefit Organizations
260 Fraternal beneficiary society, order, or association
261 Improvement of conditions of workers
262 Association of municipal employees
263 Association of employees
264 Employee or member welfare association
265 Sick, accident, death, or similar benefits
266 Strike benefits
267 Unemployment benefits
268 Pension or retirement benefits
269 Vacation benefits
279 Other services or benefits to members or employees

Sports, Athletic, Recreational and Social Activities
280 Country club
281 Hobby club
282 Dinner club
283 Variety club
284 Dog club
285 Women's club
.... Garden club (use 356)
286 Hunting or fishing club
287 Swimming or tennis club
288 Other sports club
.... Boys Club, Little League, etc. (use 321)
296 Community center
297 Community recreational facilities (park, playground, etc.)
298 Training in sports
299 Travel tours
300 Amateur athletic association
.... School or college athletic association (use 038)
301 Fundraising athletic or sports event
317 Other sports or athletic activities
318 Other recreational activities
319 Other social activities

Youth Activities
320 Boy Scouts, Girl Scouts, etc.
321 Boys Club, Little League, etc.
322 FFA, FHA, 4-H club, etc.
323 Key club
324 YMCA, YWCA, YMHA, etc.
325 Camp
326 Care and housing of children (orphanage, etc.)
327 Prevention of cruelty to children
328 Combat juvenile delinquency
349 Other youth organization or activities

Conservation, Environmental and Beautification Activities
350 Preservation of natural resources (conservation)
351 Combating or preventing pollution (air, water, etc.)
352 Land acquisition for preservation
353 Soil or water conservation
354 Preservation of scenic beauty
.... Litigation (see Litigation and Legal Aid Activities)
.... Combat community deterioration (use 402)
355 Wildlife sanctuary or refuge
356 Garden club
379 Other conservation, environmental or beautification activities

Housing Activities
380 Low-income housing
381 Low and moderate income housing
382 Housing for the aged (see also 153)
.... Nursing or convalescent home (use 152)
.... Student housing (use 042)
.... Orphanage (use 326)
398 Instruction and guidance on housing
399 Other housing activities

Inner City or Community Activities
400 Area development, redevelopment or renewal
.... Housing (see Housing Activities)
401 Homeowners association
402 Other activity aimed at combating community deterioration
403 Attracting new industry or retaining industry in an area
404 Community promotion
.... Community recreational facility (use 297)
.... Community center (use 296)
405 Loans or grants for minority businesses
.... Job training, counseling, or assistance (use 566)
.... Day care center (use 574)
.... Referral service (social agencies) (use 569)
.... Legal aid to indigents (use 462)
406 Crime prevention
407 Voluntary firemen's organization or auxiliary
.... Rescue squad (use 158)
408 Community service organization
429 Other inner city or community benefit activities

Civil Rights Activities
430 Defense of human and civil rights
431 Elimination of prejudice and discrimination (race, religion, sex, national origin, etc.)
432 Lessen neighborhood tensions
449 Other civil rights activities

Litigation and Legal Aid Activities
460 Public interest litigation activities
461 Other litigation or support of litigation
462 Legal aid to indigents
463 Providing bail
465 Plan under IRC section 120

Legislative and Political Activities
480 Propose, support, or oppose legislation
481 Voter information on issues or candidates
482 Voter education (mechanics of registering, voting, etc.)
483 Support, oppose, or rate political candidates
484 Provide facilities or services for political campaign activities
509 Other legislative and political activities

Advocacy
Attempt to influence public opinion concerning:
510 Firearms control
511 Selective Service System
512 National defense policy
513 Weapons systems
514 Government spending
515 Taxes or tax exemption
516 Separation of church and state
517 Government aid to parochial schools
518 U.S. foreign policy
519 U.S. military involvement
520 Pacifism and peace
521 Economic-political system of U.S.
522 Anti-communism
523 Right to work
524 Zoning or rezoning
525 Location of highway or transportation system
526 Rights of criminal defendants
527 Capital punishment
528 Stricter law enforcement
529 Ecology or conservation
530 Protection of consumer interests
531 Medical care service
532 Welfare system
533 Urban renewal
534 Busing students to achieve racial balance
535 Racial integration
536 Use of intoxicating beverage
537 Use of drugs or narcotics
538 Use of tobacco
539 Prohibition of erotica
540 Sex education in public schools
541 Population control
542 Birth control methods
543 Legalized abortion
559 Other matters

Other Activities Directed to Individuals
560 Supplying money, goods or services to the poor
561 Gifts or grants to individuals (other than scholarships)
.... Scholarships for children of employees (use 039)
.... Scholarships (other) (use 040)
.... Student loans (use 041)
562 Other loans to individuals
563 Marriage counseling
564 Family planning
565 Credit counseling and assistance
566 Job training, counseling, or assistance
567 Draft counseling
568 Vocational counseling
569 Referral service (social agencies)
572 Rehabilitating convicts or ex-convicts
573 Rehabilitating alcoholics, drug abusers, compulsive gamblers, etc.
574 Day care center
575 Services for the aged (see also 153 and 382)
.... Training of or aid to the handicapped (see 031 and 160)

Activities Directed to Other Organizations
600 Community Chest, United Way, etc.
601 Booster club
602 Gifts, grants, or loans to other organizations
603 Non-financial services or facilities to other organizations

Other Purposes and Activities
900 Cemetery or burial activities
901 Perpetual care fund (cemetery, columbarium, etc.)
902 Emergency or disaster aid fund
903 Community trust or component
904 Government instrumentality or agency (see also 254)
905 Testing products for public safety
906 Consumer interest group
907 Veterans activities
908 Patriotic activities
909 4947(a)(1) trust
910 Domestic organization with activities outside U.S.
911 Foreign organization
912 Title holding corporation
913 Prevention of cruelty to animals
914 Achievement prizes or awards
915 Erection or maintenance of public building or works
916 Cafeteria, restaurant, snack bar, food services, etc.
917 Thrift shop, retail outlet, etc.
918 Book, gift or supply store
919 Advertising
920 Association of employees
921 Loans or credit reporting
922 Endowment fund or financial services
923 Indians (tribes, cultures, etc.)
924 Traffic or tariff bureau
925 Section 501(c)(1) with 50% deductibility
926 Government instrumentality other than section 501(c)
927 Fundraising
928 4947(a)(2) trust
930 Prepaid legal services plan exempt under IRC section 501(c)(20)
931 Withdrawal liability payment fund
990 Section 501(k) child care organization

*U.S. GOVERNMENT PRINTING OFFICE : 1990 719-026/10851

§ 2.3 SUGGESTIONS FOR COMPLETING FORM 1023

p. 64. *Add after first paragraph of section:*

Except for new Part III, there are few substantive changes to Form 1023. Part III significantly expands and improves public charity classifications. The basic strategies for obtaining IRS approval of exempt status and the explanations for most of the form have not changed. Exhibit 2-1A is a completed version of the new form. The original attachments on pages 80–92 are still valid. The budget on page 93 is now presented on Part IV.

To assist in associating the new form with the original text, Exhibit 2-1B correlates the old and new form. The new part numbers are identified with the book page where the specific answers are discussed. The book's discussion is still relevant for most part. New information in this supplement is identified with a letter and follows the Exhibit. The Exhibit 2–1B also furnishes a reference to other pages of the book that explain why the IRS is requesting the information. This should prove a very useful tool in evaluating proper answers.

The chief improvement in Form 1023 concerns public status. For private foundations, churches, schools, hospitals, supporting organizations, and others completing the schedules on pages 11–25 of the new form, the filing is virtually the same. Those organizations for which the form is particularly helpful are those seeking classification as a publicly supported organization due to their sources of support.

Exhibit 2–1B
CHART TO CORRELATE PARTS/LINES OF NEW/OLD FORM 1023

Old Form	New Form	Discussion on Book Page
Part I, 2	Part I, 2	94
Part I, 4	Part I, 3	95
Part I, 5	Part I, 4	95
Part I, 7	Part I, 6	96
Part II	Part I, 10	10, 23, 96
Part III, 3	Part II, 1	26–38, 99
Part III, 1	Part II, 2	98
Part III, 2	Part II, 3	37, 98, 218, 268–272
Part III, 4a & b	Part II, 4a & b	101, 310–320
Part III, 4c	Part II, 4c	25, 102
Part III, 4d	Part II, 4d	103, 339–344

Exhibit (*continued*)

Old Form	New Form	Discussion on Book Page
Part III, 4e	dropped	104
Part III, 5	Part II, 5	104, § 3.8A
none	Part II, 6 (new)	see § 2.3A
Part III, 6	Part II, 7	104, § 3.5A
Part III, 7a	Part II, 8	105
Part III, 7b	dropped	105
Part III, 8	Part II, 9	107, 268, § 3.8A
Part III, 9	Part II, 11	28–38, 107
Part III, 10	Part II, 10	13, 108, 269, 317
Part III, 11	Part II, 12	109, 294–307
Part III, 11	Part II, 13	25, 286–294
Part III, 12	dropped	
Part III, 13a	Part III, 1	59
Part III, 13b	Part III, 2	62
Part III, 13c	Part III, 3	61
Part III, 13d	Part III, 4	61
Part III, 13e	Part III, 5	see § 2.3B
none	Part III, 6 (new)	see § 2.3C
Part IV, 1	Part III, 7	113, 336–337
Part IV, 2	Part III, 8	114, 363
Part VI, A	Part III, 9 (expanded)	§ 3.5A
Part IV, 3a	Part III, 10	110
none	Part III, 11	114, § 3.5A
Part VI, B, 13a	Part III, 12	110, § 3.5A
Part VI, B, 13b	Part III, 13	110, § 3.5A
Part V	Part IV (two pages)	111, see § 2.3D
none	Schedule A (churches)	27
Schedule A	Schedule B (schools)	35, 231
Schedule D	Schedule C (hospitals)	31, 313–317
Part VI, C	Schedule D (page 19)	§ 3.5A
Part VII	Schedule E (page 21)	114
Schedule E	Schedule F (homes/aged)	32
none	Schedule G (Child Care)	
Schedule B	Schedule H (scholarships)	373–378
Schedule C	Schedule I (successors)	315–316, 348
Schedule F	deleted (litigating)	307
Schedule G	deleted (amateur sports)	36

The new three-page Part III, "Technical Requirements," which replaces old Part IV, "Statement as to Private Foundation Status," is very helpful.

Special Note (New)

There is no page 10 in the new Form 1023.

p. 94.   *Delete first four paragraphs:*
See new comments.

p. 104.   *Add at end of Item 5:*

§ 2.3A   COMMENTS ON NEW FORM 1023, PART II, 6 (NEW)

This question seeks information to determine if the proposed (c)(3) organization has a relationship with another non-(c)(3) entity that creates private inurement or some other prohibited activity. A "yes" answer bodes caution. The last two sections of § 3.8A explore the issues of shared facilities and other costs and must be read in detail if the answer is "yes."

Also see the comments on page 291 regarding a possible relationship between a (c)(3) and a political organization and comments on page 230 regarding the companion page in Form 990.

p. 111.   *Add at end of Item 3b:*

§ 2.3B   COMMENTS ON NEW FORM 1023, PART III, 5 (NEW)

A "no" answer to this question is tantamount to withdrawing the application for exemption and results in the organization being classified as a nonexempt organization. See comments on page 129 for alternatives regarding an adverse determination.

§ 2.3C   COMMENTS ON NEW FORM 1023, PART III, 6 (NEW)

Proper timing is essential. Where the Form 1023 is filed more than fifteen months after the entity is "organized" and relief is not granted under Section 9100, the (c)(3) status is recognized as effective from the date the application is filed. This question addresses the status of the organization prior to the filing. It is highly desirable in such a situation to be classified as a Section 501(c)(4) organization for the initial period before filing.

Although the contribution deduction is lost for any gifts the organization has received (before filing date), at least none of the income will be taxable. See page 39 for comments on similarities between (c)(3)s and (c)(4)s to understand why this temporary classification is possible.

p. 111. *Replace comments for Part V at bottom of page with:*

§ 2.3D COMMENTS ON NEW FORM 1023, PART IV (NEW)

The new financial statement accomplishes three laudable goals, particularly regarding revenues: (1) It provides a financial history on one page; (2) for new organizations, the projected financial information is presented in the same format (prior form asked for an attachment); and (3) it contains the categories of support needed to calculate public status previously reported separately in Part VI. See the instructions for Form 990 on pages 207–215 for explanations of some of the categories.

p. 116. *Replace text of Form 8718: User Fee with:*
The IRS user fee scheduled to expire September 29, 1990 under the sunset provisions was extended by OBRA for five years to October 1, 1995. The IRS obviously didn't expect the fee to lapse because they announced increased fees in February 1990. According to Rev. Proc. 90-17,[6] the charges for submitting Applications for Exemption, effective September 30, 1990, are as follows:

Organizations with gross receipts averaging not more than $10,000 annually	$ 150
Gross annual receipts exceed $10,000	$ 375
Group Exemption	$ 500
Final letter of termination of private foundation status	$ 200

[6] Rev. Proc. 90-17, 1990-12 I.R.B. 9.

Note Form 1023 issued by the IRS does not contain Form 8718, User Fee, which must be attached to the form for approval.

§ 2.4 NEGOTIATING WITH THE IRS FOR A POSITIVE ANSWER

* **p. 118.** *Add after third paragraph:*
The processing of an application for exemption submitted to a Key District Office is graphically portrayed in Exhibit 2–3A, a chart prepared by Jeanne S. Gessay, Chief of Exempt Organizations Rulings Branch II of the IRS National Office in Washington, DC.

§ 2.5 RELIANCE ON DETERMINATION LETTER

p. 130. *Replace first full paragraph with:*
A critical question for givers and grant makers, particularly private foundations, is whether the exempt status of an organization is intact. One cannot necessarily rely on the original determination letter. Does it make any difference if the organization has started new projects? Has exempt status been revoked? Has a publicly supported organization become a private foundation? How can one find out? What can the contributor do to independently verify an organization's current exempt status?

Revocation of exemption is reported, as a general rule, in the "Deletions List" of the weekly Internal Revenue Bulletin. *Publication 78*, Cumulative List of Organizations Described in Section 170 (C) of the Internal Revenue Code of 1986, issued annually with two biannual updates, lists qualifying organizations according to the IRS master file. Until the IRS communicates notice of revocation to the public, contributors are entitled to rely upon the determination letter.[7] Where the IRS failed to publish such notice when it revoked a school's exemption, the Tax Court ruled that omission of the school's name from *Publication 78* was sufficient notice.[8]

---

[7] Rev. Proc. 82-39, 1982-27 I.R.B. 18., and Treas. Reg. § 1.170A.9(e)(5).
[8] *Estate of Sally H. Clopton*, 93 T.C. 25 (1989).

Exhibit 2–3A

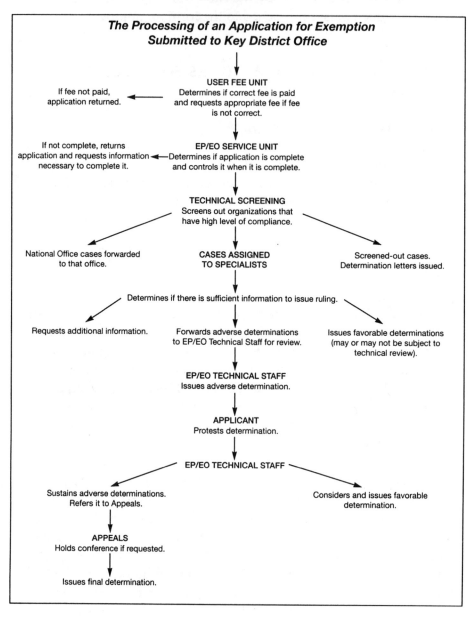

The Processing of an Application for Exemption Submitted to Key District Office

USER FEE UNIT
Determines if correct fee is paid and requests appropriate fee if fee is not correct.

If fee not paid, application returned.

EP/EO SERVICE UNIT
Determines if application is complete and controls it when it is complete.

If not complete, returns application and requests information necessary to complete it.

TECHNICAL SCREENING
Screens out organizations that have high level of compliance.

National Office cases forwarded to that office.

CASES ASSIGNED TO SPECIALISTS

Screened-out cases. Determination letters issued.

Determines if there is sufficient information to issue ruling.

Requests additional information.

Forwards adverse determinations to EP/EO Technical Staff for review.

Issues favorable determinations (may or may not be subject to technical review).

EP/EO TECHNICAL STAFF
Issues adverse determination.

APPLICANT
Protests determination.

EP/EO TECHNICAL STAFF

Sustains adverse determinations. Refers it to Appeals.

Considers and issues favorable determination.

APPEALS
Holds conference if requested.

Issues final determination.

For determinations issued by the Dallas Key District Office, there is a simpler way to find answers. By calling the taxpayer information line (214-767-3526), the current status of an organization, according to the IRS master file, can be verified over the phone. Presumably all Key District Offices can furnish similar information.

It is important to state that the reliance cushion, however, is different for insiders or donors who are in a position to be aware of organizational changes. The change in status is effective for them retroactively to the time the change occurred.

This raises another important issue: What is IRS policy concerning those organizations not included in the publication, despite the fact that they are exempt? Automatically excluded from the book are organizations not filing annual Form 990s (for two years), such as churches and their affiliates and charities whose annual gross revenue is under $25,000. Individuals and organizations must complete a thorough investigation of a proposed grant recipient's tax status and cannot rely totally upon *Publication 78.* In G.C.M. 39809, the IRS reinforced its policy that omission from the publication is sufficient notice of loss of exemption. The omission of nonfilers will continue and the burden to prove exemption on those organization's behalf remains.

See § 3.11A for consequences to donors and tax filing status of an organization that loses its exemption.

p. 130. *Add after fifth full paragraph:*

It is important to emphasize the temporary nature of an *advanced* determination for two different reasons. As discussed, contributors to an organization must be alert to ascertain the current status of an organization's exempt status. The second and more critical reason in terms of timing is the report due five years after the initial determination is received.

In their report entitled *"Tax Administration: IRS Can Improve Its Process of Recognizing Tax-Exempt Organizations* (GAO/GGD-90-55), the GAO suggests the IRS expand its advance ruling followups to include consideration of activities. At the present time, a newly recognized publicly supported organization reports back to the Key District Office at the end of its first five years of operation. The report focuses only on sources of support to allow the IRS to verify that the organization has received its revenues from public sources. (See

§ 3.5A for discussion of public charity support characteristics.) If the amounts of contributions or exempt function revenues are sufficient, the IRS issues a definitive or permanent ruling. Failure to report causes a public charity to be reclassified as a private foundation.

In its reports, the GAO comments it regrets the fact that the IRS makes no effort to look at the manner in which the charities use their support and recommends the advance ruling process be expanded to include a review of activities. The GAO recommended "the expenditures data as well as revenue data could provide IRS insight into whether the organization is fulfilling its exempt purpose and whether there are other potential issues, such as private inurement or unreported unrelated business income."

§ 2.6   REPORTING BACK TO THE KEY DISTRICT

p. 132.   *Add at the end of section:*
The procedures described in this section concern reporting changes to the IRS after a change has already occurred. In terms of the IRS procedures, it is important to distinguish between gaining approval in advance of the change rather than sanction for a fait acccompli.

Once a change has occurred in the form of organization or a major new activity is undertaken, the organization chooses the best method to inform the IRS. (See the checklist at Exhibit 2–7 and discussion in § 2.6.) Such action is taken where the tax laws are clear and established precedents exist and there is little, or no, doubt that the change is acceptable. There may be, however, proposed changes about which the organization wishes advanced approval for the change because there is a lack of published rulings or other authoritative opinions on the subject.

The procedure for obtaining sanction for prospective changes is to request a "ruling" from the Assistant Commissioner for Employee Plans and Exempt Organizations in the IRS National Office. Where significant funds are involved or the disapproval of the action would mean the organization could lose its exemption, filing of a ruling request may be warranted. A decision to request a ruling is made in view of the cost and time frame of the process. As of March 31, 1990, the user fee is $1,250 ($500 for organizations whose gross receipts are under $150,000) according to Rev. Proc. 90-17.[9] The guidelines for seeking a ruling were updated in Rev. Proc. 91-4.[10]

See § 3.7 for guidance on changing tax reporting methods. Permission to change the EOS tax accounting methods or the fiscal reporting year is obtained from the District Director rather than the Key District Office.

*   The guidelines for seeking technical advice were updated in Rev. Proc. 91-5.[11]

§ 2.7 OTHER EXEMPTIONS

p. 132. *Add after the fourth full paragraph:*
There have been two significant cases to be considered in evaluating eligibility for exemption from local sales taxes. The Supreme Court decided in *Jimmy Swaggart Ministries v. Board of Equalization of California*[12] that a sales tax could be imposed upon the sale of religious articles where it is equally imposed on other nonprofit organizations. The arguments focused primarily upon the separation of church and state and contravening the First Amendment protecting the free exercise of religion.

In *Texas Monthly, Inc. v. Bullock* (Comptroller of State of Texas) in 1989, the Supreme Court held state sales tax exemption for religious publications violated the establishment clause of the First Amendment where the religious organizations are the only beneficiaries of the exemption.

p. 132. *Add at the end of section:*
YWCAs and YMCAs have faced challenges to their local property tax exemptions in California (Supreme Court of Alameda County ruled in favor of the Y) and Oregon (State Supreme Court ruled against two Portland Ys). The primary issue has been the level of free services furnished to the needy. In Utah, a hospital system conglomerate's local property tax exemption was revoked.

---

[9] Rev. Proc. 90-17, 1990-12, I.R.B. 9.
[10] Rev. Proc. 91-4, 1991-2, I.R.B. 10.
[11] Rev. Proc 91-5, 1991-4, I.R.B. 44.
[12] January 17, 1990.

§ 2.8   FORM 1024: FOR EOs OTHER THAN 501(c)(3)s

p. 135.   *Add after the second full paragraph:*

A revised version of Form 1024 was issued in December, 1989, and again in September, 1990. The changes are minimal, therefore the revised version is not included in this supplement. The financial data has been improved (similar to the 1023) to allow submission of either actual operation information for existing organizations or the required two-year budget for a newly formed organization.

The stringent new disclosure requirements outlined on the Annual Tax Compliance Checklist on pp. 180–181 are scrutinized with a new question. Brochures, pamphlets, newsletters, journals, or similar printed materials must be attached in response to new Question 16. Questions 12 and 13 are eliminated. In Question 5 (new 3) annual compensation for officers and directors is now requested.

Maintaining Exempt Status

* **p. 163.** *Add new checklist (see pp. 70–71).*

CHECKLIST (NEW)
ANNUAL TAX COMPLIANCE—501(c)(3)s

p. 173. *Add items 3 and 4 under Group Exemptions:*

3. For parent: At least 90 days before close of fiscal year, file annual report of subsidiary changes. _____

4. For subsidiaries: In time to allow the parent to timely file annual group member changes, furnish parent the following: _____

   a. Changes in name or address. _____

   b. Notice of withdrawal as member of group. _____

   c. Intention to become new member of group (furnish organizational documents for filing with IRS). _____

   d. Description of changes in purpose, method of operations, or other "substantial" changes in activities. _____

p. 181. *Add items 3 and 4 under Group Exemptions:*

3. Same as above for page 173.

4. Same as above for page 173.

CHECKLIST (NEW)
EXEMPT ORGANIZATION—SHORT FORM FOR
ANNUAL TAX COMPLIANCE

Organizational Test

1. Have all exemptions been applied for in timely manner?

    a. Federal final determination received. _____

    b. State franchise, income, sales, or other exemptions. _____

    c. Local property taxes. _____

2. Were there changes to charter, bylaws, or purposes? _____

Operational Test

1. Were there any insider transactions causing private inurement? _____

2. Are activities in furtherance of exempt purposes?

    a. Started new activities to report to IRS? _____

    b. Are files maintained to document nature of activities? _____

    c. If EO lobbies, should Form 5768 be filed? _____

    d. Any political activity? _____

    e. Is there excessive unrelated business income? _____

    f. Is payroll tax withholding required? _____

3. Are exempt disbursements sufficient for commensurate test? _____

4. Are fund balances excessive? _____

Filing Requirements

1. Form 990 required? And if so, can and should EZ be filed? _____

2. Is Form 99T required? (complete UBI checklist). _____

3. Are payroll and information returns filed? (complete checklist).   _____

4. Should extension of time to file be requested?   _____

5. Has change of accounting method occurred?   _____

6. Should tax filing year be changed?   _____

7. Is Form 4720 required for excise taxes?   _____

8. Is Form 8283 or 8282 due for property gifts received?   _____

9. Do fund solicitations reveal FMV or nondeductibility (non c-3s) of benefits to donors?   _____

10. Are Forms 990 and 1023 made available for public inspection?   _____

11. If EO is part of a group, should group exemption be obtained?   _____

12. Has there been an IRS exam? Changes to consider?   _____

13. Is there a signed engagement letter in the file?   _____

14. If PF, complete private foundation checklist.   _____

15. If social club, complete (c)(7) checklist.   _____

Social Clubs

1. Can the organization meet the 35/15 gross revenue tests? _____

   a. No more than 35 percent of receipts from nonmember sources. _____

   b. No more than 15 percent of total use of club facilities and services by general public. _____

2. Does the club lose money on its provision of nonmember services? _____

   a. Do accounting records allow identification of direct and indirect costs? _____

   b. Are fixed club expenses charged against nonmember income? (See *Portland Golf Club* case.) _____

* **p. 182.** *Insert new checklist item:*
   1. f. Is a signed Form W-9 on file for all independent contractor withholding exemptions? (Exhibit 3–1A) _____

* **p. 183.** *Insert new checklist items:*

9. Verify timely filing of the following IRS reports: _____

    g. Form W-2G, Prizes and awards and withholding. _____

    h. Form W-2P, Statement of Recipients of Pensions. _____

* **p. 189.** *Add after item 5:*

* **§ 3.1A EMPLOYMENT TAXES (NEW)**

Employment taxes and associated payroll costs, such as workers' compensation and health insurance, equal to between 10 to 30% of an organization's payroll and represents a substantial expense to most EOs. Accordingly, there is always the temptation to classify a worker as an independent contractor to avoid such costs.

Change in IRS Examination Policy

Until 1983, exempt organizations were exempt from social security taxes and their employees were only eligible if the organization made an election to participate in the system. Until 1989, the IRS Exempt Organization examiners had no authority to look at employment taxes. For both of these reasons, EOs could ignore the complexities of employment taxes until recently when the IRS announced its intention to emphasize employment tax issues.

Since 1978, the IRS' hands have been tied by a Congressional mandate providing a safe harbor that prevents IRS reclassification of workers for an entity that uses some reasonable basis for its policy and files information returns reporting compensation to nonemployees. The organization is presumed to be correct if it was relying upon IRS precedent, long-standing industry practice, or a prior IRS audit. EOs generally have operated under this safe harbor. However, the General Accounting Office and the Treasury are actively looking for ways to enhance collections of income taxes from independent contractors and new legislation and/or new IRS pronouncements should be expected.

Definition of Employee vs. Independent Contractor

The distinction between an employee and independent contractor is a factual question based on common law requiring a detailed analysis in many cases. The case law and rulings provide some guidance and the IRS has developed a twenty-factor test.[1] Specific criteria have been developed by the courts and the IRS as reflected in Exhibit 3–1, *Employee Versus Independent Contractor Status.* There are a variety of complex factors involved.

Employees typically are subject to tighter controls by the employer: hours of work are regular and specified; place of work is the employer's; compensation is regular and continuing; and tools, training, and work supplies are normally furnished by the employer among

---

[1] Rev. Rul. 87-41, 1987-1 C.B. 296, Treas. Reg. § 31.3401(c)-1(a) and (d), and *Revival of the Independent Contractor Issue,* Tax Division of American Institute of Certified Public Accountants, September, 1991.

other benefits and advantages. Employees are given paid vacations and accrue pension and sick pay benefits and generally are thought to have a more secure position.

The term "contract worker" misleads many exempts. Typically, workers hired on a part time or temporary basis are given this title and too often not treated as employees partly because they do not possess or experience many of the advantages of employees. Nonetheless, the fact that a worker is not hired for a permanent position does not determine their status as an employee and in most cases such workers are employees subject to withholding.

Independent contractors, on the other hand, work when they please, use their own tools, have independent professional standing, and bear a risk of loss if the job is not completed satisfactorily or within the prescribed time. The CPA, the computer consultant, the fund-raising advisor, and the consulting psychologist are typical examples of independent workers. No vacation or sick pay is provided and the engagement has a limited time period for a specific task.

Form SS-8 (Exhibit 3–1A) (pp. 81–84) is to be used to determine whether a worker can be classified as independent. The form's length and the variety of criteria developed by the IRS indicates the subjective nature of the distinction and the difficulty that may occur in identifying the proper category for a worker.

For those persons classified as independent contractors, an organization must minimally have three important documents in the files to evidence the arrangement and prove the person is not an employee; they are:

- A contract or other type of engagement letter with the contractor describing the respective responsibilities and terms of the contract, including three important elements:

  1. Engaging company essentially does not control the work product of the independent contractor.

  2. The contractor cannot be fired as long as the work is performed and the obligations met.

  3. Contractor has the right to hire and fire assistants.

- A signed Form W-9, *Request for Taxpayer Identification Number and Certification,* (Exhibit 3–1B) (pp. 85–86) must be obtained to show that the contractor claims exemption from withhold-ing and that the organization is therefore not responsible to backup withholding.

- An invoice or other billing issued on a periodic basis that evi-dences the independence of the contractor. The billing should appear professional and support the organization's position that the worker is independent.

Reporting Requirements

Whether paid to employees, individual contractors, or individual grant recipients, almost all payments made by an exempt organization to individuals or unincorporated entities are reportable to the IRS. An-nual W-2 Forms are filed for employees. Forms 1099, also called infor-mation returns, are filed for most other payments to independent contractors and other nonemployees.

The penalty for failure to file an information return is $50. How-ever, if the IRS determines that a contractor should have been classi-fied as an employee, all employment taxes that would have been payable if the worker had been classed as an employee, plus interest and penalties, would be due.

Fellowships and Scholarship Grants and Awards

Although it seems incongruous and not in keeping with the motiva-tion for making grants to individuals, certain individual grants may need to be reported to the IRS on the federal information returns, Form 1099 or Form W-2 and taxes withheld as outlined below.

- *Tuition and fees:* That portion of a scholarship grant paid for tuition, books, fees, supplies and equipment required for en-rollment in an educational institution is not taxable to the recipient and are not reportable by the organization to the IRS. Such payments are called "Qualified Scholarship" payments by Section 117 and are specifically excluded by the code from gross income of a person that is a candidate for a degree.

- *Room and board:* Payments for room, board, and travel and any other expense is includable in income after the 1986 Tax Reform Act. For what appear to be inexplicable reasons, however, such taxable payments are not reported as income to the IRS.

The 1990 instructions to Form 1099 clearly states, "DO NOT use this form to report scholarship or fellowship grants." They follow by saying "Other taxable scholarship or fellowship payments are not required to be reported by you to IRS on any form. See Notice 87-13, 1987-17, I.R.B. 13, for more information."

Notice 87-13 concurs with the instructions and says the IRS "intends to promulgate regulations on the matter." To date no such regulation has been written.

- *Teaching fellowships:* Scholarships or fellowships paid to recipients with the condition that they teach, perform research, or other services for the institution granting the scholarship do earn taxable income according to Section 117(c). Such income is considered wages and reportable on Form W-2. Income tax withholding is required although students are eligible to claim a student exemption. Social security taxes are likewise due to be withheld, matched, and paid unless the institution is a state or federal agency that does not participate in the social security system.

- *Foreign grant recipients:* For foreign recipients, the IRS has taken the position that all payments made by U.S. grantors to persons outside the United States must be treated as U.S. based income, subject to the 20% withholding. Accordingly, based upon currently prevailing rules for foreign based individuals, the backup withholding rules described next will apply.[2] A broad range of grantmaking organizations are lobbying to overturn this ruling.

[2] Rev. Rul. 89-67, superseding Rev. Rul. 66-292.

Ordained Ministers

Duly ordained ministers of a church hold a special place in the employment tax procedures because the clergy of some sects take vows of poverty and as a matter of religious conscience take no compensation for their work. The procedures have also evolved in respect of a need to maintain separation of church and state. Therefore, ministers are exempt from income and social security tax withholding and are not treated as employees. The income may or may not be taxable, however, under an array of provisions that apply as follows:

- *Income tax:* Any amounts paid as compensation for services are subject to income tax the same as other individual taxpayers. The income tax liability, however, is paid individually by the minister through the estimated income tax system and the church reports the compensation on Form 1099. The minister can voluntarily have income tax withheld, but not social security tax.

- *Housing allowances:* Amounts designated by the church as housing allowance are not taxable under Section 107 for income tax purposes but are subject to self-employment tax (unless the minister is conscientiously objecting—see below). The taxable amount is equal to the fair rental value of housing (including utilities and other costs).

- *Self employment tax:* A minister is subject to the self-employment tax, except for the following persons:

  — Members of a religious order whose members have taken vows of poverty according to Section 1402(c).

  — Duly ordained ministers who have not taken a vow of poverty but make an individual election out of the social security system on Form 4361 (Exhibit 3–1C). A statement indicating he/she is opposed by conscience or religious principle to the acceptance of any public insurance and is so informing his/her church must be signed.

  — Clergy members of a church or church-controlled organizations that itself as a whole makes the election for its employees to be exempt from social security coverage pursuant to Section 3121(w). This exemption only applies, however, to remuneration of less than $100 per year and generally applies to vow of poverty situations.

Conscientious Objectors

Religious organizations, peace groups, and other types of exempt organizations employ or engage individuals other than their ministers who are nonprofit-minded and protest payment of federal income taxes for spiritual reasons. These conscientious objectors have traditionally protested moneys allocated to armaments and harm to human beings caused by wars and abortions. How does the organization that is asked to not levy taxes against such an employee respond? What is the responsibility of the organization to the IRS?

The Quakers provided some answers to the questions as they faced a district court in Pennsylvania in December, 1990. The judges decided that the collection of taxes applied to all citizens equally across the board and did not specifically regulate religious practice or beliefs. The church was required to withhold the full amount of taxes from regular employees' wages. Due to their exercise of religious freedom, however, the court imposed no penalties upon the church for failure to withhold the taxes in question.[3]

Backup Withholding

A "backup withholding" system allows the U.S. Treasury to collect funds upfront from independent contractors who potentially will not pay their taxes. Form W-9, *Request for Taxpayer Identification Number and Certification*, (Exhibit 3–1B) is furnished by organizations to payment recipients to request their social security number and to claim exemption from backup withholding. Under the same system used by financial institutions, such as banks and brokers, to ask individuals to verify their federal identification numbers, exempt organizations are subject to backup withholding rules.

[3] *United States v. Philadelphia Yearly Meeting, Religious Society of Friends*, No. 88-6386 (E.D.) Pa. Dec., 19901.

Unless the organization receives a correct social security number from nonemployees receiving payments for services and individuals receiving taxable grant or fellowship payments, income tax must be withheld from the payments. Absent completion of Form W-9 and the certificate that withholding is not required or where there is some reason to believe the social security number furnished is incorrect, a flat 20% of the amounts paid must be withheld and remitted. If the individual is unable or fails to pay the withholding, the exempt must do so.

Payroll Depository Requirements

Another aspect of the employment tax question is the temptation sometimes faced by charities with tight cash flow to pay the employees the net amount (salary less taxes) and use the tax money to pay the rent or some other pressing expense. Taxes withheld are due to be deposited in as few as three days from the date wages are paid. The checklist on pages 182–185 can be used to verify timeliness and compliance.

The amounts withheld from an employee's salary are held in trust on behalf of the workers. The moneys don't belong to the organization. The penalties for failure to pay over such taxes are steep and the organization's board members are held ultimately responsible for payment of the taxes if the organization is unable to do so. The first question the examiner will ask and all board members should ask themselves is whether the employee's withheld taxes have been matched and deposited in a timely fashion.

Other Withholding Requirements

Income taxes are imposed on gambling winnings, including prizes of all sorts won in a raffle, sweepstakes, lottery, or other contest. The rules for exempts are the same as those applying to nonexempts.[4] A serious trap for the unsuspecting exempt lurks in the requirement that a 20% withholding requirement is placed upon an organization

[4] Section 3402.

(exempt or nonexempt) awarding any prize with a value in excess of $1000 and Form W-2G is due to be filed reporting the winnings.

Cash Prizes

In the case of a cash prize, the organization must withhold the tax liability from the prize and make a net payment. For example, $200 would be withheld from a $1000 prize resulting in a $800 cash payment. If the organization pays the recipient the full $1000 without withholding the $200 tax, the organization still has to pay the tax. Unless the cash is collected up front in such a case, the reported prize is increased by the imputed compensation resulting from the organization's payment of the winner's tax liability. The amount is calculated under an algebraic formula found in the regulations.[5]

Noncash Prizes

Cars, trips, paintings, or other tangible merchandise won as prizes are also taxed and income tax must be withheld if the value exceeds $1000. The value is equal to the amount a "willing buyer would pay a willing seller in the normal marketplace in which such goods are sold." The car donated to the charity auction by the car dealer is not valued at the dealer cost, but instead at the price the dealer normally sells the car.

The charity should require the winner of a prize having a value which exceeds $1000 to deposit 20% of the prize's value with the awarding organization before release of the prizes. The organization is again obligated to pay taxes as described under cash prizes whether or not the prize winner furnishes the cash.

Free admission, tuition, or other valuable services must also be valued with income taxes paid as described above. A private school conducting a raffle to award a year of free tuition to a parent is faced with diluting the gift by requiring the parent to pay the 20% tax or increasing its fund-raising budget by the amount of tax it must pay on behalf of the winner.

[5] Treas. Reg. § 31.3402(q)-1(d).

Exhibit 3–1A

Form **SS-8**
(Rev. October 1990)
Department of the Treasury
Internal Revenue Service

Determination of Employee Work Status
for Purposes of Federal Employment Taxes
and Income Tax Withholding

OMB No. 1545-0004
Expires 10-31-93

Paperwork Reduction Act Notice.—We ask for the information on this form to carry out the Internal Revenue laws of the United States. You are required to give us this information. We need it to ensure that you are complying with these laws and to allow us to figure and collect the right amount of tax.

The time needed to complete and file this form will vary depending on individual circumstances. The estimated average time is: **recordkeeping,** 34 hrs., 41 min., **learning about the law or the form,** 6 min. and **preparing and sending the form to IRS,** 40 min. If you have comments concerning the accuracy of these time estimates or suggestions for making this form more simple, we would be happy to hear from you. You can write to both the **Internal Revenue Service,** Washington, DC 20024, Attention: IRS Reports Clearance Officer, T:FP, and the **Office of Management and Budget,** Paperwork Reduction Project (1545-0004), Washington, DC 20503. **DO NOT** send the tax form to either of these offices. Instead, see the instructions for information on where to file.

Instructions

This form should be completed carefully. If the firm is completing the form, it should be completed for **ONE** individual who is representative of the class of workers whose status is in question.

If a written determination is desired for more than one class of workers, a separate Form SS-8 should be completed for one worker from each class whose status is typical of that class. A written determination for any worker will apply to other workers of the same class if the facts are not materially different from those of the worker whose status was ruled upon.

Please return Form SS-8 to the Internal Revenue Service office that provided the form. If the Internal Revenue Service did not ask you to complete this form but you wish a determination on whether a worker is an employee, file Form SS-8 with your District Director.

Caution: *Form SS-8 is **not** a claim for refund of social security tax or Federal income tax withholding. Also, a determination that an individual is an employee does not necessarily reduce any current or prior tax liability.*

Name of firm (or person) for whom the worker performed services

Name of worker

Address of firm (include street address, apt. or suite no., city, state, and ZIP code)

Address of worker (include street address, apt. or suite no., city, state, and ZIP code)

Trade name

Telephone number

Worker's social security number

Telephone number

Firm's taxpayer identification number

Check type of firm:

☐ **Individual** ☐ **Partnership** ☐ **Corporation** ☐ **Other** (specify) ▶

This form is being completed by: ☐ **FIRM** ☐ **WORKER**

If the form is being completed by the worker, do you object to disclosing your name or the information on this form to the firm? . . . . ☐ **Yes** ☐ **No**

(If your answer is "Yes," we cannot furnish you a determination on the basis of this form. You may write to your District Director for further information. **Do not complete the rest of the form, unless the IRS requests it.**)

All items must be answered or marked "Unknown" or "Not Applicable" (NA). **If you need more space, attach another sheet.** This form is designed to cover many work activities, so some of the questions may not pertain to you.

Total number of workers in this class (if more than one, please see item 19) ▶ --

This information is about services performed by the worker from ▶ ----------------------- to ----------------------
                                                                                    (Month, day, year)   (Month, day, year)

What was the first date on which the worker performed services of any kind for the firm? ▶ --------------------------
                                                                                                                      (Month, day, year)

Is the worker still performing services for the firm? . . . . ☐ **Yes** ☐ **No**

If "No," what was the date of termination? ▶ --
                                                                          (Month, day, year)

In which IRS district are you located? --

1a Describe the firm's business --
----

b Describe the work done by the worker --

2a If the work is done under a written agreement between the firm and the worker, attach a copy.

b If the agreement is not in writing, describe the terms and conditions of the work arrangement -----------------
----

Form **SS-8** (Rev. 10-90)

Exhibit 3–1A (*continued*)

Form SS-8 (Rev. 10–90)   Page **2**

c If the actual working arrangement differs in any way from the agreement, explain the differences and why they occur . . . .

....

....

3a Is the worker given training by the firm? . . . . □ **Yes**   □ **No**

    If "Yes":

        What kind? ....

        How often? ....

b Is the worker given instructions in the way the work is to be done? . . . . □ **Yes**   □ **No**

    If "Yes," give specific examples. ....

c Attach samples of any written instructions or procedures.

d Does the firm have the right to change the methods used by the worker or direct that person on how to do the work?   □ **Yes**   □ **No**

    Explain your answer ....

    ....

e Does the operation of the firm's business require that the worker be supervised or controlled in the performance of

    the service? . . . . □ **Yes**   □ **No**

    Explain your answer ....

    ....

4a The firm engages the worker:

    □ To perform and complete a particular job only

    □ To work at a job for an indefinite period of time

    □ Other (explain) ....

b Is the worker required to follow a routine or a schedule established by the firm? . . . . □ **Yes**   □ **No**

    If "Yes," what is the routine or schedule? ....

    ....

    ....

c Does the worker report to the firm or its representative? . . . . □ **Yes**   □ **No**

    If "Yes":

        How often? ....

        For what purpose? ....

        In what manner (in person, in writing, by telephone, etc.)? ....

        Attach copies of report forms used in reporting to the firm.

d Does the worker furnish a time record to the firm? . . . . □ **Yes**   □ **No**

    If "Yes," attach copies of time records.

5a State the kind and value of tools and equipment furnished by:

    The firm ....

    ....

    The worker ....

b State the kind and value of supplies and materials furnished by:

    The firm ....

    ....

    The worker ....

c What expenses are incurred by the worker in the performance of services for the firm?

    ....

d Does the firm reimburse the worker for any expenses? . . . . □ **Yes**   □ **No**

    If "Yes," specify the reimbursed expenses ....

    ....

6a Will the worker perform the services personally? . . . . □ **Yes**   □ **No**

b Does the worker have helpers? . . . . □ **Yes**   □ **No**

    If "Yes": Are the helpers hired by: □ Firm   □ Worker

    If hired by the worker, is the firm's approval necessary? . . . . □ **Yes**   □ **No**

    Who pays the helpers? □ Firm   □ Worker

    Are social security taxes and Federal income tax withheld from the helpers' wages? . . . . □ **Yes**   □ **No**

    If "Yes": Who reports and pays these taxes? □ Firm   □ Worker

    Who reports the helpers' incomes to the Internal Revenue Service?   □ Firm   □ Worker

    If the worker pays the helpers, does the firm repay the worker? . . . . □ **Yes**   □ **No**

    What services do the helpers perform? ....

■ **82** ■

Exhibit 3–1A *(continued)*

Form SS-8 (Rev. 10-90)   Page **3**

7 At what location are the services performed? ☐ Firm's   ☐ Worker's   ☐ Other (specify) ....

8a Type of pay worker receives:

    ☐ Salary   ☐ Commission   ☐ Hourly wage   ☐ Piecework   ☐ Lump sum   ☐ Other (specify) ....

  b Does the firm guarantee a minimum amount of pay to the worker? . . . . ☐ **Yes** ☐ **No**

  c Does the firm allow the worker a drawing account or advances against pay? . . . . ☐ **Yes** ☐ **No**

    If "Yes": Is the worker paid such advances on a regular basis?   . . . . ☐ **Yes** ☐ **No**

  d How does the worker repay such advances? ....

9a Is the worker eligible for a pension, bonuses, paid vacations, sick pay, etc.? . . . . ☐ **Yes** ☐ **No**

    If "Yes," specify ....

  b Does the firm carry workmen's compensation insurance on the worker? . . . . ☐ **Yes** ☐ **No**

  c Does the firm deduct social security tax from amounts paid the worker? . . . . ☐ **Yes** ☐ **No**

  d Does the firm deduct Federal income taxes from amounts paid the worker? . . . . ☐ **Yes** ☐ **No**

  e How does the firm report the worker's income to the Internal Revenue Service?

    ☐ Form W-2   ☐ Form 1099   ☐ Does not report   ☐ Other (specify) ....

  f Does the firm bond the worker? . . . . ☐ **Yes** ☐ **No**

10a Approximately how many hours a day does the worker perform services for the firm? ....

  b Does the worker perform similar services for others? . . . . ☐ **Yes** ☐ **No** ☐ **Unknown**

    If "Yes": Are these services performed on a daily basis for other firms? . . . . ☐ **Yes** ☐ **No** ☐ **Unknown**

    Percentage of time spent in performing these services for:

    This firm ....%   Other firms...........%   ☐ **Unknown**

    Does the firm have priority on the worker's time? . . . . ☐ **Yes** ☐ **No**

    If "No," explain...

  c Is the worker prohibited from competing with the firm either while performing services or during any later period? . . ☐ **Yes** ☐ **No**

11a Can the firm discharge the worker at any time without incurring a liability? . . . . ☐ **Yes** ☐ **No**

    If "No," explain...

  b Can the worker terminate the services at any time without incurring a liability? . . . . ☐ **Yes** ☐ **No**

    If "No," explain...

12a Does the worker perform services for the firm under:

    ☐ The firm's business name   ☐ The worker's own business name   ☐ Other (specify) ....

  b Does the worker advertise or maintain a business listing in the telephone directory, a trade journal, etc.? ☐ **Yes** ☐ **No** ☐ **Unknown**

    If "Yes," specify..

  c Does the worker represent himself or herself to the public as being in business to perform the

    same or similar services? . . . . ☐ **Yes** ☐ **No** ☐ **Unknown**

    If "Yes," how?..

  d Does the worker have his or her own shop or office? . . . . ☐ **Yes** ☐ **No** ☐ **Unknown**

    If "Yes," where?..

  e Does the firm represent the worker as an employee of the firm to its customers? . . . . ☐ **Yes** ☐ **No**

    If "No," how is the worker represented? ....

  f How did the firm learn of the worker's services? ....

13 Is a license necessary for the work? . . . . ☐ **Yes** ☐ **No** ☐ **Unknown**

    If "Yes," what kind of license is required?...

    By whom is it issued? ....

    By whom is the license fee paid?..

14 Does the worker have a financial investment in a business related to the services performed? . . . . ☐ **Yes** ☐ **No** ☐ **Unknown**

    If "Yes," specify and give amounts of the investment ....

15 Can the worker incur a loss in the performance of the service for the firm? . . . . ☐ **Yes** ☐ **No**

    If "Yes," how?..

16a Has any other government agency ruled on the status of the firm's workers? . . . . ☐ **Yes** ☐ **No**

    If "Yes," attach a copy of the ruling.

  b Is the same issue being considered by any IRS office in connection with the audit of the worker's tax return or the

    firm's tax return, or has it recently been considered? . . . . ☐ **Yes** ☐ **No**

    If "Yes," for which year(s)?..

17 Does the worker assemble or process a product at home or away from the firm's place of business? . . . . . . ☐ **Yes** ☐ **No**

    If "Yes":

      Who furnishes materials or goods used by the worker?   ☐ Firm   ☐ Worker

      Is the worker furnished a pattern or given instructions to follow in making the product? . . . . ☐ **Yes** ☐ **No**

      Is the worker required to return the finished product to the firm or to someone designated by the firm? . . . . ☐ **Yes** ☐ **No**

Exhibit 3–1A *(continued)*

Answer items 18a through n if the worker is a salesperson or provides a service directly to customers.

18a Are leads to prospective customers furnished by the firm? . . . . ☐ Yes ☐ No ☐ **Does not apply**

b Is the worker required to pursue or report on leads? . . . . ☐ Yes ☐ No ☐ **Does not apply**

c Is the worker required to adhere to prices, terms, and conditions of sale established by the firm? . . . . ☐ Yes ☐ No

d Are orders submitted to and subject to approval by the firm? . . . . ☐ Yes ☐ No

e Is the worker expected to attend sales meetings? . . . . ☐ Yes ☐ No

If "Yes": Is the worker subject to any kind of penalty for failing to attend? . . . . ☐ Yes ☐ No

f Does the firm assign a specific territory to the worker? . . . . ☐ Yes ☐ No ☐ **Does not apply**

g Who does the customer pay? ☐ Firm ☐ Worker

If worker, does the worker remit the total amount to the firm? . . . . ☐ Yes ☐ No

h Does the worker sell a consumer product in a home or establishment other than a permanent retail establishment? . ☐ Yes ☐ No

i List the products and/or services distributed by the worker, such as meat, vegetables, fruit, bakery products, beverages (other than milk), or laundry or dry cleaning services. If more than one type of product and/or service is distributed, specify the principal one. ....

j Did the firm or another person assign the route or territory and a list of customers to the worker? . . . . ☐ Yes ☐ No

If "Yes," please identify the person who made the assignment. ....

k Did the worker pay the firm or person for the privilege of serving customers on the route or in the territory? . . . . ☐ Yes ☐ No

If "Yes," how much did the worker pay (not including any amount paid for a truck or racks, etc.)? $ ....

What factors were considered in determining the value of the route or territory? ....

l How are new customers obtained by the worker? Explain fully, showing whether the new customers called the firm for service, were solicited by the worker, or both. ....

m Does the worker sell life insurance? . . . . ☐ Yes ☐ No

If "Yes":

Is the selling of life insurance or annuity contracts for the firm the worker's entire business activity? . . . . . ☐ Yes ☐ No

If "No," state the extent of the worker's other business activities ....

Does the worker sell other types of insurance for the firm? . . . . ☐ Yes ☐ No

If "Yes," state the percentage of the worker's total working time spent in selling such other types of insurance .... %

At the time the contract was entered into between the firm and the worker, was it their intention that the worker sell life insurance for the firm: ☐ on a full-time basis ☐ on a part-time basis

State the manner in which such intention was expressed. .... ☐ Yes ☐ No

n Is the worker a traveling salesperson or city salesperson? . . . . ☐ Yes ☐ No

If "Yes":

Specify from whom the worker principally solicits orders on behalf of the firm. ....

If the worker solicits orders from wholesalers, retailers, contractors, or operators of hotels, restaurants, or other similar establishments, specify the percentage of the worker's time spent in such solicitation. .... %

Is the merchandise purchased by the customers for resale, or is it purchased for use in their business operations? If used by the customers in their business operations, describe the merchandise and state whether it is equipment installed on their premises or a consumable supply. ....

19 Attach the names and addresses of the total number of workers in this class from page 1, or the names and addresses of 10 such workers if there are more than 10.

20 Attach a detailed explanation for any other reason why you believe the worker is an independent contractor or is an employee of the firm.

IMPORTANT INFORMATION NEEDED TO PROCESS YOUR REQUEST

Under section 6110 of the Internal Revenue Code, the text and related background file documents of any ruling, determination letter, or technical advice memorandum will be open to public inspection. This section provides that before the text and background file documents are made public, identifying and certain other information must be deleted.

Are the names, addresses, and taxpayer identifying numbers the only items you want deleted? . . . . ☐ Yes ☐ No

If you checked "No," and believe additional deletions should be made, we cannot process your request unless you submit a copy of this form and copies of all supporting documents indicating, in brackets, those parts you believe should be deleted in accordance with section 6110(c) of the Code. Attach a separate statement indicating which specific exemption provided by section 6110(c) applies to each bracketed part.

Under penalties of perjury, I declare that I have examined this request, including accompanying documents, and to the best of my knowledge and belief, the facts presented are true, correct, and complete.

Signature ▶	Title ▶	Date ▶

If this form is used by the firm in requesting a written determination, the form should be signed by an officer or member of the firm.
If this form is used by the worker in requesting a written determination, the form should be signed by the worker. If the worker wants a written determination with respect to services performed for two or more firms, a separate form should be furnished for each firm.
Additional copies of this form may be obtained from any Internal Revenue Service office.

*U.S. GPO:1990-518-282/20301

Exhibit 3–1B

Form **W-9** (Rev. April 1990) Department of the Treasury Internal Revenue Service	**Request for Taxpayer Identification Number and Certification**	Give this form to the requester. Do NOT send to IRS.

Please print or type

Name (If joint names, list first and circle the name of the person or entity whose number you enter in Part I below. **See instructions under "Name"** if your name has changed.)	
Address (number and street)	List account number(s) here (optional)
City, state, and ZIP code	

Part I Taxpayer Identification Number (TIN)	**Part II** For Payees Exempt From Backup Withholding (See Instructions)
Enter your taxpayer identification number in the appropriate box. For individuals and sole proprietors, this is your social security number. For other entities, it is your employer identification number. If you do not have a number, see *How To Obtain a TIN,* below. **Social security number** [| | | + | | + | | |] **OR** **Employer identification number** [| + | | | | | |] **Note:** *If the account is in more than one name, see the chart on page 2 for guidelines on whose number to enter.*	Requester's name and address (optional)

Certification.—Under penalties of perjury, I certify that:

(1) The number shown on this form is my correct taxpayer identification number (or I am waiting for a number to be issued to me), **and**

(2) I am not subject to backup withholding because: **(a)** I am exempt from backup withholding, or **(b)** I have not been notified by the Internal Revenue Service (IRS) that I am subject to backup withholding as a result of a failure to report all interest or dividends, or **(c)** the IRS has notified me that I am no longer subject to backup withholding.

Certification Instructions.—You must cross out item (2) above if you have been notified by IRS that you are currently subject to backup withholding because of underreporting interest or dividends on your tax return. For real estate transactions, item (2) does not apply. For mortgage interest paid, the acquisition or abandonment of secured property, contributions to an individual retirement arrangement (IRA), and generally payments other than interest and dividends, you are not required to sign the Certification, but you must provide your correct TIN. (Also see *Signing the Certification* under *Specific Instructions,* on page 2.)

Please Sign Here	Signature ▶	Date ▶

Instructions

(Section references are to the Internal Revenue Code.)

Purpose of Form.—A person who is required to file an information return with IRS must obtain your correct taxpayer identification number (TIN) to report income paid to you, real estate transactions, mortgage interest you paid, the acquisition or abandonment of secured property, or contributions you made to an individual retirement arrangement (IRA). Use Form W-9 to furnish your correct TIN to the requester (the person asking you to furnish your TIN), and, when applicable, (1) to certify that the TIN you are furnishing is correct (or that you are waiting for a number to be issued), (2) to certify that you are not subject to backup withholding, and (3) to claim exemption from backup withholding if you are an exempt payee. Furnishing your correct TIN and making the appropriate certifications will prevent certain payments from being subject to the 20% backup withholding.

Note: *If a requester gives you a form other than a W-9 to request your TIN, you must use the requester's form.*

How To Obtain a TIN.—If you do not have a TIN, apply for one immediately. To apply, get **Form SS-5,** Application for a Social Security Number Card (for individuals), from your local office of the Social Security Administration, or **Form SS-4,** Application for Employer Identification Number (for businesses and all other entities), from your local Internal Revenue Service office.

To complete Form W-9 if you do not have a TIN, write "Applied For" in the space for the TIN in Part I, sign and date the form, and give it to the requester. Generally, you will then have 60 days to obtain a TIN and furnish it to the requester. If the requester does not receive your TIN within 60 days, backup withholding, if applicable, will begin and continue until you furnish your TIN to the requester. For reportable interest or dividend payments, the payer must exercise one of the following options concerning backup withholding during this 60-day period. Under option (1), a payer must backup withhold on any withdrawals you make from your account after 7 business days after the requester receives this form back from you. Under option (2), the payer must backup withhold on any reportable interest or dividend payments made to your account, regardless of whether you make any withdrawals. The backup withholding under option (2) must begin no later than 7 business days after the requester receives this form back. Under option (2), the payer is required to refund the amounts withheld if your certified TIN is received within the 60-day period and you were not subject to backup withholding during that period.

Note: *Writing "Applied For" on the form means that you have already applied for a TIN OR that you intend to apply for one in the near future.*

As soon as you receive your TIN, complete another Form W-9, include your TIN, sign and date the form, and give it to the requester.

What Is Backup Withholding?—Persons making certain payments to you are required to withhold and pay to IRS 20% of such payments under certain conditions. This is called "backup withholding." Payments that could be subject to backup withholding include interest, dividends, broker and barter exchange transactions, rents, royalties, nonemployee compensation, and certain payments from fishing boat operators, but do not include real estate transactions.

If you give the requester your correct TIN, make the appropriate certifications, and report all your taxable interest and dividends on your tax return, your payments will not be subject to backup withholding. Payments you receive will be subject to backup withholding if:

(1) You do not furnish your TIN to the requester, or

(2) IRS notifies the requester that you furnished an incorrect TIN, or

(3) You are notified by IRS that you are subject to backup withholding because you failed to report all your interest and dividends on your tax return (for reportable interest and dividends only), or

(4) You fail to certify to the requester that you are not subject to backup withholding under (3) above (for reportable interest and dividend accounts opened after 1983 only), or

(5) You fail to certify your TIN. This applies only to reportable interest, dividend, broker, or barter exchange accounts opened after 1983, or broker accounts considered inactive in 1983.

Except as explained in (5) above, other reportable payments are subject to backup withholding only if (1) or (2) above applies.

Certain payees and payments are exempt from backup withholding and information reporting. See *Payees and Payments Exempt From Backup Withholding,* below, and *Exempt Payees and Payments* under *Specific Instructions,* on page 2, if you are an exempt payee.

Payees and Payments Exempt From Backup Withholding.—The following is a list of payees exempt from backup withholding and for which no information reporting is required. For interest and dividends, all listed payees are exempt except item (9). For broker transactions, payees listed in (1) through (13) and a person registered under the Investment Advisers Act of 1940 who regularly acts as a broker are exempt. Payments subject to reporting under sections 6041 and 6041A are generally exempt from backup withholding only if made to payees described in items (1) through (7), except that a corporation that provides medical and health care services or bills and collects payments for such services is

Form **W-9** (Rev. 4-90)

Exhibit 3–1B (continued)

not exempt from backup withholding or information reporting. Only payees described in items (2) through (6) are exempt from backup withholding for barter exchange transactions, patronage dividends, and payments by certain fishing boat operators.

(1) A corporation.

(2) An organization exempt from tax under section 501(a), or an individual retirement plan (IRA), or a custodial account under 403(b)(7).

(3) The United States or any of its agencies or instrumentalities.

(4) A state, the District of Columbia, a possession of the United States, or any of their political subdivisions or instrumentalities.

(5) A foreign government or any of its political subdivisions, agencies, or instrumentalities.

(6) An international organization or any of its agencies or instrumentalities.

(7) A foreign central bank of issue.

(8) A dealer in securities or commodities required to register in the U.S. or a possession of the U.S.

(9) A futures commission merchant registered with the Commodity Futures Trading Commission.

(10) A real estate investment trust.

(11) An entity registered at all times during the tax year under the Investment Company Act of 1940.

(12) A common trust fund operated by a bank under section 584(a).

(13) A financial institution.

(14) A middleman known in the investment community as a nominee or listed in the most recent publication of the American Society of Corporate Secretaries, Inc., Nominee List.

(15) A trust exempt from tax under section 664 or described in section 4947.

Payments of **dividends** and **patronage dividends** generally not subject to backup withholding also include the following:

● Payments to nonresident aliens subject to withholding under section 1441.

● Payments to partnerships not engaged in a trade or business in the U.S. and that have at least one nonresident partner.

● Payments of patronage dividends not paid in money.

● Payments made by certain foreign organizations.

Payments of **interest** generally not subject to backup withholding include the following:

● Payments of interest on obligations issued by individuals. **Note:** *You may be subject to backup withholding if this interest is $600 or more and is paid in the course of the payer's trade or business and you have not provided your correct TIN to the payer.*

● Payments of tax-exempt interest (including exempt-interest dividends under section 852).

● Payments described in section 6049(b)(5) to nonresident aliens.

● Payments on tax-free covenant bonds under section 1451.

● Payments made by certain foreign organizations.

● Mortgage interest paid by you.

Payments that are not subject to information reporting are also not subject to backup withholding. For details, see sections 6041, 6041A(a), 6042, 6044, 6045, 6049, 6050A, and 6050N, and the regulations under those sections.

Penalties

Failure To Furnish TIN.—If you fail to furnish your correct TIN to a requester, you are subject to a penalty of $50 for each such failure unless your failure is due to reasonable cause and not to willful neglect.

Civil Penalty for False Information With Respect to Withholding.—If you make a false statement with no reasonable basis that results in no imposition of backup withholding, you are subject to a penalty of $500.

Criminal Penalty for Falsifying Information.—Willfully falsifying certifications or affirmations may subject you to criminal penalties including fines and/or imprisonment.

Specific Instructions

Name.—If you are an individual, you must generally provide the name shown on your social security card. However, if you have changed your last name, for instance, due to marriage, without informing the Social Security Administration of the name change, please enter your first name and both the last name shown on your social security card and your new last name.

Signing the Certification.—

(1) Interest, Dividend, and Barter Exchange Accounts Opened Before 1984 and Broker Accounts That Were Considered Active During 1983.—You are not required to sign the certification; however, you may do so. You are required to provide your correct TIN.

(2) Interest, Dividend, Broker and Barter Exchange Accounts Opened After 1983 and Broker Accounts That Were Considered Inactive During 1983.—You must sign the certification or backup withholding will apply. If you are subject to backup withholding and you are merely providing your correct TIN to the requester, you must cross out item (2) in the certification before signing the form.

(3) Real Estate Transactions.—You must sign the certification. You may cross out item (2) of the certification if you wish.

(4) Other Payments.—You are required to furnish your correct TIN, but you are not required to sign the certification unless you have been notified of an incorrect TIN. Other payments include payments made in the course of the requester's trade or business for rents, royalties, goods (other than bills for merchandise), medical and health care services, payments to a nonemployee for services (including attorney and accounting fees), and payments to certain fishing boat crew members.

(5) Mortgage Interest Paid by You, Acquisition or Abandonment of Secured Property, or IRA Contributions.—You are required to furnish your correct TIN, but you are not required to sign the certification.

(6) Exempt Payees and Payments.—If you are exempt from backup withholding, you should complete this form to avoid possible erroneous backup withholding. Enter your correct TIN in Part I, write "EXEMPT" in the block in Part II, sign and date the form. If you are a nonresident alien or foreign individual not subject to backup withholding, give the requester a completed **Form W-8**, Certificate of Foreign Status.

(7) TIN "Applied For."—Follow the instructions under *How To Obtain a TIN*, on page 1, sign and date this form.

Signature.—For a joint account, only the person whose TIN is shown in Part I should sign the form.

Privacy Act Notice.—Section 6109 requires you to furnish your correct taxpayer identification number (TIN) to persons who must file information returns with IRS to report interest, dividends, and certain other income paid to you, mortgage interest you paid, the acquisition or abandonment of secured property, or contributions you made to an individual retirement arrangement (IRA). IRS uses the numbers for identification purposes and to help verify the accuracy of your tax return. You must provide your TIN whether or not you are required to file a tax return. Payers must generally withhold 20% of taxable interest, dividend, and certain other payments to a payee who does not furnish a TIN to a payer. Certain penalties may also apply.

What Name and Number To Give the Requester

For this type of account:	Give the name and SOCIAL SECURITY number of:
1. Individual	The individual
2. Two or more individuals (joint account)	The actual owner of the account or, if combined funds, the first individual on the account[1]
3. Custodian account of a minor (Uniform Gift to Minors Act)	The minor[2]
4. a. The usual revocable savings trust (grantor is also trustee)	The grantor-trustee[1]
b. So-called trust account that is not a legal or valid trust under state law	The actual owner[1]
5. Sole proprietorship	The owner[3]

For this type of account:	Give the name and EMPLOYER IDENTIFICATION number of:
6. A valid trust, estate, or pension trust	Legal entity (Do not furnish the identification number of the personal representative or trustee unless the legal entity itself is not designated in the account title.)[4]
7. Corporate	The corporation
8. Association, club, religious, charitable, educational, or, other tax-exempt organization	The organization
9. Partnership	The partnership
10. A broker or registered nominee	The broker or nominee
11. Account with the Department of Agriculture in the name of a public entity (such as a state or local government, school district, or prison) that receives agricultural program payments	The public entity

[1] List first and circle the name of the person whose number you furnish.

[2] Circle the minor's name and furnish the minor's social security number.

[3] Show the individual's name.

[4] List first and circle the name of the legal trust, estate, or pension trust.

Note: *If no name is circled when there is more than one name, the number will be considered to be that of the first name listed.*

★U.S.GPO:1990-0-265-091

Exhibit 3–1C

Form **4361** (Rev. June 1991) Department of the Treasury Internal Revenue Service	**Application for Exemption From Self-Employment Tax for Use by Ministers, Members of Religious Orders and Christian Science Practitioners**	OMB No. 1545-0168 Expires 6-30-94 **File Original and Two Copies**

File original and two copies and attach supporting documents. This exemption is granted only if the IRS returns a copy to you marked "approved."

Please type or print	1 Name of taxpayer shown on Form 1040	Social security number
	Number and street (including apt. no.)	Telephone number (optional) ( )
	City or town, state, and ZIP code	

2 Check ONE box: ☐ Christian Science practitioner ☐ Ordained minister, priest, rabbi
☐ Member of religious order not under a vow of poverty ☐ Commissioned or licensed minister (see line 6)

3 Date ordained, licensed, etc. (Attach supporting document. See instructions.) / /

4 Legal name of ordaining, licensing, or commissioning body or religious order

Number, street, and room or suite no.

Employer identification number

City or town, state, and ZIP code

5 Enter the first 2 years, after the date shown on line 3, that you had net self-employment earnings of $400 or more, any of which came from services as a minister. priest, rabbi, etc.; member of a religious order; or Christian Science practitioner ▶ 19____ 19____

6 If you apply for the exemption as a licensed or commissioned minister, and your denomination also ordains ministers, please indicate how your ecclesiastical powers differ from those of an ordained minister of your denomination. Attach a copy of your denomination's by-laws relating to the powers of ordained, commissioned, or licensed ministers.

7 I certify that I am conscientiously opposed to, or because of my religious principles I am opposed to, the acceptance (for services I perform as a minister, member of a religious order not under a vow of poverty, or a Christian Science practitioner) of any public insurance that makes payments in the event of death, disability, old age, or retirement; or that makes payments toward the cost of, or provides services for, medical care. (Public insurance includes insurance systems established by the Social Security Act.)

I certify that as a duly ordained, commissioned, or licensed minister of a church or a member of a religious order not under a vow of poverty, I have informed the ordaining, commissioning, or licensing body of my church or order that I am conscientiously opposed to, or because of religious principles, I am opposed to the acceptance (for services I perform as a minister or as a member of a religious order) of any public insurance that makes payments in the event of death, disability, old age, or retirement; or that makes payments toward the cost of, or provides services for, medical care, including the benefits of any insurance system established by the Social Security Act.

I certify that I did not file an effective waiver certificate (Form 2031) electing social security coverage on earnings as a minister, member of a religious order not under a vow of poverty, or a Christian Science practitioner.

I request to be exempted from paying self-employment tax on my earnings from services as a minister, member of a religious order not under a vow of poverty, or a Christian Science practitioner, under section 1402(e) of the Internal Revenue Code. I understand that the exemption, if granted, will apply only to these earnings. Under penalties of perjury, I declare that I have examined this application and to the best of my knowledge and belief, it is true and correct.

Signature ▶   Date ▶

Caution: Form 4361 is **not proof** of the right to an exemption from Federal income tax withholding or social security tax, the right to a parsonage allowance exclusion (section 107), assignment by your religious superiors to a particular job, or the exemption or church status of the ordaining, licensing, commissioning body, or religious order.

For Internal Revenue Service Use

☐ Approved for exemption from self-employment tax on ministerial earnings
☐ Disapproved for exemption from self-employment tax on ministerial earnings

By ....
                              (Director's signature)   (Date)

General Instructions

(Section references are to the Internal Revenue Code.)

Paperwork Reduction Act Notice.—We ask for the information on this form to carry out the Internal Revenue laws of the United States. You are required to give us the information. We need it to ensure that you are complying with these laws and to allow us to figure and collect the right amount of tax.

The time needed to complete and file this form will vary depending on individual circumstances. The estimated average time is:

Recordkeeping, 7 minutes; **Learning about the law or the form,** 19 minutes; **Preparing the form,** 16 minutes; **Copying, assembling, and sending the form to IRS,** 17 minutes.

If you have comments concerning the accuracy of these time estimates or

suggestions for making this form more simple, we would be happy to hear from you. You can write to both the **Internal Revenue Service,** Washington, DC 20224, Attention: IRS Reports Clearance Officer, T:FP; and the **Office of Management and Budget,** Paperwork Reduction Project (1545-0168), Washington, DC 20503. **DO NOT** send the form to either of these offices. Instead, see **Where To File** on page 2.

Purpose of Form.—File Form 4361 to apply for an exemption from self-employment tax if you are:

● An ordained, commissioned, or licensed minister of a church;

● A member of a religious order who has not taken a vow of poverty;

● A Christian Science practitioner; or

● A commissioned or licensed minister of a church or church denomination that

ordains ministers, if you have authority to perform substantially all religious duties of your church or denomination.

This application must be based on your religious or conscientious opposition to the acceptance (for services performed as a minister, member of a religious order, or Christian Science practitioner) of any public insurance that makes payments for death, disability, old age, or retirement; or that makes payments for the cost of, or provides services for, medical care, including any insurance benefits established by the Social Security Act.

If you are a duly ordained, commissioned, or licensed minister of a church or a member of a religious order not under a vow of poverty, prior to filing this form you must inform the ordaining, commissioning, or

(continued on page 2)

Cat. No. 41586H   Form **4361** (Rev. 6-91)

Exhibit 3–1C *(continued)*

licensing body of your church or order that you are opposed to the acceptance of public insurance benefits based on ministerial service on religious or conscientious grounds.

Do not file Form 4361 if:

• You ever filed a waiver certificate (Form 2031); or

• You belong to a religious order and took a vow of poverty. You are automatically exempt from self-employment tax on earnings for services you perform for your church or its agencies. No tax exemption applies to earnings for services you perform for any other organization.

Additional Information.—For more information, get **Pub. 517,** Social Security for Members of the Clergy and Religious Workers.

When To File.—File Form 4361 by the date your tax return is due, including extensions, for the second tax year in which you had at least $400 of net earnings from self-employment, any of which came from services performed as a minister, member of a religious order, or Christian Science practitioner.

Effective Date of Exemption.—An exemption from self-employment tax is effective for all tax years ending after 1967 in which you have net self-employment earnings of $400 or more, if you derive any of it from ministerial services. For example, if you had qualified net earnings of $400 or more in 1968 and not again until 1991, a valid Form 4361 filed by April 15, 1992, would apply to 1968 and all later years. Refer to Pub. 517 to see if you are entitled to a refund of self-employment tax paid in earlier years.

Where To File.—Mail the original and two copies of this form to the **Internal Revenue Service Center** for the place where you live.

If you live in:	Use this address:
Florida, Georgia, South Carolina	Atlanta, GA 39901
New Jersey, New York City and counties of Nassau, Rockland, Suffolk, and Westchester	Holtsville, NY 00501
Connecticut, Maine, Massachusetts, New Hampshire, New York (all other counties), Rhode Island, Vermont	Andover, MA 05501
Delaware, District of Columbia, Maryland, Pennsylvania, Virginia	Philadelphia, PA 19255
Illinois, Iowa, Minnesota, Missouri, Wisconsin	Kansas City, MO 64999
Indiana, Kentucky, Michigan, Ohio, West Virginia	Cincinnati, OH 45999
Kansas, New Mexico, Oklahoma, Texas	Austin, TX 73301
Alaska, Arizona, California (counties of Alpine, Amador, Butte, Calaveras, Colusa, Contra Costa, Del Norte, El Dorado, Glenn, Humboldt, Lake, Lassen, Marin, Mendocino, Modoc, Napa, Nevada, Placer, Plumas, Sacramento, San Joaquin, Shasta, Sierra, Siskiyou, Solano, Sonoma, Sutter, Tehama, Trinity, Yolo, and Yuba), Colorado, Idaho, Montana, Nebraska, Nevada, North Dakota, Oregon, South Dakota, Utah, Washington, Wyoming	Ogden, UT 84201
California (all other counties), Hawaii	Fresno, CA 93888
Alabama, Arkansas, Louisiana, Mississippi, North Carolina, Tennessee	Memphis, TN 37501

American Samoa	Philadelphia, PA 19255
Guam	Commissioner of Revenue and Taxation 855 West Marine Drive Agana, GU 96910
Northern Mariana Islands (Commonwealth of the)	Philadelphia, PA 19255
Puerto Rico (or if excluding income under section 933) Virgin Islands: Nonpermanent residents	Philadelphia, PA 19255
Virgin Islands: Permanent residents	V.I. Bureau of Internal Revenue Lockharts Garden No. 1A Charlotte Amalie St. Thomas, VI 00802
Foreign country: U.S. citizens and those filing Form 2555 or Form 4563	Philadelphia, PA 19255
All A.P.O. or F.P.O. addresses	Philadelphia, PA 19255

Approval of Application.— Before your application can be approved, the IRS must verify that you are aware of the grounds for exemption and that you want the exemption on that basis. When your completed Form 4361 is received, the IRS will mail you a statement that describes the grounds for receiving an exemption under section 1402(e). You must certify that you have read the statement and seek exemption on the grounds listed on the statement. The certification must be made by signing a copy of the statement under penalties of perjury and mailing it to the IRS service center that issued it, not later than 90 days after the date the statement was mailed to you. If it is not mailed by that time, your exemption will not be effective until the date the signed copy is received by the service center.

If your application is approved, a copy of Form 4361 will be returned to you marked "approved." Once the exemption is approved, you cannot revoke it.

Earnings To Which Exemption Applies.— Only earnings from ministerial services are exempt from self-employment tax.

Conducting a religious worship services or ministering sacerdotal functions are ministerial services whether or not performed for a religious organization.

Ministerial services also include those performed under the authority of a church or church denomination. Examples are controlling, conducting, and maintaining religious organizations, including religious boards, societies, and other agencies integral to these organizations.

If your church assigns or designates you to perform services for an organization that is neither a religious organization nor an integral agency of a religious organization, you are performing ministerial services, even though they may not involve conducting religious worship or ministering sacerdotal functions. Your services are ordinarily not considered assigned or designated by your church if any of the following is true:

• The organization for which you perform the services did not arrange with your church for your services.

• You perform the same services for the organization as other employees not designated as you were.

• You perform the same services before and after the designation.

Earnings To Which Exemption Does Not Apply.—Exemption from self-employment tax does not apply to earnings from services that are not ministerial.

Earnings from the following entities are not exempt even if religious services are conducted or sacerdotal functions are ministered: the United States; a state, territory, or possession of the U.S.; the District of Columbia; a foreign government; or a subdivision of any of these bodies. For example, chaplains in the U.S. Armed Forces are considered commissioned officers, not ministers. Similarly, chaplains in state prisons or universities are considered civil servants.

Indicating Exemption on Form 1040.—If the IRS returned your application marked "approved" and your only self-employment income was from ministerial services, write "Exempt—Form 4361" on the self-employment line in the **Other Taxes** section of Form 1040. If you had other self-employment income, see **Schedule SE** (Form 1040).

Specific Instructions

Line 1—Social Security Number.—Enter your social security number. If you do not have one, file **Form SS-5,** Application for a Social Security Card, with your local Social Security Administration office. If you do not receive your card in time, file Form 4361 and enter "applied for" in the space for your social security number.

Line 3.—Enter the date you were ordained, commissioned, or licensed as a minister of a church; became a member of a religious order; or began practice as a Christian Science practitioner. Do not file Form 4361 before this date. Attach a copy of the certificate (or, if you did not receive one, a letter from the governing body of your church) that establishes your status as an ordained, commissioned, or licensed minister; a member of a religious order; or a Christian Science practitioner.

Line 4.—If you are a minister or belong to a religious order, enter the legal name, address, and employer identification number of the denomination that ordained, commissioned, or licensed you, or the order to which you belong. Get the employer identification number from your church or order.

You must be able to show that the body that ordained, commissioned, or licensed you, or your religious order, is exempt from Federal income tax under section 501(a) as a religious organization described in section 501(c)(3). You must also be able to show that the body is a church (or convention or association of churches) described in section 170(b)(1)(A)(i). To assist the service center in processing your application, you can attach a copy of the exemption letter issued to the organization by the IRS. If that is not available, you can attach a letter signed by an individual authorized to act for the organization stating that the organization meets both of the above requirements.

*U.S. Government Printing Office: 1991 — 299-982/49197

§ 3.2 FILING FORM 990

p. 190. *Add at the end of the second paragraph:*
The various Forms 990 are designed by the IRS to accomplish two purposes. The basic financial information—the revenues, disbursements, assets and liabilities—are classified into meaningful categories to allow the IRS to statistically evaluate the scope and type of EO activity. Second, questions are directly asked and analyses completed to fish for failures to comply with the federal requirements for maintenance of tax exempt status. Do the fundraising costs equal too high a percentage of the total expenses? Are officers paid excessive salaries? Does the EO operate to benefit private individuals? Examples of this second purpose are found throughout the explanations of the form on pages 207–230.

p. 190. *Replace § 3.3 Updated Forms with:*

§ 3.3 WHO'S REQUIRED TO FILE?

Exempt organizations have many different possibilities for annual information return filing for fiscal years beginning after January 1, 1989.

Types of Exempt Organization Annual Reports to IRS

The different types of forms and their basic requirement are:

No Form Filed	Gross annual receipts "normally" under $25,000, churches and certain of their affiliates and other types of organizations listed below. (See "why to file" note below.)
Form 990EZ	Gross annual receipts between $25,000 and $100,000, total assets less than $250,000.
Form 990	Gross annual receipts over $100,000 or assets over $250,000 with gross annual receipts between $25,000 and $100,000.
Form 990PF	All private foundations (PF) file annually regardless of gross annual receipts (even if the PF has no gross receipts).

Form 990T   Any organization exempt under 501(a) (includes IRAs and other pension plans) with $1,000 or more gross income from unrelated trade or business file Form 990T.

Form 990BL   Black lung trusts (Section 501(c)(21)) file an annual Information and Initial Excise Tax Return for Black Lung Benefit Trusts and Certain Related Persons.

Form 5500   One of several Forms 5500 are filed annually by pension, profit-sharing, and stock bonus plans whose assets exceed $100,000. Form 5500EZ is filed for a one-participant pension benefit plan and 5500 C/R is filed for organizations with fewer than 100 participants in the employee plans.

Organizations not required to file include:

- Church affiliates including an interchurch organization of local units of a church, a convention or association of churches, an integrated auxiliary of a church, such as a men's or women's society, religious school, mission society, or youth group, or an internally supported, church-controlled organization.

- School below college level affiliated with a church or operated by a religious order.

- Mission society sponsored by or affiliated with one or more churches or church denominations, if more than one-half of the society's activities are conducted in, or directed at persons in, foreign countries.

- An exclusively religious activity of any religious order.

- A state institution whose income is excluded from gross income under Section 115.

- Section 501(c)(1) organizations organized under an Act of Congress that are instrumentalities of the United States.

Definition of Gross Receipts (New)

The definition of gross receipts is all cash receipts of the organization during a year not including borrowing, interfund transfers, and expense reimbursements. For purpose of determining annual filing requirements for Forms 990, the calculation can be tied to the front page of the form itself. For Form 990, the following lines are added:

Line 1:   Contributions, gifts and grants

Line 2:   Program service revenue

Line 3:   Membership dues and assessments

Line 4:   Interest on savings and investments

Line 5:   Dividends and interest from securities

Line 6a: Gross rent

Line 7:   Other investment income

Line 8a: Gross amount from sale of assets other than inventory

Line 9a: Gross revenue from special fund-raising events and activities

Line 10a: Gross sales less returns and allowances

Line 11:   Other revenue.

The total can be checked by adding back all the costs deducted on page one on lines 6b, 8b, 9b, and 10b to line 12 (total revenue).

For Form 990EZ, follow the same pattern using the somewhat different designations on fewer lines, adding all gross income before the expenses deductions.

Why to File Even if Not Required

Organizations not filing annual Forms 990 are removed from *Publication 78*, the master list of qualifying charitable organizations published by the IRS. This IRS policy came to light recently in connection with a disallowed charitable deduction as discussed in § 2.5 concerning reliance on determination letters. Prudence dictates that any organization that seeks donations assure that its name is listed in the publication.

Annual filings are advisable also for organizations whose annual gross receipts hover around the $25,000 mark to assure that the organization remains on the IRS mailing list to receive the forms for annual filing and other announcements issued by the IRS every year or so. Form 990EZ can be filed with the simple notation, "gross receipts under $25,000," with no other information being completed.

p. 191. *Add after third paragraph:*

* § 3.3A STRATEGIES FOR FILLING OUT PAGE 5 (NEW)

The Statistics of Income Division of the IRS will begin to compile statistics from 1989 and 1990 Form 990, page 5s in October, 1991, and would expect to complete the study within about three years (apparently meaning sometime in 1992).

The new page 5 added to Form 990 in 1989 (Exhibit 3–3A) contains a host of pitfalls and traps for the unwary. At the behest of Congress, the IRS designed this form as an audit trail to find unrelated business income (UBI). Selection of the appropriate code to identify income is difficult in some cases and can have adverse consequences. Some choices are not absolute and discretion can be important. For example, code 40 highlights activities being conducted for nonexempt purposes and operated at a loss—potentially representing use of EO funds for private purposes and the possibility that the IRS should revoke the EO's exemption. Such losses in the IRS's opinion are also not available to offset against profit-motivated UBI. (See the Portland Golf Club supplement discussion on page 51 regarding limitations on a social club's activities not entered into to produce a profit.)

A thorough review of the unrelated business income provisions discussed in § 3.8 is useful. An understanding of the terms "regularly carried on," "member convenience," "related and unrelated," and "fragmented" are absolutely necessary for correct completion of this page. The form forces the organization to report items of income

Exhibit 3-3A

Part VII — Analysis of Income-Producing Activities

Enter gross amounts unless otherwise indicated.

93 Program service revenue:	Unrelated business income		Excluded by section 512, 513, or 514		(e) Related or exempt function income
	(a) Business code	(b) Amount	(c) Exclusion code	(d) Amount	
(a) _____					
(b) _____					
(c) _____					
(d) _____					
(e) _____					
(f) _____					
(g) Fees from government agencies					
94 Membership dues and assessments					
95 Interest on savings and temporary cash investments					
96 Dividends and interest on securities					
97 Net rental income (loss) from real estate:					
(a) debt-financed property					
(b) not debt-financed property					
98 Net rental income (loss) from personal property					
99 Other investment income					
100 Gain (loss) from sales of assets other than inventory					
101 Net income from special fundraising events					
102 Gross profit (loss) from sales of inventory					
103 Other revenue: (a) _____					
(b) _____					
(c) _____					
(d) _____					
(e) _____					
104 Subtotal (add columns (b), (d), and (e))					

105 TOTAL (add line 104, columns (b), (d), and (e)) . . . . ▶

(Line 105 plus line 1d, Part I, should equal the amount on line 12, Part I.)

Part VIII — Relationship of Activities to the Accomplishment of Exempt Purposes

Line No. ▼   Explain below how each activity for which income is reported in column (e) of Part VII contributed importantly to the accomplishment of your exempt purposes (other than by providing funds for such purposes).

Part IX — Information Regarding Taxable Subsidiaries (Complete this Part if you answered "Yes" to question 78c)

Name, address, and employer identification number of corporation or partnership	Percentage of ownership interest	Nature of business activities	Total income	End-of-year assets

Please Sign Here

Under penalties of perjury, I declare that I have examined this return, including accompanying schedules and statements, and to the best of my knowledge and belief, it is true, correct, and complete. Declaration of preparer (other than officer) is based on all information of which preparer has any knowledge.

▶ Signature of officer   Date   ▶ Title

Paid Preparer's Use Only

Preparer's signature ▶	Date	Check if self-employed ▶ ☐
Firm's name (or yours if self-employed) and address ▶	ZIP code	

appearing on page 1, line 2 through 11 (except for contributions) in one of three categories by columns.

Columns of Page 5

UBI—Columns (a) and (b)

Income from unrelated business activities is reported in column (b). Any amounts included here must be reported on Form 990T and is subject to income tax if a profit is generated from the activity. Column (a) codes are those used in Form 990T (Exhibit 3–3B) to identify the type of business conducted—mining, construction, manufacturing, services, and so on. The codes are very similar to those used in Forms 1120 and 1065 for corporate and partnership income tax returns.

UBI, Excluded, or Modified from Tax—Columns (c) and (d)

Income from investments, fund-raising events, and business activities statutorily excluded from tax are included in these columns. The reason for exclusion of the income from tax is claimed by inserting one of forty code numbers (explained below under line numbers) in column (c) (Exhibit 3–3C). If more than one code applies, the lowest applicable code number is used according to the instructions. Certain codes, such as bingo (9), membership lists (13), and royalties (15), that are the particular subjects of current IRS/taxpayer battles as described in § 3.8 may be troublesome as the IRS uses this page to choose EOs it will examine.

Related or Exempt Function Income—Column (e)

Income generated through charges for services rendered or items sold in connection with the EO's underlying exempt, or program, activities are entered in column (e). Student tuition and fees, hospital charges, admissions, publication sales, handicraft or other byproduct sales, seminar registrations, and all other revenues received in return for providing exempt functions are included. A code definition of exempt function income is found in Section 512(a)(3)(B). This column is a

Exhibit 3–3B

Codes for Unrelated Business Activity

(If engaged in more than one unrelated business activity, select up to three codes for the principal activities. List first the largest in terms of unrelated income, then the next largest, etc.)

AGRICULTURE, FORESTRY, AND FISHING

Code
0400	Agricultural production
0600	Agricultural services (except veterinarians), forestry, fishing, hunting and trapping
0740	Veterinary services

MINING

Code
1330	Crude petroleum, natural gas and natural gas liquids
1399	All other mining

CONSTRUCTION

Code
1510	General building contractors
1798	All other construction

MANUFACTURING

Code
2000	Food and kindred products
2100	Tobacco manufacturers
2200	Textile mill products
2300	Apparel and other textile products
2400	Lumber and wood products, except furniture
2500	Furniture and fixtures
2600	Paper and allied products

Printing, publishing and allied industries
2710	Newspapers
2720	Periodicals
2730	Books
2750	Commercial printing (except advertising)
2770	Greeting cards
2799	All other printing and printing trade services
2800	Chemicals and allied products
2900	Petroleum refining and related industries (including those integrated with extraction)
3000	Rubber and miscellaneous plastics products
3100	Leather and leather products
3200	Stone, clay, glass and concrete products
3300	Primary metal industries
3400	Fabricated metal products, except machinery and transportation equipment
3500	Industrial and commercial machinery and computer equipment
3600	Electronic and other electrical equipment and components, except computer equipment
3700	Transportation equipment

Measuring, analyzing, and controlling instruments; photographic, medical and optical goods; watches and clocks
3841	Surgical and medical instruments and apparatus
3842	Orthopedic, prosthetic, and surgical appliances and supplies
3899	Other instruments, photographic and optical goods; watches and clocks
3900	Miscellaneous manufacturing industries

TRANSPORTATION, COMMUNICATIONS, ELECTRIC, GAS AND SANITARY SERVICES

Code

Transportation
4117	Sightseeing buses
4118	Ambulance service (local)
4140	Bus charter service
4199	Other local and suburban transit and interurban highway passenger transportation
4724	Travel agencies
4725	Tour operators
4799	All other transportation

Communication
4830	Radio and television broadcasting
4898	Other communication services
4900	Electric, gas and sanitary services

WHOLESALE TRADE

Code
5000	Durable goods
5100	Nondurable goods

RETAIL TRADE

Code
5200	Building materials, hardware, garden supply and mobile home dealers
5300	General merchandise stores

Food stores
5410	Grocery stores
5460	Bakeries
5495	Health food stores
5498	Other food stores
5500	Automotive dealers and gasoline service stations
5600	Apparel and accessory stores

Home furniture, furnishings, and equipment stores
5734	Computer and computer software stores
5799	Home furniture, furnishings, and other equipment stores

Eating and drinking places
5811	Caterers
5812	Other eating places
5813	Drinking places (alcoholic beverages)

Miscellaneous retail
5910	Drugstores and proprietary stores
5930	Used merchandise stores
5941	Sporting goods stores and bicycle shops
5942	Book stores
5947	Gift, novelty, and souvenir shops
5961	Catalog and mail order houses
5992	Florists
5994	News dealers and newsstands
5995	Optical goods
5996	Hearing aids
5997	Orthopedic and artificial limbs stores
5998	Miscellaneous retail stores

FINANCE, INSURANCE AND REAL ESTATE

Code

Depository institutions
6020	Commercial banks, including bank holding companies
6030	Savings institutions
6060	Credit unions
6098	Other depository institutions

Nondepository credit institutions
6140	Personal credit institutions, including mutual benefit associations
6199	Other nondepository credit institutions
6200	Security, commodity brokers, dealers, exchanges and services

Insurance
6310	Life insurance
6321	Accident and health insurance
6324	Hospital and medical service plans
6330	Fire, marine and casualty insurance
6370	Pension, health and welfare funds
6398	All other insurance carriers
6410	Insurance agents, brokers and services

Real estate
6512	Operators of nonresidential buildings
6513	Operators of apartment buildings
6515	Operators of residential mobile home sites
6518	All other real estate operators (except developers) and lessors
6530	Real estate agents and managers
6550	Land subdividers and developers
6599	Other real estate

Holding and other investment companies, except bank holding companies
6730	Trusts
6797	Investment clubs
6798	Miscellaneous holding and investment offices

SERVICES

Code

Hotels, rooming houses, camps, and other lodging places
7010	Hotels and motels
7020	Rooming and boarding houses
7030	Camps and recreational vehicle parks
7040	Organization hotels and lodging houses, on membership basis

Code

Personal services
7210	Laundry, cleaning and garment services
7298	Miscellaneous personal services

Business services
7310	Advertising (including printing)
7331	Direct mail advertising services
7334	Photocopying and duplicating services
7345	Building cleaning and maintenance services
7352	Medical equipment rental and leasing
7360	Personnel supply services
7371	Computer programming services
7374	Computer processing and data preparation, and processing services
7377	Computer rental and leasing
7378	Computer maintenance and repair
7388	Other business services
7500	Automotive repair, services, and parking
7600	Miscellaneous repair services
7800	Motion pictures

Amusement and recreation services
7910	Dance studios, schools, and halls
7920	Theatrical producers (except motion pictures), bands, orchestras, and entertainers
7933	Bowling centers
7940	Commercial sports
7991	Physical fitness facilities
7992	Public golf courses
7996	Amusement parks
7997	Membership sports and recreation clubs
7998	Amusement and recreation services, not elsewhere classified

Health services
8010	Offices and clinics of doctors
8020	Offices and clinics of dentists
8045	Offices and clinics of other health practitioners
8050	Nursing and personal care facilities
8060	Hospitals
8071	Medical laboratories
8072	Dental laboratories
8080	Home health care services
8094	Specialty outpatient facilities
8095	Blood banks
8096	Invitro fertilization
8097	Family planning clinics
8098	Health and allied services, not elsewhere classified
8100	Legal services

Educational services
8210	Elementary and secondary schools
8220	Colleges, universities, and professional schools
8240	Vocational schools
8298	Schools and educational services, not elsewhere classified

Social services
8320	Individual and family social services
8330	Job training and vocational rehabilitation services
8351	Child day care services
8361	Residential care
8399	Social services, not elsewhere classified
8400	Museums, art galleries and botanical and zoological gardens

Engineering, accounting, research, management, and related services
8712	Architectural services
8715	Engineering and surveying services
8720	Accounting, auditing and bookkeeping services
8734	Testing laboratories
8735	Research and development
8745	Management and management consulting services
8980	Miscellaneous services

OTHER

Code
9000	Unrelated debt-financed activities other than rental of real estate
9100	Investment activities by section 501(c)(7), (9), (17), or (20) organizations
9200	Rental of personal property
9300	Passive income activities with controlled organizations
9400	Exploited exempt activities

Exhibit 3-3C

Exclusion Codes

General Exceptions

01— Income from an activity that is not regularly carried on (section 512(a)(1))

02— Income from an activity in which labor is a material income-producing factor and substantially all (at least 85%) of the work is performed with unpaid labor (section 513(a)(1))

03— Section 501(c)(3) organization— Income from an activity carried on primarily for the convenience of the organization's members, students, patients, visitors, officers, or employees (hospital parking lot or museum cafeteria, for example) (section 513(a)(2))

04— Section 501(c)(4) local association of employees organized before 5/27/69—Income from the sale of work-related clothes or equipment and items normally sold through vending machines; food dispensing facilities; or snack bars for the convenience of association members at their usual places of employment (section 513(a)(2))

05— Income from the sale of merchandise, substantially all of which (at least 85%) was donated to the organization (section 513(a)(3))

Specific Exceptions

06— Section 501(c)(3), (4), or (5) organization conducting an agricultural or educational fair or exposition—Qualified public entertainment activity income (section 513(d)(2))

07— Section 501(c)(3), (4), (5), or (6) organization—Qualified convention and trade show activity income (section 513(d)(3))

08— Income from hospital services described in section 513(e)

09— Income from noncommercial bingo games that do not violate state or local law (section 513(f))

10— Income from games of chance conducted by an organization in North Dakota (section 311 of the Deficit Reduction Act of 1984, as amended)

11— Section 501(c)(12) organization— Qualified pole rental income (section 513(g))

12— Income from the distribution of low-cost articles in connection with the solicitation of charitable contributions (section 513(h))

13— Income from the exchange or rental of membership or donor list with an organization eligible to receive charitable contributions by a section 501(c)(3) organization; by a war veterans' organization; or an auxiliary unit or society of, or trust or foundation for, a war veterans' post or organization (section 513(h))

Modifications and Exclusions

14— Dividends, interest, or payments with respect to securities loans, and annuities excluded by section 512(b)(1)

15— Royalty income excluded by section 512(b)(2)

16— Real property rental income that does not depend on the income or profits derived by the person leasing the property and is excluded by section 512 (b)(3)

17— Rent from personal property leased with real property and incidental (10% or less) in relation to the combined income from the real and personal property (section 512(b)(3))

18— Proceeds from the sale of investments and other non-inventory property (capital gains excluded by section 512(b)(5))

19— Income (gains) from the lapse or termination of options to buy or sell securities (section 512(b)(5))

20— Income from research for the United States; its agencies or instrumentalities; or any state or political subdivision (section 512(b)(7))

21— Income from research conducted by a college, university, or hospital (section 512(b)(8))

22— Income from research conducted by an organization whose primary activity is conducting fundamental research, the results of which are freely available to the general public (section 512(b)(9))

23— Income from services provided under license issued by a federal regulatory agency and conducted by a religious order or school operated by a religious order, but only if the trade or business has been carried on by the organization since before May 27, 1959 (section 512 (b)(15))

Foreign Organizations

24— Foreign organizations only—Income from a trade or business NOT conducted in the United States and NOT derived from United States sources (patrons) (section 512(a)(2))

Social Clubs and VEBAs

25— Section 501(c)(7), (9), (17), or (20) organization—Non-exempt function income set aside for a charitable, etc., purpose specified in section 170(c)(4) (section 512(a)(3)(B)(i))

26— Section 501(c)(7), (9), (17), or (20) organization—Proceeds from the sale of exempt function property that was or will be timely reinvested in similar property (section 512(a)(3)(D))

27— Section 501(c)(9), (17), or (20) organization—Non-exempt function income set aside for the payment of life, sick, accident, or other benefits (section 512(a)(3)(B)(ii))

Veterans' Organizations

28— Section 501(c)(19) organization— Payments for life, sick, accident, or health insurance for members or their dependents that are set aside for the payment of such insurance benefits or for a charitable, etc., purpose specified in section 170(c)(4) (section 512(a)(4))

29— Section 501(c)(19) organization—Income from an insurance set-aside (see code 28 above) that is set aside for payment of insurance benefits or for a charitable, etc., purpose specified in section 170(c)(4) (Regs. 1.512(a)- 4(b)(2))

Debt-financed Income

30— Income exempt from debt-financed (section 514) provisions because at least 85% of the use of the property is for the organization's exempt purposes (**Note:** *This code is only for income from the 15% or less non-exempt purpose use.*) (section 514(b)(1)(A))

31— Gross income from mortgaged property used in research activities described in section 512(b)(7), (8), or (9) (section 514(b)(1)(C))

32— Gross income from mortgaged property used in any activity described in section 513(a)(1), (2), or (3) (section 514(b)(1)(D))

33— Income from mortgaged property (neighborhood land) acquired for exempt purpose use within ten years (section 514(b)(3))

34— Income from mortgaged property acquired by bequest or devise (applies to income received within ten years from the date of acquisition) (section 514(c)(2)(B))

35— Income from mortgaged property acquired by gift where the mortgage was placed on the property more than five years previously and the property was held by the donor for more than five years (applies to income received within ten years from the date of gift (section 514(c)(2)(B))

36— Income from property received in return for the obligation to pay an annuity described in section 514(c)(5)

37— Income from mortgaged property that provides housing to low and moderate income persons, to the extent the mortgage is insured by the Federal Housing Administration (section 514(c)(6)) (**Note:** *In many cases, this would be exempt function income reportable in column (e). It would not be so in the case of a section 501(c)(5) or (6) organization, for example, that acquired the housing as an investment or as a charitable activity.*)

38— Income from mortgaged real property owned by: a school described in section 170(b)(1)(A)(ii); a section 509(a)(3) affiliated support organization of such a school; a section 501(c)(25) organization, or by a partnership in which any of the above organizations owns an interest if the requirements of section 514(c)(9)(B)(vi) are met (section 514(c)(9))

Special Rules

39— Section 501(c)(5) organization— Farm income used to finance the operation and maintenance of a retirement home, hospital, or similar facility operated by the organization for its members on property adjacent to the farm land (section 1951(b)(8)(B) of Public Law 94-455)

Trade or Business

40— Gross income from an unrelated activity that is regularly carried on but, in light of continuous losses sustained over a number of tax periods, cannot be regarded as being conducted with the motive to make a profit (not a trade or business)

Page 16

■ 96 ■

safe harbor because it contains income not potentially subject to the UBI tax—that income which is generated by "substantially related" activities (those with a causal relationship, contributing importantly to the EO's programs). Note an explanation of the related aspect of each number in this column must be entered in Part VIII.

Some exempt function income is also described by specific exclusion codes. Rentals from low income housing fits into code 16 and therefore, could also properly be placed in column (c)/(d). It is preferable to place such an item in column e because the taint of UBI character is removed. Interest income earned under a student loan program or by a credit union or royalties from scientific research patents are other examples of potential dual classifications.

Line-by-Line Description

First note that for certain lines gross income before any deductions is reported and for others (lines 97, 98, 100, and 101) net income is reported.

Line 93: Program Service Revenue

Revenues produced from activities forming the basis for exemption described above under column (e), are considered program service revenues. As a general rule all revenues on this line would be reportable in column (e). One important exception is fees for social club services charged to nonmembers, which must be reported in column (b) and labeled with UBI code 7997 or 7998.

A short description of the type of income—student tuition, admission fees, and so on—is entered under line 93 a-f. Program service revenue in the form of interest, dividend, rent, or royalty is entered on this line. Sales of goods or "inventory items," such as student books, blood bank sales, or museum gift shop items are not entered here but on line 102, except for hospitals and colleges. According to the page 1 instructions, they may include inventory sales items as program services revenue where it is consistent with their overall reporting system under GAAP.

Governmental grants for services rendered, not entered as contributions on line 1c of page 1, are entered on line 93g. Contractual services, such as research, student testing, medical or food services, child welfare program fees, and similar services performed on a fee basis for governmental agencies is to be included here.

Line 94: Membership Dues and Assessments

As the title connotes, dues and other charges for services rendered to members are included on this line. When a member pays dues primarily to support the organization's activities, rather than to derive benefits of more than nominal monetary benefit, that dues payment represents a contribution. To the extent a (c)(3) EO's membership dues are treated as a contribution because they have no monetary value, they are not included here. See § 3.4A for a description of member items to be included such as "commercial quality publications," discounts on admission or store purchases, free admission, educational classes, referral services, and any other items of value given to members in return for their dues.

A business league, labor union, social club, veterans organization, or similar organizations would report their members' dues, not including any portion allocable to inventory items sold or program services, such as decals or group insurance. Varying levels of memberships with different amounts of dues, such as associates or junior members, raise a question. The IRS in Priv. Ltr. Rul. 8515061 decided that, as long as the privileges given to a different class of member did not provide special benefit to individual, all types of dues can be aggregated.

Dues would be most commonly placed in column (e). To the extent member services, such as group insurance or job placement services, are considered UBI, they would be included in column (b) and labeled with UBI code (6310-6330 for insurance and 7338 for placement services).

Line 95: Interest on Savings and Temporary Cash Investment

Payments from savings and loan, bank, or credit union cash deposits are entered on this line. Typically this income is entered in column (d) and identified with code 14. Interest income on student, low income housing, or other program related loans are reported on line 93. Interest on a loan to an officer or employee would be reported as other revenue, line 103, in column (d), unless the loan is in the nature of compensation (as temporary loan to buy new home) when it could be reported in column (e).

Line 96: Dividends and Interest from Securities

Dividends earned on common or preferred stock, money market accounts, mutual fund shares, U.S. or local government and corporate bonds, and any other securities are usually reported on this line in column (d) and also labeled with code 14. Dividends received from an 80 percent owned for-profit subsidiary would also be reported in column (d) (interest, rent, or other payments deductible to the sub go in column (b)). Capital gains distributed by a mutual fund are reported on line 100.

Securities purchased with borrowed funds, either through a margin account or other debt, called "acquisition indebtedness," produce UBI. Income from such indebted securities are reported in column (b); in the case of partial indebtedness, only a portion, calculated in the ratio of the cost to the debt would be reported in (b) (UBI code 9000) with the balance reported in (d).

Line 97: Net Rental Income (Loss) from Real Estate

The net income, calculated after deduction of expenses such as depreciation, interest on debt, and other direct costs of maintaining real property, are reported on line 97 (code 16). This line does not come directly off of page 1; on page 5, real estate and personal property rentals are separated. Also this is the first line on page 5 where the net income, instead of gross, is entered in column (b), (d), or (e).

Real estate rentals can be classified under one of ten codes and careful studying of IRC Sections 512-514 may be necessary to assure property classification under a particular fact or circumstance. The majority of real property rentals are received on unindebted property held for investment the income from which is reported in column (d) and identified with code 16. Note lease rentals dependent upon the tenants profits are classed as UBI and must be reported in column (b). Rents on program related real estate properties are placed in column (e) on line 93.

Codes 30-38 apply specifically to debt-financed income reportable in column (d) but excludable from UBI classification due to a statutory exception. The portion of income attributable to acquisition indebtedness which is not excluded (see pp. 275-276) is reported in column (b), line 97a (UBI code 6512-6599).

Rents paid by an 80 percent or more owned subsidiary are reported in column (b) as taxable UBI and identified with UBI code 9300. If services are rendered to benefit the individual occupant, such as in a hotel, boarding house, parking lot, or storage facility, the rental is also classed as UBI (codes 7010, 7020, 7500, 7388). Services customarily provided for all tenants, such as utilities, security, cleaning of public entrances, elevators, and other common areas do not constitute services rendered to individual tenants.

Line 98: Net Rental Income (Loss) from Personal Property

Rentals from personal property earned for purely investment purposes create UBI (whether indebted or not) and are reported in column (b) and identified with the appropriate business code such as 7353, 7377, or 9200. Such rentals could be program related in which case they are reported on line 93 in column (e) with no code.

If more than 50 percent of a combined real and personal property lease revenue is attributable to personal property, the rental is reported on line 98, column (b), and is subject to UBI. A manufacturing or printing plant, scientific research facility, or an exhibition hall with booths are examples of the types of rentals which might fall into this category. A Form 990T code again applies and this income, net of directly allocable expenses, is entered in column (b) (UBI code 6512).

Line 99: Other Investment Income

Royalty income from mineral or intellectual property interests are entered on this line. In most cases such income is entered in column (d) and identified with modification code 15. Royalties from educational publications or research patents might be classed as program service revenue on line 93 and entered in column (e) instead. (See line 103 for certain royalties.)

Unrealized gain or loss on the investment portfolio is not considered as current income on page 1 or 5, but is entered as a surplus adjustment on line 20 of page 1.

Line 100: Gain (Loss) from Sales of Assets Other Than Inventory

Capital gains and losses reported on line 8 of page 1 from the disposition of all EO assets, other than inventory, are reported on this line (code 18). Gains and losses from the sale of investment portfolio assets, real estate, office equipment, program related assets, partnership interest, and all sorts of property are included.

As a general rule, most gains or losses will be reportable in column (d), except for debt-financed property that must be shown in column (b). EOs with sophisticated UBI activity may realize gain from sale of assets used in that business also reportable in column (b). Gain (loss) from the sale of program related assets is reported in column (e).

Gain or loss or purchase, sale, and lapse of security options can be reported on this line (code 19). It has been suggested that revenue attributable to lapsed options, as distinguished from options sold or "covered" before maturity, should be reportable on line 99; the IRS instructions are silent and for convenience all option activity can be combined.

Line 101: Net Income from Special Fund-Raising Events

Fund-raising event net income, excluding any portion allocated to donations (included in contributions), is technically UBI. The typical charitable event is excepted from UBI under the irregular (code 01) or volunteer exception (code 02) and the net profit is reported in column (d). Where the primary purpose of the event is educational or exempt, such as a cultural festival, it is conceivable that the profits could be reported as related income in column (e). Any other fund-raising profits must be reported as UBI in column (b) (code 7998). (See § 3.4A for more information about fund-raising events revenue calculations.)

Line 102: Gross Profit (Loss) from Sales of Inventory

Gross revenues from the sale of inventory, less returns and allowances and cost of goods sold (line 10c on page 1) is entered here. Inventory includes objects purchased or made for resale, rather than to hold as an investment. Contrary to the instruction for rents and interest produced from program-related investments, exempt function inventory sales are to be reported on this line, rather than on line 93.

Line 103: Other Revenue

Revenues not suitable for inclusion on lines 93-102 are entered here. Two particular types of revenues that fit on this line are the subject of current battles between the IRS and EOs. Advertising revenues not classified as program related can be entered in either column (b) or (d). Ads produce unrelated income (column (b)—code 7310) unless the irregular or the volunteer exception apply. Likewise, royalties from use of the EO's name, logo, mailing list could be entered in either. If the EO disagrees with the IRS's current position that such income is unrelated (see new materials for § 3.8), such revenue would be entered in column (d) with the modification code 15. See code 13 for the narrow exception available to (c)(3)s and certain veterans organizations for exchanges or rentals of lists between similar types of organizations.

Some have speculated that use of code 15 is an invitation to be examined because the IRS will be scrutinizing EOs claiming modification of royalties despite the fact that some royalties are clearly passive income.

Recoveries of prior year expenditures, interest on loans not made for investment or program purposes (employees or managers), and any other items of revenue not properly reported elsewhere would also be entered on this line.

For further information on specific lines on this page, consult the instructions for the page 1 lines that provide the best IRS guidance.

Rationale for Column (e)

Part VII, *Relationship of Activities to the Accomplishment of Exempt Purposes,* asks that the EO explain how each activity for which income is reported in column (e) contributes importantly to the accomplishment of its exempt purposes (other than by providing funds for such purposes). Although it seems contradictory, dues payments providing funds to support the organization's exempt activities are included in column (e). Not much room is provided and the debate for the past year has been how much to submit. There are two answers to this question dependent upon the nature of the income.

For clearly and unquestionably related types of revenue, such as student tuition, hospital room fees, symphony performance admission tickets, and member dues, the answer can simply be such a description. For revenues received in activities which might arguably produce UBI, such as charges for computer services, sale of standard forms, advertising, or logo sales, a more convincing description is recommended.

The IRS SAMPLE contained in the instructions suggest sentences like: "Fee from county for finding foster homes for 2 children —this furthers our exempt purpose of ensuring qualify care for foster children" and "Members are social services workers who receive information and advice on problem cases from our staff as part of our counseling, adoption, and foster care programs."

The explanation here need not repeat the same information and can be coordinated and tied by direct reference back to Part III, *Statement of Program Service Accomplishments*, where a very similar question is asked.

Consideration can also be given to combinations of similar types of revenue, such as student fees and tuition, rather than a tuition on a separate line for student fees. A social club reporting only members fees and services in column (e) (nonmember reported in column (b)), must clearly indicate this dichotomy.

The Codes

Each numerical entry on page 5 is individually explained either with a code or literal description (suggestions above).

Column (b) is described by column (a) codes (Exhibit 3–3B) which mimic those used for the unrelated business income tax return, Form 990T. The codes describe the type of business and are fairly easy to assign because they are literal—dance studio, or physical fitness facilities, for example. Each major category has a miscellaneous number. There is little harm from a mistake because the EO is already admitting that the income is UBI.

Column (d) is described by "exclusion" codes the correct choice of which is very important. These codes explain that while the EO is admitting it has unrelated business income, it claims that the UBI is not taxable for one of forty different reasons. A review of pages 267–286 will be useful in making the choices.

Part IX   Information Regarding Taxable Subsidiaries

Again with this schedule, the IRS is gathering information to report back to Congress. In this case they will quantify EO ownership of taxable subsidiaries. This part is completed if the EO owns a 50 percent or more interest in a taxable corporation or partnership as asked in Question 78c on page 4. Total assets and income of the sub is reported.

The subsidiary's statistics will presumably be added to those of the parent to allow the IRS to assess the extent to which the sub is being used to avert a primary purpose challenge for excessive business income on the part of the parent. For (c)(3) organizations, transactions between the EO and its relatives are further explored in Part VII, page 5 of Schedule A, Form 990 as shown on page 224 and discussed on page 230. Similar questions are asked on Form 990PF, Part XVIII on page 244.

p. 191.   *Delete the paragraph in § 3.4 and replace with:*

§ 3.4   1990 FORMS UPDATE

* In most respects, the 1990 and 1991 Forms 990 are virtually the same as the 1988 and 1989 forms included in the book. To review the changes that occurred in 1988, the following chart explains the significant ones and identifies the book page where the form explanation can be found.

Form 990, page 1, Part I.   The optional columns to distinguish unrestricted and restricted revenues was eliminated. The last line 21 has been retitled, "Net assets or fund balances at end of year" to conform with the AICPA exposure draft on accounting principles.

Form 990, page 3, Part IV.   The Program Service Revenue detail eliminated because it is now included in Part VII, page 5.

Form 990, page 4, Part VII.   These questions are now Part VI and contain two significant new questions as described on page 218. In Question 83, compliance with public inspection requests must be revealed. In Question 84, the EO must inform the IRS whether it is complying with the voluntary solicitation disclosure program reviewed in § 3.4A.

Form 990, page 5, Part VII (new).   See § 3.3A suggestions for completion of the "Analysis of Income-Producing Activities."

Form 990, page 5, Part IX.   "Information regarding Taxable Subsidiaries" must now be submitted. See § 3.8A for discussion of relationships to other organizations.

Form 990EZ.   The final version was slightly different from the draft included on pages 216–217. The approved 1990 version is shown on pages 74–75 of this supplement and replaces Exhibit 3–4 of the main volume.

p. 218.   *Add comment for Line 83 (1989):*
   Over 58 percent of randomly selected Washington, DC. EOs failed to make their Forms 990 and 1023 available to staff investigators of Congressman Richard Schulze during the summer of 1989 and 1990. In 1990, of the 24 nonprofits sampled, 5 flatly refused to allow public access to their forms; 5 denied access unless staff investigators disclosed their names, employers, and survey purpose; and 3 delayed disclosure for over two months.
   Apparently some EOs are defying the disclosure requirements. Two important factors should influence an organization's decision to refuse an inspection request: (1) The penalty is $10 a day, up to a maximum penalty of $5,000, and (2) although no legislative plans have been advanced to date, continued failure by EOs to allow public reviewing of their financial information may instigate enhanced sanctions.

Exhibit 3-4

Form **990EZ**	**Short Form** **Return of Organization Exempt From Income Tax**		OMB No. 1545-1150
Department of the Treasury Internal Revenue Service	Under section 501(c) of the Internal Revenue Code (except black lung benefit trust or private foundation) or section 4947(a)(1) charitable trust ► For organizations with gross receipts less than $100,000 and total assets less than $250,000 at end of year **Note :** You may have to use a copy of this return to satisfy state reporting requirements. See instruction E.		19**90**

For the calendar year 1990, or fiscal year beginning _____ , 1990, and ending _____ , 19 ____

	Name of organization DISPOSABLE BOTTLE ACTION COMMITTEE	A Employer identification number (see instruction R2) 42 : 2222222
Use IRS label. Otherwise, please print or type.	Number, street, and room (If P.O. box number, see instruction R1) 1111 ANY STREET	B State registration number(s) (see instruction E) none
	City or town, state, and ZIP code HOMETOWN, STATE 44444	C If application for exemption is pending, check here ► . . . . ☐

D Check type of organization—Exempt under section ► ☒ 501(c)(4) (insert number), OR ► ☐ section 4947(a)(1) trust (see instruction C7 and question 42)

E Accounting method: ☒ Cash   ☐ Accrual   ☐ Other (specify) ►

F Check here ► ☐ if your gross receipts are normally not more than $25,000. You need not file a completed return with IRS; but if you received a
Form 990 Package in the mail, you should file a return without financial data (see instructions A4 and B11). **Some states require a completed return.**

G Enter your 1990 gross receipts (add lines 5b, 6b, 7b, and 9) . . . . ► $ _____ 75,500
If $100,000 or more, you must file Form 990 instead of Form 990EZ.

Part I   Statement of Revenue, Expenses, and Changes in Net Assets or Fund Balances

Revenue	1	Contributions, gifts, grants, and similar amounts received (attach schedule—see instructions) .	1	
	2	Program service revenue	2	25,000
	3	Membership dues and assessments (see instructions)	3	50,000
	4	Investment income	4	500
	5a	Gross amount from sale of assets other than inventory . . . [5a]		
	b	Less: cost or other basis and sales expenses . . . . . [5b]		
	c	Gain or (loss) (line 5a less line 5b) (attach schedule)	5c	
	6	Special events and activities (attach schedule—see instructions):		
	a	Gross revenue (not including $_____ of contributions reported on line 1) . . . . [6a]		
	b	Less: direct expenses . . . . [6b]		
	c	Net income or (loss) (line 6a less line 6b)	6c	
	7a	Gross sales less returns and allowances . . . . . . [7a]		
	b	Less: cost of goods sold . . . . [7b]		
	c	Gross profit or (loss) (line 7a less line 7b)	7c	
	8	Other revenue (describe ► _____)	8	
	9	**Total revenue** (add lines 1, 2, 3, 4, 5c, 6c, 7c, and 8) . . . . ►	9	75,500
Expenses	10	Grants and similar amounts paid (attach schedule)	10	
	11	Benefits paid to or for members	11	
	12	Salaries, other compensation, and employee benefits	12	30,000
	13	Professional fees and other payments to independent contractors	13	
	14	Occupancy, rent, utilities, and maintenance	14	15,000
	15	Printing, publications, postage, and shipping	15	24,000
	16	Other expenses (describe ► Cost of buttons, posters, & stickers)	16	6,000
	17	**Total expenses** (add lines 10 through 16). . . . . ►	17	75,000
Net Assets	18	Excess or (deficit) for the year (line 9 less line 17)	18	500
	19	Net assets or fund balances at beginning of year (from line 27, column (A)) (must agree with end-of-year figure reported on prior year's return).	19	7,000
	20	Other changes in net assets or fund balances (attach explanation)	20	
	21	Net assets or fund balances at end of year (combine lines 18 through 20) (must agree with line 27, column (B)). . . . . ►	21	7,500

Part II   Balance Sheets—If Total assets on line 25, Column (B) are $250,000 or more, you must file Form 990 instead of Form 990EZ.

		(A) Beginning of year		(B) End of year
22	Cash, savings, and investments.	7,000	22	7,500
23	Land and buildings.		23	
24	Other assets (describe ► _____)		24	
25	**Total assets**.	7,000	25	7,500
26	Total liabilities (describe ► _____)		26	
27	**Net assets or fund balances** (Column (B) must agree with line 21.)	7,000	27	7,500

For Paperwork Reduction Act Notice, see page 1 of the separate Instructions.   Form **990EZ** (1990)

Exhibit 3–4 *(continued)*

DISPOSABLE BOTTLE ACTION COMMITTEE · · · · · · · 42-2222222 · · · · · · · · Page **2**

Part III	Statement of Program Service Accomplishments—(See instructions.)				Expenses

Describe what was achieved in carrying out your exempt purposes. Fully describe the services provided, the number of persons benefited, or other relevant information for each program title. Section 501(c)(3) and (4) organizations must also enter the amount of grants to others.

Required for section 501(c)(3) and (4) organizations; optional for others.

28 Disposable Bottle Action Committee (DBAC) conducts a nationwide campaign to propose and pass legislation to eliminate disposable containers and reward recycling efforts. Model (Grants $)

29 legislation was prepared this year and introduced in two state legislatures. Committees were formed in four target states and volunteer coordinators have been named. (Grants $) **45,000**

30 Public information brochures, posters, and buttons were designed; over 300,000 copies were distributed in schools and communities in the four target states. (Grants $) **30,000**

31 Other program services (attach schedule) . . . . (Grants $)

32 Total program service expenses (add lines 28 through 31) . . . . ▶ **75,000**

Part IV	List of Officers, Directors, and Trustees (List each one even if not compensated. See instructions.)				

(A) Name and address	(B) Title and average hours per week devoted to position	(C) Compensation (if not paid, enter zero)	(D) Contributions to employee benefit plans	(E) Expense account and other allowances
Gary G. Generous 222 Fifth St., Hometown, St. 44444	President Part-time	–0–	–0–	–0–
Samantha Zealot 404 University Dr., Austin, St. 45555	Vice President Part-time	–0–	–0–	–0–
Linda Lockard 982 Pine Valley, Dallas, St. 46666	Secretary/Treas. Part-time	10,000	–0–	–0–
Jane D. Environmentalist 333 First Street, Hometown, St. 44444	Director Part-time	–0–	–0–	–0–

Part V	Other Information—Section 501(c)(3) organizations and section 4947(a)(1) charitable trusts must also complete and attach Schedule A (Form 990). (See instruction C1.)	Yes	No

33 Did the organization engage in any activity not previously reported to the Internal Revenue Service? . . . . . . | | x
If "Yes," attach a detailed description of each activity.

34 Were any changes made to the organizing or governing documents, but not reported to IRS? . . . . . | | x
If "Yes," attach a conformed copy of the changes.

35 If the organization had income from business activities, such as those reported on lines 2, 6, and 7 (among others), but NOT reported on Form 990-T, attach a statement explaining your reason for not reporting the income on Form 990-T.

  a Did the organization have unrelated business gross income of $1,000 or more during the year covered by this return? . | | x

  b If "Yes," have you filed a tax return on **Form 990-T**, Exempt Organization Business Income Tax Return, for this year? | - - - | - -

36 Was there a liquidation, dissolution, termination, or substantial contraction during the year? (See instructions.) . . | | x
If "Yes," attach a statement as described in the instructions.

37a Enter amount of political expenditures, direct or indirect, as described in the instructions. ▶ | 37a | –0– |

  b Did you file Form 1120-POL, U.S. Income Tax Return for Certain Political Organizations, for this year? . . . . . | | x

38a Did you borrow from or make any loans to any officer, director, trustee, or key employee OR were any such loans made in a prior year and still unpaid at the start of the period covered by this return? . . . . . | | x

  b If "Yes," attach the schedule specified in the instructions and enter the amount involved . | 38b |

39 Section 501(c)(7) organizations.—Enter:

  a Initiation fees and capital contributions included on line 9 . . . . | 39a |

  b Gross receipts, included on line 9, for public use of club facilities (see instructions) . . . | 39b |

  c Does the club's governing instrument or any written policy statement provide for discrimination against any person because of race, color, or religion? (see instructions) . . . . . .

40 List the states with which a copy of this return is filed. ▶ none

41 The books are in care of ▶ John Mockingbird Telephone no. ▶ 444-444-4444
Located at ▶ 222 Fifth St., Hometown, St. 44444

42 Section 4947(a)(1) charitable trusts filing Form 990EZ in lieu of Form 1041, U.S. Fiduciary Income Tax Return.—Check here ▶ ☐
and enter the amount of tax-exempt interest received or accrued during the tax year . . . . . . ▶ | 42 |

Please Sign Here	Under penalties of perjury, I declare that I have examined this return, including accompanying schedules and statements, and to the best of my knowledge and belief, it is true, correct, and complete. Declaration of preparer (other than officer) is based on all information of which preparer has any knowledge.

▶ *Gary Generous* (Signature of officer)   14.7.91 (Date) ▶ President (Title)

Paid Preparer's Use Only	Preparer's signature ▶ *Joan Jones* CPA	Date 4.1.91	Check if self-employed ▶ ☐
	Firm's name (or yours if self-employed) and address	Jones & Brown, CPAs ein55-5555555 234 Fifth St., Hometown, St.	ZIP code 44444

p. 218. *Add new section at the end of § 3.4:*

§ 3.4A IRS SPECIAL EMPHASIS PROGRAM (NEW)

Phase I   Education and Disclosure

During 1990, the IRS continued its Exempt Organization Charitable Solicitations Compliance Improvement Study (CSCI) on deductibility of payments made for participating in charitable fund-raising events, a program which began in August 1988 with public education and the issuance of Publication 1391 (discussed in detail on page 208 and reproduced on page 331). This program was initiated to quantify the perceived abuses in claimed deductions for gifts to charity.

What Is a Charitable Contribution?

A charitable contribution is very simply defined by Section 170 as a gift to or for the use of a qualified organization. The courts have further provided that a "charitable contribution is a gift motivated by detached and disinterested generosity with no expectation of receiving financial benefit commensurate with the amount of the transfer."[6] When the charity offers premiums, prizes, privileges, membership, and other benefits to its contributors, the amount given is not entirely a deductible gift. The fair market value of the inducement or return gift reduces the amount given to calculate the net amount of the actual gift for income tax purposes.

Until 1988, a charity was neither expected nor required to assign such value or inform the givers of the amount. The program asks charities to voluntarily furnish the appropriate valuations to contributors.

The Dilemma: To Disclose or Not

The only sanction for failure to inform contributors is imposition of a penalty for "aiding and abetting" the understatement of the contributor's income tax and the IRS indicates they don't anticipate

---

[6] *Duberstein v. Commissioner*, 363 S.Ct. 278 (1960).

this step. Because there is no specific requirement to furnish donor information, some organizations are choosing not to do so. The sentiment is usually fear that the organization will raise less money when donors discover their deduction is reduced. Some organizations look at the issue as an ethical one. State fund-raising statutes may be decisive. The Texas Attorney General's office is of the opinion that donors should be informed of the amount of their gift that is actually used for charitable purposes. To the extent the organization expends part of the donation to purchase the gifts returned to the givers, the state is concerned that such information be revealed.

The dilemma starts when, as is typical, many of the goods and services furnished to donors cost the organization nothing. Restaurants, merchants, manufacturers, and others are very generous and respond often to appeals (despite the fact that they receive no tax advantage from such gifts). Many charity events and programs are run by volunteers. Often the benefits provided to the givers cost the charity nothing. Why then should they be, and how can they be, valued?

Determining the Value of Benefits

The general rule is the value of the benefit equals its fair market value (FMV). FMV equals the amount a "willing buyer would pay a willing seller" in the normal marketplace for the property being valued in a situation where there was no compulsion to sell. For some benefits, FMV is easily ascertainable: posted price of admission to noncontributors, listed price of the catalog or subscription, or the actual amount of discount. However, many times it is not so easy. The IRS fortunately has adopted a policy that any good-faith, reasonable method of valuation will be acceptable. Evidence of the factors used, hopefully independent information, is to be maintained by the charity.

Note that the definition of FMV is not related to the cost which the organization pays for the object or benefit. In many circumstances, though, similar objects or services are not commercially available and a comparable price cannot be found. In such cases, the actual expenditures, including the value of donated goods and services, may be the only valid indication of value. The task is often difficult and charities trying to comply find that ascribing value to benefits furnished is a "difficult and burdensome" task.

De Minimus Rule

The IRS responded to the complaints of valuation difficulties by issuing Rev. Proc. 90-12 in February, 1990.[7] The procedure describes de minimus rules for fund-raising premiums having insubstantial value.

The *guidelines* provide that a gift is fully deductible and the value of the premiums or benefits can be ignored in the following circumstances:

> The payment occurs in the context of a fund-raising campaign in which the charity informs patrons how much of their payment is a deductible contribution, and either
>
> (a) The fair market value of all of the benefits received in connection with the payment is not more than 2 percent of the payment, or $50, whichever is less, or
>
> (b) The payment of $28.59 during 1991 ($27.26 for 1990, $26.03 for 1989 and $25.00 for 1988) or more (adjusted annually for inflation), and the benefits received are token items (bookmarks, calendars, key chains, mugs, posters, tee shirts, and so on) and bear the organization's name or logo with a cost (as opposed to fair market value) of no more than $5.72 (during 1991; $5.45 for 1990, $5.21 for 1989 and $5.00 for 1988).

A *qualifying fund-raising campaign* for purposes of this procedure has three elements:

1. It is designed to raise tax-deductible contributions.

2. The charity determines the fair market value of the benefits offered in return for contributions using a reasonable estimate if an exact determination is not possible.

3. It states in its solicitations (whether written, broadcast, telephoned, or in person)—as well as in tickets, receipts, or other documents issued in connection with contributions—how much is deductible under Section 170 *and how much is not.*

---

[7] Rev. Proc. 90-12, IRS News Release IR-90-20, February 1990.

Publications, such as newsletters and program guides, may or may not be treated as having measurable fair market value that reduce the deductible portion of the gift. If the primary purpose of the publication is to inform members about the activities of the organization and it is not available to nonmembers by paid subscription or through newsstand sales, the publication is *not* considered to be a "commercial quality publication (CQP)." CQPs are assigned value and reduce the value of the gift. The procedure states, "Whether a publication is considered a CQP depends upon all of the facts and circumstances. Generally publications that contain articles written for compensation and that accept advertising will be treated as CQPs having measurable fair market value or costs. Professional journals (whether or not articles are written for compensation and advertising is accepted) will normally be treated as CQPs."

Organizations furnishing benefits deemed insubstantial under this procedure are advised by the IRS to include on their fund-raising materials "a statement to the effect that: Under IRS guidelines, the estimated value of (the benefits received) is not substantial; therefore the full amount of your payment is a deductible contribution."

Phase II   IRS Examinations

The Checksheet

Phase II of the Special Emphasis Program began in the spring of 1990. To determine the extent of unallowable contributions being claimed by participants in charitable fund-raising campaigns, the IRS began examinations of organizations and their contributors. The checksheet (Exhibit 3–4A) reflects the broad extent of the examinations. Examination objectives, according to the Internal Revenue Manual (Manual Supplement 7(10)G-59), are to exhaustively look at all aspects of fund-raising and charitable solicitations.

Based upon the initial findings, the IRS plans to complete this checksheet for all (c)(3)s examined during 1991.

The agents are directed to review disclosure of deductibility information to ascertain whether it is misleading. Information about individual donors is gathered for referral to the income tax examination

Exhibit 3-4A

Exempt Organizations Charitable Solicitations Compliance Improvement
Program Study Checksheet – Phase II

I. Entity Data	National Office Hotline Phone for:

National Office Hotline Phone for:

• **Project and Checksheet Questions – 566–6181**
• **Technical (fundraising) Questions – 566–4332**

1. Name of Organization:

2. Street Address:

3. City, State, ZIP Code:

4. EIN: |___|___|___|–|___|___|___|___|___|___|___| 5. Type of Return: ☐ Form 990   ☐ Form 990–PF

6. Tax Period: |___|___|___|___| 7. Foundation Code: |___|___| 8. Classification Code: |___|___|___|___|

9. Activity Codes   Per EO/BMF: _____ _____ _____   10. Income/Asset   Per EO/BMF: ____/____
                     Per Exam: _____ _____ _____   Codes   Per Exam: ____/____

II. Fundraising Activities Present?

11. Did you find the organization was involved in fundraising activities?   ☐ Yes   ☐ No
[Based upon the response to this Item, please refer to "Note 2" in Attachment 5 of the Manual Supplement for further Instruction for the completion of this checksheet.)

12. What was the nature of the fundraising activities? [Check the applicable activities listed below and give a brief description of the activities in the space below or complete the descriptive "Items" mentioned which appear later on this checksheet.]:

Auction	☐	Fashion Show	☐
Musical Concert	☐	Theatrical Show	☐
Spectator Sporting Event	☐	Thrift Store [or similar activity (Items 56 – 60)]	☐
Luncheon, Dinner, or Banquet	☐	Membership Drive	☐
Carnival, Bazaar, or Fair	☐	Awards Ceremony	☐
Raffle, Lottery, or Sweepstakes	☐	Cultural Exhibition	☐
Las Vegas or Monte Carlo Nights	☐	Annual Solicitation Campaign	☐
Bingo [and any other Games of Chance (Items 39–48)]	☐	Other (specify):[ ]	☐
Charity Ball	☐		

[Describe activity here.]:

	Yes	No	N/A
13. Did the organization conduct any fundraising activities designed to solicit payments which were intended to be, in part, a gift and, in part, a payment for admission to the fundraising event, participation in the fundraising event, or for other benefits conferred on the donor? [If "Yes", please refer to Items 62–67].	☐	☐	☐
14. Did the charity receive any "noncash" contributions with a fair market value greater than $500 from any donor(s)? [If "Yes", please refer to Items 70 – 76].	☐	☐	☐
15. Did the charity sell, exchange, consume or otherwise dispose of any "noncash" contribution(s) within two years of receipt of the "noncash" property? [If "Yes", please refer to Items 78–80].	☐	☐	☐

III. General Information on Fundraising Activities

	Yes	No	N/A
16. If the charity engaged in fundraising activities, complete Items 17–25. Otherwise, enter an "X" in "N/A".		☐	N/A
17. Did the charity acknowledge receipt of the cash donation in writing?	☐	☐	☐
18. Did the charity acknowledge receipt of the noncash donation in writing?	☐	☐	☐
19. Was an outside/professional fundraiser hired to conduct the fundraising program? [If "Yes", please refer to Items 27–37].	☐	☐	☐

Exhibit 3–4A *(continued)*

Charitable Solicitations Compliance Improvement Program Study Checksheet – Phase II

III. General Information on Fundraising Activities (Continued)

	Yes	No	N/A
20. Did the charity maintain any record(s) of the names and addresses of the donors?	☐	☐	☐
21. Did the charity maintain sample copies of the solicitation materials, advertisements of the fundraising event(s), tickets, receipts, or other evidence of payment received in connection with the fundraising activity(ies)?	☐	☐	☐
22. Did the charity maintain copies of script, transcripts, or other evidence of on–air solicitations for TV and/or radio fundraising solicitations?	☐	☐	☐
23. Did the charity indicate in membership literature or other written evidence that the "cost" of membership dues was tax deductible?	☐	☐	☐
24. If "Yes" to Item 23, were there any benefits associated with joining the charity as a member?	☐	☐	☐

25. Describe in the space below the benefits that a new member would receive in return for his/her membership contribution:

IV. Outside/Professional Fundraiser

26. If the charity hired an outside/professional fundraiser, complete Items 27–37. Otherwise, enter an "X" in "N/A", and go to Item 38. . . . . ☐ N/A

27. Who was the professional fundraiser? [Check the box at the right that best applies and provide the name and address]:

For–Profit Entity . . . ☐
Individual . . . . ☐
Tax Exempt Entity . . ☐
Other . . . . ☐
N/A . . . . ☐

28. Please provide the following information, as it relates to the fundraising activities of the "outside" fundraiser:

28(a). Total number of mailings . . . . _____

28(b). Total aggregate cost of the mailings . . . . $_____

28(c). Total number of donor responses to the mailings . . . . _____

28(d). Total dollar amount of contributions generated from the mailings . . . . $_____

	Yes	No
29. Was there a written agreement between the charity and the professional fundraiser? If "Yes", attach a copy of the agreement.	☐	☐
30. If "Yes" to Item 29, was the compensation arrangement based upon a flat fee or as a percentage of the income generated by the professional fundraiser? Please describe the arrangement in the space provided:	☐	☐
31. Was the charity created by an owner, officer, director, trustee, or employee of the professional fundraiser? If "Yes", please specify in the space provided:	☐	☐
32. Is any officer, director, trustee, or employee of the charity employed by or connected with the professional fundraiser in any ownership of business, investment venture, or family relationship? If "Yes", please explain in the space below:	☐	☐

Exhibit 3–4A *(continued)*

Charitable Solicitations Compliance Improvement Program Study Checksheet – Phase II

IV. Outside/Professional Fundraiser (Continued)

	Yes	No
33. Did the charity have "approval" rights, as client of the professional fundraiser, over any of the fundraising program implemented by the professional fundraiser?	☐	☐
34. Did the professional fundraiser have check "writing" authority?	☐	☐
35. Did the professional fundraiser have check "cashing" authority?	☐	☐
36. Did the charity retain copies of fundraising materials prepared by the professional fundraiser? If "Yes", please attach copies of the fundraising materials.	☐	☐
37. Did the charity meet the "commensurate test" as set forth in Rev. Rul. 64–182?	☐	☐

V. Bingo and Other Games of Chance

	Yes	No	N/A
38. If the charity conducted bingo or other games of chance, complete items 39–48. Otherwise, enter an "X" in "N/A", then go to item 49.			☐ N/A
39. Did the bingo activity meet the tests of IRC 513(f)(2), specifically including the requirements that the activity meet the definition of a "Bingo game"; the conduct of which is not an activity ordinarily carried out on a commercial basis; and the conduct of which does not violate any state or local law?	☐	☐	☐
40. If the tests under IRC 513(f)(2) were not met, did the charity timely file Form 990–T?	☐	☐	☐
41. If "No" to Item 40, did you secure the delinquent Form 990–T?	☐	☐	☐
42. Did the games of chance, other than bingo, take place in North Dakota? If "Yes", go to Item 43. If "No", go to Item 44.	☐	☐	☐
43. If the games of chance, other than bingo, were conducted in North Dakota, and the gross income was not reported on a filed Form 990–T, did the organization meet all the tests set forth in Section 311 of the Deficit Reduction Act of 1984? If "No", go to Item 44. [These tests specifically include the requirements that the games must be conducted by non-profit entities; that there must have been a state law (originally enacted on 4-22-77) in effect on 10-5-83, which permitted the conduct of such games of chance; and the games must not violate state or local law.]	☐	☐	☐
44. Did the charity timely file Form 990–T?	☐	☐	☐
45. If "No" to Item 44, did you secure the delinquent Form 990–T?	☐	☐	☐
46. Was the income from either bingo or any other games of chance subject to any of the UBI exceptions, e.g. volunteer labor, as described in IRC 513(a)? If "Yes", please specify the exception in the space provided.	☐	☐	☐
47. Did the charity timely file the proper information returns (Form 1099–MISC) and withholding returns (Form W2–G) for the winners of bingo and other games of chance?	☐	☐	☐
48. Did the charity hire outside contractors to specifically operate bingo and other games of chance?	☐	☐	☐

Exhibit 3–4A *(continued)*

Charitable Solicitations Compliance Improvement Program Study Checksheet – Phase II

VI. Travel Tours

	Yes	No	N/A
49. If the charity conducted travel tours, complete items 50–54. Otherwise, enter an "X" in "N/A", then go to item 55.			☐ N/A
50. Did the promotional travel literature and/or other written documentation indicate that the tours were educational? [Please attach copies of the tour literature or documentation.]	☐ Yes	☐ No	☐ N/A
51. Did the promotional travel literature and/or other written documentation contain discussions of any social/recreational aspects of the tour?	☐ Yes	☐ No	☐ N/A
52. Did the charity have a contract or do business with a for–profit travel agency?	☐ Yes	☐ No	☐ N/A
53. If "Yes" to Item 52, did the charity receive any fee from the travel agency? If "Yes", please explain in the space below:	☐ Yes	☐ No	☐ N/A

54. Please indicate if the charity was related to the for–profit travel agency by means of:

54(a). Sharing the same address or building . . . . ☐

54(b). Sharing the same office space, equipment, or personnel . . . . ☐

54(c). Creator of charity and owner of for–profit entity . . . . ☐

54(d). Officer, director, trustee, or employee of the charity and the travel agency . . . . ☐

54(e). Presence of family ties between the charity and travel agency . . . . ☐

54(f). No Relationship exists between charity and travel agency . . . . ☐

54(g). Other, specify:[   ] . . . . ☐

VII. Thrift Store or Similar Type Activity

	Yes	No	N/A
55. If the charity operated a thrift or "second–hand" store, complete items 56–60. Otherwise, enter an "X" in "N/A", then go to item 61.			☐ N/A
56. Did the charity solicit used clothing, furniture, etc. from donors for resale by a for–profit entrepreneur?	☐ Yes	☐ No	☐ N/A
57. Did the charity receive compensation from the for–profit entrepreneur? If "Yes", please describe the terms of the compensation agreement in the space below, i.e. flat fee, percent of revenues, etc.:	☐ Yes	☐ No	☐ N/A
58. Was there a co–venture, partnership, or similar type arrangement between the charity and the thrift store or similar type operation? If "Yes", please describe the arrangement in the space below and provide the name and address of the other entity:	☐ Yes	☐ No	☐ N/A
59. Did the charity receive any new goods from corporate inventories designated as surplus or not saleable by the corporation?	☐ Yes	☐ No	☐ N/A
60. If "Yes" to Item 59, please describe the goods received, including the fair market value and use made of the goods:	☐ Yes	☐ No	☐ N/A

Exhibit 3–4A (continued)

Charitable Solicitations Compliance Improvement Program Study Checksheet – Phase II

VIII. Goods or Services Received in Exchange for a Charitable Contribution

61. If the charity gives goods or services for charitable donations, complete Items 62–67. Otherwise, enter an "X" in "N/A", then go to Item 68. ..... ☐ N/A

62. What was the nature of the benefits, goods, or services given to the donor? Please indicate those goods or services that apply and give a brief description in the space below:

62(a). Retail merchandise .... ☐
62(b). New and donated merchandise received at an auction .... ☐
62(c). Tickets for a raffle, lottery, bingo, or other game of chance .... ☐
62(d). Tuition at a school or other educational institution .... ☐
62(e). Travel or other transportation .... ☐
62(f). Tickets to an athletic, cultural, entertainment, or other event .... ☐
62(g). Discounts on goods or services .... ☐
62(h). Free subscriptions to publications .... ☐
62(i). Preferential seating at a college or university athletic event .... ☐
62(j). Other, specify:[   ] .... ☐
Description:

63. Did the charity disclose the deductible amount or make reference to deductibility in its solicitations and/or promotional literature? [Please attach representative copies of the literature.] — ☐ Yes ☐ No ☐ N/A

64. Did the charity disclose the deductible amount or refer to deductibility in any thank you letter, receipt, ticket, or other written receipt? [Please attach representative copies of receipts.] — ☐ Yes ☐ No ☐ N/A

65. Did the charity disclose the deductible amount or make reference to deductibility in any other manner, e.g. via oral communication? If "Yes", please select the item that best describes the manner of oral communication: — ☐ Yes ☐ No ☐ N/A

65(a). Radio .... ☐
65(b). Television .... ☐
65(c). Door-to-door solicitation .... ☐
65(d). Other, specify:[   ] .... ☐

66. Was the charity aware of Rev. Rul. 67–246 prior to the examination? — ☐ Yes ☐ No ☐ N/A

67. Did the charity receive Publication 1391 in the mail in 1988? If "No", please provide a copy of the publication to the charity. — ☐ Yes ☐ No ☐ N/A

IX. Noncash Contributions

68. If the charity received or disposed of any noncash charitable contributions, complete Items 69–80. Otherwise, enter an "X" in "N/A", then go to Item 81. ☐ N/A

69. If the charity received any noncash contributions in the year examined, complete Items 70–76. Otherwise, enter an "X" in "N/A". .... ☐ N/A

70. Please attach a listing (if more than one item) of all noncash charitable contributions, whose fair market value (FMV) exceeded $500, given to the charity during the year examined. The listing should include the following:

70(a). Name and Address of donor:
70(b). Item Name:
70(c). Description of Item:
70(d). Date Item Received:
70(e). FMV: $

71. Who determined the FMV of the contributed noncash property? Select one below:

71(a). Donor .... ☐
71(b). Charity .... ☐
71(c). Independent Appraiser .... ☐
71(d). Other, specify:[   ] .... ☐

Form 9215 (1-90) · Page –5– · Department of the Treasury – Internal Revenue Service

■ 116 ■

Exhibit 3-4A *(continued)*

IX. Noncash Contributions (Continued)

	Yes	No	N/A
72. For contributed noncash property with a FMV of $5,000 or less, did the charity provide the donor with a receipt containing the following information? 72(a). Donee name, 72(b). Date and location of the contributed property, and 72(c). A description of the property in detail, including its value.	☐	☐	☐
73. Was there any kind of an agreement between the charity and donor concerning the use, sale, or other disposition of the property? If "Yes", please explain below:	☐	☐	☐
74. Did the charity complete Section B, Part I of Form 8283? (If "No", please explain below. If "Yes", complete Items 75 and 76.)	☐	☐	☐
75. Was Form 8283 signed by a properly authorized official of the charity?	☐	☐	☐
76. Did the charity retain a copy of Form 8283?	☐	☐	☐

77. If the charity disposed of any noncash property within two years of its receipt, complete Items 78–80. Otherwise, enter an "X" in "N/A". . . . . ☐ N/A

78. Please attach a listing (if more than one item) of all noncash donated property, valued at $500 or more, that was sold, exchanged, consumed, or otherwise disposed of during the year under examination, which the charity received within two years of the disposal date. The listing should include:

78(a). Description of the donated noncash property disposed of:
78(b). Date the charity received the property:
78(c). Date the property was disposed of:

	Yes	No	N/A
79. Did the charity timely file Form 8282, Noncash Charitable Contributions Donee Information?	☐	☐	☐
80. Did the charity furnish a copy of Form 8282 to the donor of the noncash property?	☐	☐	☐ N/A

X. Penalty Assessments

81. If any penalty was assessed against the charity, complete Item 82. Otherwise, enter an "X" in "N/A", then go to Item 83. . . . . ☐ N/A

82. Select the penalty(ies) which you assessed against the charity and give a brief explanation below:

82(a). § 6651(a)(1) – Failure to file tax return . . . . ☐
82(b). § 6652(a)(2) – Failure to pay tax . . . . ☐
82(c). § 6652(c)(1)(A)(ii) – Failure to file complete or accurate EO information return . . . . ☐
82(d). § 6661 – Substantial understatement of liability . . . . ☐
82(e). § 6700 – Promoting abusive tax shelters . . . . ☐
82(f). § 6701 – Aiding and abetting understatements of tax liability . . . . ☐
82(g). § 6721 – Failure to file certain information returns . . . . ☐
82(h). § 6722 – Failure to file certain payee statements . . . . ☐
82(i). § 6723 – Failure to include correct information on an information return or payee statement . . . . ☐
82(j). Other, specify:{§   } . . . . ☐

Please explain the reason for the assessment and state the amount of the penalty:

Exhibit 3–4A *(continued)*

XI. Form 990/990–PF Return Information

REVENUE			Per Return	Per Exam
83. Contributions, gifts, and grants received:			$	$
84. Membership dues and assessments:			$	$
85. Special fundraising events & activities:	Per Return	Per Exam		
85(a). Gross Revenue:	$	$		
85(b). Minus – Direct Expenses:	$	$		
85(c). Net Income:			$	$
86. Total Revenue:			$	$

EXPENSES	Per Return	Per Exam
87. Program services:	$	$
88. Management and General:	$	$
89. Fundraising:		
89(a). Professional fundraising:	$	$
89(b). Total Fundraising:	$	$
90. Total Expenses:	$	$
91. Excess (deficit) for the year:	$	$

XII. Control Data

92. Project Code: |9 |0 |2 | 93. District Name: _____   94. KDO: |__|__|

95. Examiner Name: _____   96. Examiner Grade: |__|__| 97. Date:

98. Time on Case: _____   99. Principal Issue Code: |__|__| 100. Disposal Code: |__|__|

101. Group Manager's Name and Telephone Number: _____   102. Date:

XIII. REMARKS

103. Remarks [Enter Item Number to which remarks refer and use the space below for general remarks.]:

division. Where outside/professionals are hired to plan and/or conduct the campaign, details of the financial arrangements are studied. Is the compensation paid reasonable? Is the arrangement based upon a percentage of the funds raised or a flat hourly or monthly fee? Can the commensurate test be met?

The commensurate test was outlined by the IRS in Rev. Rul. 64-182[8] and is still used by the IRS to evaluate fund-raising arrangements where the promoter keeps a major share of the proceeds. Unless a minimal percentage (say 25 percent) of the gross receipts of a fund-raiser is actually paid over to the organization for its charitable purposes, the activity fails this test. Contributors are misinformed and mislead unless a "commensurate part" of their gifts are actually used for the charitable purposes to which they are giving.

The private inurement/benefit issues discussed in § 3.10 may also apply and should be reviewed.

Unrelated Business Income Aspect

If part of the money received from contributors in connection with a benefit or other fund raiser is not a donation, what is it? Does the event constitute a trade or business activity carried on for the production of income from the sale or goods or performance of services? If so, trade or business income is potentially taxable unless the organization can prove that the activity is accomplishing an exempt purpose other than the need for funds, or related income. This aspect of the special emphasis program may prove the most costly to EOs. Unless the exceptions or modifications discussed on pages 269–272 are applicable, profits from fund-raising events conceivably could be subject to the unrelated business income tax.

One such situation has already been reviewed in T.A.M. 9029001 issued March 21, 1990. An organization conducted travel tours that the IRS determined were not as educational as claimed. Instead the tours were unrelated to the organizations underlying exempt status and therefore produced unrelated business income. The "so-called contribution" requested from each individual participating in the tour program, in addition to the quoted price of the trip, was also classified as UBI, not a donation revenue.

[8] Rev. Rul. 64-182, 1964-1 C.B. (Part 1), 186.

Bingo Controversy

Bingo and other games of chance are also a topic to be examined. Agents in the Dallas Key District conducted a special study of bingo-sponsoring organizations during 1990. Their primary concern was to enforce their narrow definition of bingo. Pull-tabs and other forms of "instant bingo" are not bingo in their opinion and therefore produce unrelated business income despite the fact that such variations of the bingo game are so classified by the state bingo authority. Section 513(f) defines bingo as any game of bingo of a type in which usually:

1. The wagers are placed,

2. The winners are determined, and

3. The distribution of prizes or other property is made, in the presence of all persons placing wagers in such game.

The argument starts in the regulations that explicitly say, "A bingo game is a game of chance played with cards that are generally printed with five rows of five squares each. Participants place markers over randomly called numbers on the cards in an attempt to form a preselected pattern such as a horizontal, vertical, or diagonal line, or all four corners. The first participant to form the preselected pattern wins the game." Any other game of chance, including but not limited to, keno, dice, cards, and lotteries, is not bingo (and will create UBI).

The code definition would encompass some of the game variations excluded by the regulations and numbers of groups raising funds in this fashion are now (fall, 1990) preparing to battle with the IRS in the courts.

§ 3.5 SCHEDULE A: FOR 501(c)(3)s ONLY

p. 219. *Add at the end of first paragraph Reasons for Non-Private Foundation Status:*
See § 3.5A for definition of Public Charities.

p. 228. *Correct the numerator of investment income test to add "and UBI less UBIT."*

p. 230. *Add at bottom of the page:*
See § 3.8A for significance of these relationship questions.

p. 230. *Add new section at end of § 3.5:*

§ 3.5A DEFINITION OF PUBLIC CHARITIES (NEW)

The significance of the "public charity" category is multifaceted and of utmost importance to EOs in and out of the classification. Section 509 provides that all Section 501(c)(3) organizations, other than those listed in 509(a)(1), (2), and (3) are private foundations. The specific requirements for each of the 509 categories are described next.

The breadth of Chapter Four indicates both the complicated nature and the extent of the special rules and sanctions placed upon private foundations. Thus, obtaining and maintaining public status, when possible, is useful. A brief list of the important attributes of private foundations (PFs), compared to public charities (in parentheses) includes:

1. Percentage limitation for allowable contribution deduction for individuals under Section 170 is only 30 percent of adjusted gross income for cash gifts and 20 percent for appreciated property gifts (not 50 and 30 percent).

2. An excise tax of 2 percent must be paid on a PF's investment income (versus none).

3. A PF cannot enter into transactions with related parties under any circumstances (see § 3.10).

4. Annual returns (11 pages, rather than 4) must be filed regardless of support levels and value of assets (no return required for certain public organizations, see § 3.3).

5. Fund raising from other PFs is constrained by "expenditure responsibility" requirements (none, see p. 367).

6. Absolutely no lobbying activity is permitted (see § 3.9 for lobbying activity allowed by public charities.) No political activity for any category of (c)(3).

Broad Public Support Category: 509(a)(1)

A wide variety of organizations qualify under this category, which is defined to include all those organizations described in Section 170(b)(1)(A), a rather unwieldy definition that actually includes six categories. The first three 509(a)(1) categories achieve public status because of the nature of their activities, even if they are privately supported. The qualification for public status under the next three categories is measured by the organization's contribution base. Many organizations qualify under the "vi" category. As shown in Exhibit 3–6 on page 227, such organizations must receive at least one-third of their donations from public sources. The categories of Section 170(b)(1)(A) are:

(i)   Church, convention, or association of churches.

(ii) Educational organization that normally maintains a regular faculty and curriculum and normally has a regularly enrolled body of pupils or students in attendance at the place where its educational activities are regularly carried on.

(iii) Hospital providing medical care, medical education or medical research, or an organization performing medical research in conjunction with a hospital.

(iv) Organization supported by governmental units or public contributions and operated to benefit state-controlled colleges and universities.

(v)   The United States, District of Columbia, a state, a possession of the United States, or their political subdivisions (governmental units).

(vi) Organization that receives a substantial part (over one-third) of its annual support (not including fees and charges for performing exempt functions) from the general public.

* A governmental unit for purposes of category "v" is defined by Section 170(c) to include a state, a possession of the United States, or any political subdivision of any of the forgoing, or the United States or the District of Columbia and not defined any further by the regulations.

Such a unit qualifies as a public charity regardless of its sources of support.

An unincorporated intergovernmental cooperative organization established by an act of the Texas legislature on behalf of a consortium of 11 Texas public school districts was found to be a private foundation, not a governmental unit, for two reasons.[9]

1. Its source of support was a particular private foundation that granted it the money to undertake its curriculum research and development.

2. It was not a governmental unit. Although the cooperative arguably was an instrumentality of the State, it had no sovereign powers, such as right of eminent domain, tax assessment and collection or police powers. The fact that it was an integral part of a group of governmental units—the public schools by which it was established—also did not make it a governmental unit itself.

Service Providing Organizations: 509(a)(2)

The second major category of public charity is measured again by sources of revenue, but the significant difference is the inclusion of "exempt function income" in the support base as shown in Exhibit 3–7 on page 228.

This category has a two-part support test. Its investment income cannot exceed one-third of its total support and it must receive over one-third of its total support from a combination of:

- Admissions (theater, ballet, museums, historic sites, seminar, lecture).

- Fees for performance of services (school tuition, day care fees, hospital room and expenses, psychiatric counseling, testing, scientific laboratory fees, library fines, animal neutering charge, athletic facility fees).

---

[9] *Texas Learning Technology Group v. Commissioner*, 96 T.C. 28 (April 30, 1991).

- Merchandise sales (books and educational literature, pharmaceuticals and medical devices, handicrafts, reproductions and copies of original works or art, byproducts of blood bank, goods produced by handicapped).

- Contributions and membership dues.

- Investment income.

Difference between Section 509(a)(1) and (a)(2)

Some organizations can qualify for public status under both of the Section 509 categories including, for example, the typical church, school, or hospital. In such cases, an (a)(1) class will be assigned by the IRS in making a determination of public status.

For purposes of annual reporting, unrelated business, deductibility of contributions, and most other tax purposes, the two categories are virtually the same, with one important exception. To receive a terminating distribution from a private foundation upon its dissolution, the charity must be an (a)(1) organization according to Section 507(b)(1)(A).

Definition of support is different and does not equal total revenue under either class. Support forms the basis for the public status for both and the calculations are made on a four-year moving average basis using the cash method of accounting. For (a)(1) purposes, revenues earned through exempt function activities, capital gains or losses, and unusual grants are not counted in "total support." For (a)(2) purposes, total revenue less capital gains or losses and unusual grants equals total support.

Major gifts are counted as public support differently and for planning purposes are extremely important to consider. Under the (a)(1) category, a particular giver's donations are counted only up to an amount equal to 2 percent of the total "support" for the four-year period. For example, assume an organization receives $100,000 of donations and investment income annually resulting in total base period of support is $400,000. Two percent of the total support, or $8,000, is the maximum amount of any contributor's gift deemed public support. Any gifts in excess of that amount from an individual (and related parties as described in Section 4946) is considered private support. Gifts from other public charities and governmental entities not subject to this 2 percent floor.

For (a)(2) purposes, all contributions are counted as public support, except those received from disqualified persons as defined in Section 4946 (see p. 339). The organization receiving substantial gifts from uninvolved parties that cause loss of public status under (a)(1) may instead easily qualify under (a)(2).

Facts and Circumstances Test[10] can be used as an alternative method for qualifying for public support under (a)(1) only (not available under (a)(2)), where the mathematical one-third support test is failed. IRS approval must be sought for this status. Three factors must be present to meet this test:

1. Public support must be at least 10 percent of the total support (the higher the better).

2. Organization must have an active "continuous and bonafide program" fund-raising program.

3. Members of board of directors, support from government and other public sources, availability of facilities and programs to the general public, appeal of programs to broadly based public, and other factors prove support of general public.

Community foundations are another potential (a)(1) classification. Designed to attract capital and endowment gifts for the benefit of a particular community or area by pooling donations from benevolent citizens. The requirements for qualifications and constraints on operation of community foundations are a mixture of the rules governing both private and public charities and are quite complicated in their application.[11]

A community foundation serves as a convenient receptacle for givers who do not wish to create their own private foundation, but wish to make a bequest, endowment, or other permanent charitable gift. Donors may designated the purpose for which their gift is to be used, subject to ultimate control by the foundation's board of

---

[10] Treas. Reg. § 1.170A-9(e)(3).
[11] Treas. Reg. § 1.170A-9(e)(10) and (11).

directors. "Component parts" can be established by the foundation to hold contributors gifts for restricted purposes.

Change of Category from (a)(1) to (a)(2) or vice versa is discussed in the supplemental comments for page 263.

Special Types of Support

Membership fees for both classes may represent donations or charges for services rendered and the facts in each circumstance must be examined to properly classify the revenue. A membership fee is a donation if it is paid to support the organization rather than to purchase admission, merchandise, services, or the use of facilities. Under the enhanced scrutiny of the IRS's Special Emphasis Program (see § 3.4A) on deductibility of charitable gifts, some organizations are realizing the members are not necessarily making contributions. Particularly for (a)(1) purposes, this distinction is very important because exempt function fees are not included in the public support calculations.

Grants for services to be rendered for the granting organization, such as a state government's funding for home health care, are treated under both categories are exempt function income, not donations. Under (a)(2) status, only the first $5,000 of fees for services received from a particular person or organization is includable in public support. Thus, this distinction must be carefully studied for such an organization. The regulations should be carefully studied.[12]

Pass-through grants received from another public charity are totally counted towards public support unless the gift represents an amount expressly or impliedly earmarked by a donor to be paid to a sub-grantee organization,[13] according to the regulations.

In G.C.M. 39748 (1988), however, the IRS clarified that this rule applies to grants received as "agent." Donations received under a donor-designation or donor-advised funds would qualify as public support to the inital recipients.

Unusual grants are excluded from gross revenue in calculating total support for (a)(1) and (a)(2) purposes. In a situation where inclusion of such a gift causes loss of public status, the exception is very

---

[12] Treas. Reg. § 1.509(a)(3)(f)-(m).
[13] Treas. Reg. §§ 1.170A-9(e)(6)(v), 1.509(a)-3(j)(3), and G.C.M. 39748.

important. A grant is unusual if it is an unexpected and substantial gift attracted by the public nature of the organization *and* received from a disinterested party.

In Rev. Rul. 81-7,[14] a set of "safe harbor" reliance factors were provided for the makers of unusual grants. Under this ruling an unusual grant must be:

1. Received from a person who isn't a substantial contributor, board member, manager, or related to one.

2. In the form of cash, marketable securities, or property that furthers the organization's exempt purposes.

3. Unrestricted with no material stipulations.

4. Intended to pay operating expenses, not to become part of an endowment. Cannot exceed one year's operating expense.

Supporting organization and split-interest trust gifts to (a)(2) entities may retain their character as investment income for purposes of limiting the amount of investment income an (a)(2) organization is allowed to receive.[15]

Supporting Organizations: 509(a)(3)

The third category of organizations that escape the stringent requirements placed upon private foundations is called supporting organizations (SOs). If such organizations are sufficiently responsive to and controlled or supervised by one or more public charities, they are classified as public charities themselves even if they are privately funded.

Basically, supporting organizations dedicate all of their assets to one or more public charities but may be separately controlled (although many are not). Beneficiary organization(s) may be unspecified, and under certain conditions, can be changed, making this type of foundation popular with benefactors not wanting to create a private foundation and also not wanting to make an outright gift to an

---

[14] Rev. Rul. 81-7, 1981-1 C.B. 621.
[15] Treas. Reg. § 1.509(a)-5(a)(1).

established charity. According to the Congressional Records, the SO rules were fashioned to allow a particular organization to escape PF classification. The rules are not entirely logical and the regulations are quite detailed and extensive. Anyone considering the creation of an SO must read and try to understand the regulations. An SO must meet unique organizational and operational tests.

Purpose Clause

Under Section 509(a)(3)(A), SOs must be organized, and at all times thereafter operated exclusively:

- For the benefit of,

- To perform the functions of, or

- To carry out the purposes of one or more specified organizations described in Section 509(a)(1) or (2), a "public charity."

The articles of organization must limit the purposes to those listed above in addition to the regular constraints on operations contained in the sample charter (pp. 82–85 of the main book). The categories of purpose, charitable, religious, or educational may be very broad. Classic examples of suitable SO purposes would be to raise money for the publicly supported hospitals in an urban medical center, to fund the medical library of the center, or to build and maintain a chapel for the center.

The IRS regulations specifically require the supported organization(s) be named in the articles; but in a complex labyrinth of terms, allow nondesignation where certain combinations of the control relationships are provided.

A class of beneficiary organizations, such as "Catholic churches in the city" or "institutions of higher learning in a particular state" may be named (rather than naming individual churches or schools) if the public charities are generally in control (see specifics below). The named beneficiaries may be changed if the substitution is a result of occurrences beyond the organization's control. Also the amount of support may be varied between the specified charities (if it meets the integral part test).

Operational Control

According to Section 509(a)(3)(B), the SO must be operated, supervised, controlled by, or operated in connection with a public charity. Simply turning over all of the organization's income to the specifically named charity in accordance with the SO's articles of incorporation is not sufficient to meet this operational test even though it satisfies the 501(c)(3) operational tests. The regulations, for reasons not made clear, delineate three distinct types of permissible relationships:

- *Type 1: Operated, Supervised, or Controlled By.* A SO is operated, supervised, or controlled by its beneficiary organization(s) where it essentially functions in a parent-subsidiary relationship. A substantial degree of direction is exercised by the parent over programs, policies, and activities. The SO, or subsidiary, is accountable and responsible to the parent, or supported organization. Proof of this type is found where a majority of the controlling officials of the SO are appointed by the supportees, although any one of a group of beneficiaries need not control if all are represented.

- *Type 2: Supervised or Controlled in Connection With.* This type of relationship exists when the same persons control both the supporting and the supported organization, or in other words, common control or supervision.

- *Type 3: Operated in Connection With.* This type is the most independent, may have a totally independent board with specific named beneficiary organization(s). Because of its relative freedom, it must meet two additional tests to qualify: the responsiveness and the integral part tests. To meet the responsiveness test, the supported organization must have a significant voice in the SO's governance. This voice is gained when one or more officers or directors of the SO are appointed or elected by the supported organization's board or officers. In the case of a charitable trust, the responsiveness is present where the supportee is named and the supportee has the power to enforce the trust and compel an accounting under state laws.

The integral part test essentially determines whether the supportee is dependent upon the SO. The SO must maintain a significant
involvement in the public organization's activities. The SO may meet
this test one of two ways. The SO may carry out a function or activity
which the public organization itself would normally carry out. Another way the SO meets this test is to use substantially all of its
annual income for the purposes of the supportee, either through direct expenditures for or grants to the supportee. "Income" is not defined under the regulations, although an early ruling[16] prescribes that
85 percent of the income is minimum amount to be distributed (same
rule as private operating foundations). In calculating the annual income, Priv. Ltr. Rul. 9021060 clarifies that neither long- and short-
term capital gains are considered as income required to be distributed
annually for this test.

A subset of the income test portion of the integral part test,
entitled "attentiveness," requires that the SO support be sufficient in
amount to assure the public organization will be attentive to the
operation of the SO. In other the words, the money paid must be
important enough to the charity. The regulations suggest the test is
passed where it can be shown that the funds are needed to avoid the
interruption of the supported organization's particular functions or
activities. "Actual attentiveness" in the form of required reporting,
investment oversight, or scope of accomplishments can be taken into
consideration. To read a good example of a "circumstances" application, read *Cockerline Memorial Fund.*[17] To review facts of an organization that did not meet the "in connection with" relationship test, read
Roe Foundation Charitable Trust.[18]

Disqualified Persons

A SO cannot be controlled by disqualified persons other than their
managers or the public charities which they benefit under Section
509(a)(3)(C). The control can be neither direct or indirect. For example, persons, such as a funder's employees, cannot substitute for the

[16] Rev. Rul. 76-208, 1976-1 C.B. 161.
[17] *Cockerline Memorial Fund v. Commissioner,* 86 T.C. 53 (1986).
[18] *Roe Foundation Charitable Trust v. Commissioner,* T.C.M. 1989-566 (1989).

funder. The basic concept is that substantial contributors and the persons who will act under their influence cannot control the SO. The regulations provide an organization will be considered controlled by disqualified persons if, by aggregating their votes or positions of authority in the organization, they may require the organization to perform any act which significantly affects its operations. The regulations lack such control as evidenced when the disqualified persons have under 50 percent of the voting power or lack the right to veto actions of the board.

Permissible Activities

In operating to benefit particular organization(s), the SO may conduct its own active programs to accomplish the purposes of the beneficiaries, may provide and maintain facilities or equipment, as well as make direct grants of funds to its named supportees. The SO may conduct fund-raising programs and unrelated businesses (on limited scale) to raise funds in support of its publicly supported organization.

* Conversion to Private Foundation (New)

If the circumstances of the benefited organization or the funders change, it is possible that an SO can cease to operate solely to benefit the current public charity(ies) and convert itself into a private foundation (or a public foundation for that matter). Two important questions arise in such a conversion.

1. The SO should agree to its ceasing to be supported. As a practical matter since the supported organization normally controls the SO, this factor would almost always be present.

   There might be a price for agreement. In a conversion sanctioned by a private ruling,[19] the retiring public charity supportee was given about one-half of the foundation's assets upon termination of the SO status.

[19] Priv. Ltr. Rul. 9052055, January 7, 1991.

MAINTAINING EXEMPT STATUS

2. The conversion must not be part of a prearranged plan at the time the SO was created to enable the creators or donors to circumvent some tax limitation or private foundation sanction.

For example, it is common for SOs to be created when the property to be given is closely held corporate stock. A private foundation cannot hold more than 2 percent of the shares of a company owned more than 20 percent by the persons who control or create the foundation and such "excess business holdings" must be sold by the PF within five years of their receipt. Thus the conversion of an eight-year-old SO to a private foundation the same year its stock holdings were purchased in a public offering might be asked if such conversion was originally intended.

Without question a conversion within a few years of original creation would be suspect where the SO's public status afforded the donors a contribution carryover or higher percentage limitation on deduction than that allowed to a private foundation.

Noncharitable Beneficiaries

Business leagues, chambers of commerce, civic leagues, social welfare organizations, labor unions, and agricultural and horticulture organizations are themselves publicly supported and can meet the Section 509(a)(2) support tests. For that reason, they may also be the beneficiary organization of an SO. Since the SO qualifies for receipt of deductible contributions, an SO formed with such a beneficiary must, of course, meet the organizational and operational tests of 501(c)(3). In other words, an organization performing the charitable or other Section 170(c)(2) purpose activities for a Section 501(c)(4), (5), or (6) organization and meeting the Section 509(a)(3)(B) control tests may qualify as a supporting organization under Section 509(a)(3).

Testing for Public Safety: 509(a)(4)

An organization that is organized and operated exclusively for testing for public safety is also treated as a public charity. This category is of little use, however, because the Section 170 does not provide for the deductibility of donations to such organizations. Thus, organizations seeking this status must also satisfy the requirements for a research organization (see § 1.10, p. 33) to receive donations.

§ 3.6 SPECIAL CONSIDERATIONS FOR FORM 990-PF

p. 256. *Add to Part VI Excise Tax on Investment Income:*

Penalties are also imposed for failure to deposit taxes with a Federal Tax Deposit Coupon (Form 8109) at a qualified bank or the Federal Reserve Bank. Instructions to the Form 990-W and 990PF must be carefully followed to avoid penalties.

* **p. 257.** *Replace text of Part XI with:*

Effective December 31, 1990, the limitation on Grant Administrative Expenses provided by Part XI expires. After a study of 1985 private foundation returns, the IRS concluded PFs spent a sufficient portion of their annual income on direct charitable expenditures. Consequently the limitations enacted by Congress in 1986 were unnecessary and should be allowed to expire on their sunset date.

Based upon the study, the IRS found that the limits were not effective. They were not designed to curb abusive situations often found in larger organizations, such as excessive compensation. The smaller foundations most likely to incur excessive amounts of administrative expenses (based upon their total asset ratios) usually had excess qualifying distributions based upon their earned income. Lastly, the IRS admitted the calculations were complicated and burdensome to PFs and did not recommend their continuance.

§ 3.7 CHANGES IN TAX METHODS

p. 261. *Replace text of Fiscal or Accounting Year section with:*

A common type of change that may occur during the life of an EO is a change in the tax accounting year. Although commercial, tax-paying businesses must secure advanced IRS approval under Section 446(e) to change their tax year, EOs have a streamlined system. The EO simply files a "timely filed short period" Form 990 (or 990EZ, 990PF, or 990T).

For example, say a calendar year EO wishes to change its tax year to a fiscal year spanning July 1 to June 30. A return reporting financial transactions for the short period year (the six months ending June 30 of the year of change) is filed. The June 30 return would be due to be filed by November 15, the normal due date for a full year return ending June 30 (the fifteenth day of the fifth month following the year end).

If the organization has not changed its year within the past ten years (counting backwards to include the prior short period return as a full year), the change is simply indicated on the return. The words "Change of Accounting Period" are to be written across the top of the front page. Where a prior change had occurred within ten years, Form 1128 is attached to the return and a copy is separately filed with the Service Center where the return is filed along with a user fee of $150 (as of January 1, 1991).

Late applications, due when the organization finds it wants to change its year after the short-period return filing due date has passed, can also be filed on Form 1128. The user fee of $300 must accompany the Service Center copy, along with a request for Section 9100 relief must accompany the form. See Rev. Proc. 85-37 for more details.[20]

Affiliated organizations holding a group exemption must follow Rev. Proc. 76-10 to effect a change.

p. 262. *Add after fourth paragraph:*
The current address for "simplified procedure" submissions is:

Assistant Commissioner (Employee Plans/Exempt Organizations)
Attention E/EO, Box 120, Ben Franklin Station,
Washington, DC 20044.

The normal permission procedures required by Section 446 are waived and permission is automatically granted and no user fee is due. A copy of Form 3115 must be included in the return filed for the year of accounting method change.

---

[20] Rev. Proc. 85-37, 1985-2 C.B. 438.

A special note for changing accounting method for unrelated business activities is needed. Where the change of accounting method causes reporting of previously deferred or accelerated income or expense, a tax calculation adjustment pursuant to Section 481 is made. The tax consequences of the change of accounting method are then taken into account in determining the tax due according to specific procedures outlined in the revenue procedure.

Late applications can be filed, but will only be considered upon a showing of "good cause" and it can be shown to the satisfaction of the Commissioner that granting the extension will not jeopardize the government's interests. The guidelines for showing cause are found in Section 6110. Since the EO is typically not paying tax, the possibilities for such approval are good. A user fee of $300 is paid with late forms.

p. 263. *Add at end of § 3.7:*

Change in Section 509(a) Class

Section 509(a)(1) to (a)(2) or Vice Versa

Publicly supported organizations classified under Section 509(a)(1) or (2) can often qualify for both categories and sometimes changes in the sources of support and exempt function revenues cause the organization to change from one code subsection to another. The distinction between qualification for one category or another is described in detail in § 3.5A. The qualification is based upon percentage levels of public support. The calculation is based upon a four year moving average of financial support received annually and is furnished to the IRS in filing Form 990, Schedule A.

For purposes of this discussion, the issue is what the organization must do if it experiences such a change. For purposes of being classified as a publicly supported organization and not a private foundation, passage of either tests suffices. In one narrow circumstance, it is preferable for the organization to be classified as a 509(a)(1): Only (a)(1)s qualify to receive terminating distributions from private foundations.

The question an organization has to answer is whether to report back to the EO Key District Office (in addition to the Service Center which is informed on the annual return) as discussed in § 2.6. Sometimes it is a simple question of the board's tolerance for a bit of uncertainty. When is written verification of the particular category of public charity for which the organization qualifies needed? Is a new determination letter desirable? The factors to consider include:

- The IRS does not issue amended or new determination letters when Form 990, Schedule A, indicates a change has occurred.

- PFs need not exercise expenditure responsibility (p. 367) in making a grant to either category (so that the new letter is not critical).

- *Publication 78* makes no distinction in its labeling of public charities, so the information is not entered into that IRS record.

- At this time, the Key District Office does not charge a user fee for submission of the information.

Ceasing to Qualify as a 509(a)(3) Organization

Failure to maintain qualification as a Section 509(a)(3), or supporting, organization would occur for one of two reasons:

1. The organizational documents are altered in a manner that removes the requisite relationship with another public charity(ies) and the organization becomes a private foundation supporting grantees of its choice.

2. A sufficient level of public support is obtained to allow the organization to convert to a 509(a)(1) or (2).

In the case of number 1, conversion to a private foundation (PF) again requires no IRS sanction. As of the date of conversion to a PF, a final Form 990 would be filed. A short-period Form 990PF would then be filed beginning with the date of the change. Required minimum distributions and other PF sanctions would apply as if the organization was newly created upon the date of conversion. Full disclosure of the changes would be furnished to the IRS in connection with filing both returns. Note this process also applies to failure to continue qualification under Section 509(a)(1) and (2) with resulting reclassification as a PF.

The EO's determination letter would become obsolete. If the EO anticipates receiving significant donations, it might consider submission of the information also to the Key District Office for issuance of a new determination letter.

For case 2, the EO would analyze its need to furnish evidence of its new status to potential supporters. This situation is rather unusual and prudence would dictate reporting back to the Key District Office to assure approval of the new category of public status. For more details on the different public status categories see § 3.5A.

There is some overlap and confusion in the IRS systems for dealing with changes. For some years, there has been a rumor (and a hope) that a central, and single, EO Service Center would be created to handle EO return filings and coordinate information with the Key District Offices. To date, this remains a rumor.

See § 2.6 for discussion of organizational changes.

§ 3.8 UNRELATED BUSINESS INCOME

* **p. 265.** *Delete remainder of § 3.8 (pages 265–279 and pages 284–286, item 5) and add:*

Exempt organizations (EOs) receive two types of income: earned and unearned. Unearned income comes from grants, membership fees, and donations: that income for which the EO gives nothing in return. Think of it as "one-way-street" money. The motivation for giving the money is gratuitous and/or of a nonprofit character with no expectation of gain on the part of the giver; there is donative intent.

In contrast, an EO furnishes services/goods or invests its capital in return for earned income: an opera is seen, classes are attended, hospital care is provided, or credit counseling is given, for example. The purchasers of the EO's goods and services do intend to receive something in return; they expect the street to be "two-way." An investment company holding the EO's money expects to have to pay reasonable return to the EO for using the funds. In these examples, the EO receives earned income. The important issue this chapter considers is when earned income becomes unrelated business income subject to income tax.

There are complex rules that govern when an EO's earned income becomes unrelated business income (UBI). The concepts of UBI are vague and contain many exceptions carved out by special interest groups. The House of Representatives Subcommittee on Oversight held hearings and drafted revisions over a four-year period during 1987 to 1990 and still has not proposed tax legislation (see list of proposals under *Special Interest Topics*).

IRS Scrutiny Focused on UBI

Beginning in 1989 with the addition of a new page 5 to Form 990, the IRS is studying the UBI issue. Until page 5 and its "Analysis of Revenue-Producing Activities" was added to the annual EO reporting requirements, UBI was not identified in any special way on Form 990; the income was simply included with related income of the same character. Both the Congressional representatives and the IRS agreed there was insufficient information to propose changes to the existing UBI rules.

Now EOs filing Form 990 (not including Form 990EZ filers whose gross income is less than $100,000) complete new page 5 to separate income into three categories:

1. Unrelated income (identified with a business code from Form 990T that describes its nature),

2. Unrelated income identified by the specific revenue code section by which the income is excluded from UBI, and

3. Related or exempt function income, along with a description of the relationship of the income-producing activity to the accomplishment of exempt purposes.

This statistical information is being gathered to evaluate the consequences of proposed changes to the UBIT rules. Marcus Owens of the IRS National Office announced in May, 1991, that additionally a compliance program will be initiated in the future with a public educational effort and emphasis on large case examinations.

History of the Unrelated Business Income Tax (UBIT)

A historical note helps to understand how the rules have evolved. Before 1950, an EO could conduct any income-producing activity and, in fact, did operate businesses without paying income tax. Using a "destination of income" test, as long as the income earned from the business was totally expended for grants and other exempt activities, any amount of business activity was permissible. One famous tax case involved New York University Law School's operation of a highly successful spaghetti factory.[21] In view of the extensive profits and businesslike manner in which the factory was operated, the IRS tried to impose an income tax on the profits. The courts decided, however, that no tax could be imposed under the then existing tax code as long as the profits were used to operate the school.

In response to pressure from businesses, Congress established the unrelated business income tax (UBIT) with the intention of eliminating the unfair competition charitable businesses represented, but it did not prohibit its receipt. The Congressional Committee thought that the:

> tax free status of exemption section 501 organizations enables them to use their profits tax free to expand operations, while their competitors can expand only with profits remaining after taxes. The problem. . . . is primarily that of unfair competition.[22]

The key questions in finding UBI are, then, whether the activity that produces earned income competes with commercial businesses and whether the method of operation is distinguishable from that of businesses. Another way to ask the question is, "Does it serve an exempt purpose and therefore it is related?" The distinction between for profits and nonprofits has narrowed over the years as organizations search for creative ways to pay for program services. Consider what the difference between the museum bookstore and a commercial one is, other than the absence of private ownership. Privately owned for-profit theaters operate alongside nonprofit ones. Magazines owned by nonprofits, such as *National Geographic* and *Harpers* contain advertising and appear indistinguishable from Conde Nast's *Traveler* or *Life*

---

[21] *C.F. Mueller Co. v. Commissioner,* 190 F.2d 120 (3rd Cir. 1951).
[22] House of Representatives No. 2319, 81st Cong., 2d Sess. (1950) at 36, 37.

Magazine. The health care profession is also full of indistinguishable examples.

Consequences of Receiving Unrelated Income

There are potentially several unpleasant consequences of earning unrelated income.

- *Payment of Unrelated Income Tax.* Unrelated net income may be taxed at corporate or trust rates with estimated tax payments required. Social clubs, homeowners' associations, and political organizations also pay the UBI tax on their passive investment income in addition to the business income. See *Special Interests Topics* for social club nonmember activity issues.

- *Exempt Status Revocation.* Exempt status could be revoked. Separate and apart from the UBI rules, the basic exemption status Internal Revenue Code Section (Section) 501 requires that an organization be organized and operated *exclusively* for exempt purpose, although "exclusively" has not been construed to mean 100 percent. Some commentators say any amount of UBI under 50 percent of the EO's gross income is permissible, although many others recommend no more UBI than 15 to 20 percent. The courts have allowed higher amounts; the IRS tends to vote for lower amounts in measuring whether the EO is operating "exclusively" for exempt purposes rather than to operate a business. An organization can run a business as a secondary purpose, but not as a primary purpose.

  In evaluating the amount of unrelated business activity that is permissible, not only the amount of gross revenue but other factors may be taken into consideration. Nonrevenue aspects of the activity, such as staff time devoted or value of donated services are factors in determining whether UBI is substantial.

  A complex of non-exempt activity caused the IRS to revoke the exemption of the *Orange County Agricultural Society.*[23] The unrelated business revenues represented between 29 to 34

[23] *Orange County Agricultural Society,* 55 T.C.M. 1602 (1988).

percent of the gross revenue which, although troublesome, were not the sole factor in the decision of the Tax Court to uphold the IRS's revocation. The presence of private inurement in doing business with its board of directors influenced the decision.

- *All Income Taxed.* Income from all sources will be taxed if exempt status is lost.

- *Private Foundation Issue.* Private foundation's ownership of an unrelated business would likely trigger "excess business holdings" tax and cause loss of exemption.

Definition of Trade or Business

To have UBI, the EO must first be found to be engaging in a trade or business. *Trade or business* is defined to include any activity carried on for the production of income from the sale of goods or performance of services.[24] This is a very broad, sweeping definition. The language seems pretty straightforward and, as a safe rule of thumb, would literally mean any activity for which the exempt receives revenues constitutes a business. Unfortunately, this is an area where the tax rules are very gray and the statutory history is difficult to follow. The word "income" does not mean receipts or revenue and also doesn't necessarily mean net income. Section 513(c) provides, "Where an activity carried on for profit constitutes an unrelated trade or business, no part of such trade or business shall be excluded from such classification merely because it does not result in profit."

If you delve deeper into the tax code and regulations, it becomes more difficult to find what is meant by the terms "trade or business." The regulations couch the definition in the context of unfair competition with commercial businesses, saying that "when an activity does not possess the characteristics of a trade or business within the meaning of Section 162," the unrelated business income tax (UBIT) will not apply. These regulations, however, were written before the Section 513(c) profit motive language was added to the code and are the subject of continuing arguments between taxpayers and the IRS.

[24] Regs. § 1.513-1(b)

Profit Motive Test (New)

The confusion has produced two tests: profit motive and commerciality. Under the profit motive test, an activity conducted simply to produce some revenue but without an expectation of producing a profit (similar to the hobby loss rules) is not a business.[25] This test is used by the IRS in situations where an EO has more than one unrelated business. Losses from the hobby cannot be offset against profits from other businesses. Thus the excess expenses (losses) generated in fundamentally exempt activity, such as an educational publication undertaken without the intention of making a profit, cannot be deducted against the profits from a profit-motivated project.

Commerciality Test (New)

The commerciality test looks instead to the type of operation: if the activity is carried on in a manner similar to a commercial business, it constitutes a trade or business.[26] This test poses serious problems for the unsuspecting because there are no statutory or regulatory parameters to follow. A broad range of UBI cases where the scope of sales or service activity was beyond that normally found in the exempt setting have been decided by examining the commercial taint of the activity.

Fragmentation Rule (New)

Further evidence of the overreaching scope of the term "trade or business" is found in the *Fragmentation rule.*[27] This rule carves out activity carried on alongside an exempt one and provides that unrelated business does not lose its identity and taxability when it is earned in a related setting. Take for example a museum shop. The shop itself is clearly a trade or business, often established with a

---

[25] *West Virginia State Medical Association*, 91 T.C. 651 (1988), aff'd, 89-2 U.S.T.C. § 9491 (4th Cir. 1989) and *Commissioner v. Groetzinger*, 480 U.S. 23 (1987).

[26] *Better Business Bureau v. U.S.*, 326 U.S. 279, 283 (1945), *U.S. National Water Well Association, Inc. v. Commissioner*, 92 T.C. No. 7 (1989); *Scripture Press Foundation v. U.S.*, 285 F.2d 800 (Ct. Cl. 1961), cert. denied; *Greater United Navajo Development Enterprises, Inc. v. Commissioner*, 74 T.C. 69 (1980).

[27] Section 513(c).

profit motive and operated in a commercial manner. Items sold in such shops, however, often include both educational items, such as the books, reproductions of art works, and souvenirs. The fragmentation rule requires that all items sold be analyzed to identify the equational, or related, items the profit from which is not taxable and the unrelated souvenir items that do produce taxable income. See *Special Interest Topic* section for more information about museums.

What Is Unrelated Business Income (UBI)?

UBI is defined as the gross income derived from any *unrelated trade or business regularly carried on,* less the *deductions* connected with the carrying on of such trade or business, computed with *modifications* and *exceptions.* [28] These terms are key to identifying UBI. Exhibit 3–11 shows them graphically. All the prongs of the circle must be considered to determine what earned income is to be classified as UBI.

Regularly Carried On

A trade or business regularly carried on is considered to compete unfairly with commercial business and is fair game for classification

Exhibit 3–11
COMPONENTS OF UNRELATED BUSINESS INCOME

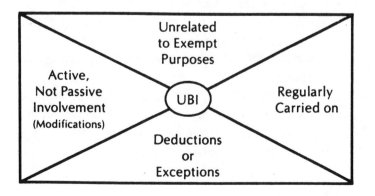

---

[28] Section 512(a)(1).

as a taxable business. In determining whether an activity is regularly carried on, the IRS looks at the *frequency and continuity* of an activity when examined by comparison to commercial enterprises. The normal time span of comparable commercial activities can also be determinative.[29] Compare the following:

Irregular	Regular
Sandwich stand at annual county fair.	Cafe open daily.
Annual golf tournament.	Racetrack operated during racing "season."
Nine-day antique show.	Antique store.
Gala Ball held annually.	Monthly dance.
Program ads for annual fund-raising event.	Advertisements in quarterly magazine.

Meaning of Irregular

Intermittent activities may be deemed "regularly carried on" or commercial unless they are discontinuous or periodic. For example, the revenue from a weekly dance would be more likely to be taxed than the profits from an annual fund-raising event. By the same token, ads sold for a monthly newsletter would more likely be classed as commercial than program ads sold for an annual ball. Where the planning and sales effort of a special event or athletic tournament is conducted over a long span of time, the IRS may argue that the activity itself becomes regularly carried on despite the fact that the event occurs infrequently. See the NCAA advertising sales discussion following under "agency theory."

In a 1981 case, the IRS lost in arguing that the engagement of professionals to stage the show and produce a program guide containing advertising caused the patrolmen's fund-raising event profits to be UBI.[30] The fact that the solicitors worked for sixteen weeks in

[29] Regs. § 1.513-1(c).
[30] *Suffolk County Patrolmen's Benevolent Association, Inc. v. Commissioner,* 77 T.CX. 1314 (1981), acq. 1999984-1 C.B. 2.

preparing and organizing the event made the activity regular in the IRS eyes; the Tax Court disagreed.

Season Activity

Activities conducted during the period traditionally identified as seasonal, such as Christmas, if conducted during the "season," will be considered regular and the income will not qualify to be excluded from UBIT. Christmas card sales during October or November or Independence Day balloons sold in June/July would be "regular."

Substantially Related

"Any business the conduct of which is not substantially related (aside from need to make money) to the performance of an organization's charitable, educational, or other purposes or function constituting the basis of its exemption is defined as unrelated," according to the IRS regulations.[31]

An activity is substantially related only when it has a causal relationship to the achievement of an EO's exempt purpose (that is, the purpose for which the EO was granted exemption according to its Form 1023 or 1024 or subsequent Form 990 filings). The IRS regulations suggest the presence of this requirement necessitates an examination of the relationship between the business activities (of producing or distributing goods or performing services) which generate the particular income in question and the accomplishment of the organization's exempt purposes.[32]

The size and extent of the activity itself and its contribution to exempt purposes is determinative. The "nexus" (association, connection or linkage) between the activity and accomplishment of exempt purposes is examined to find "relatedness." The best way to illustrate the concept is with examples.

Related income-producing activities include:

- Admission tickets for performances or lectures.

- Student or member tuition or class fees.

[31] Regs. § 1.513-1(a).
[32] Regs. § 1.513-1(d).

- Symphony society sale of symphonic musical recordings.

- Products made by handicapped workers or trainees.

- Hospital room, drug, and other patient charges.

- Agriculture college sale of produce or student work.

- Sale of educational materials.

- Secretarial and telephone answering service training program for indigent and homeless.[33]

- Operation of diagnostic health devices, such as CAT scans or magnetic imaging machines by a hospital or health care organization.[34]

- Sale of online bibliographic data from EO's central data bases.[35]

- "Public entertainment activities," or agricultural and educational fair or exposition.

- "Qualified conventions and trade shows."

Potentially unrelated categories of UBI are numerous as the following controversial types of income illustrate. The examples don't always follow a logical pattern because courts and the IRS don't always agree and the IRS has not always been consistent in its rulings.

Rental of equipment and other personal property (for example, computer or phone systems) to others are specifically listed in Section 512(b)(3) for inclusion in UBI. Such rental presumably is undertaken only to earn revenue and cover costs with no direct connection to the EO's own exempt purposes; it "exploits" the exempt holding of the property. However,

- Renting to (or sharing with) another EO (or conceivably an individual or a forprofit business) is related if the rental expressly serves the landlord's exempt purposes, such as a museum's rental of art works—that would otherwise be kept in

---

[33] IRS Priv. Ltr. Rul. 9009038.
[34] IRS T.A.M. 8932004.
[35] IRS Priv. Ltr. Rul. 9017028.

its storage—to other institutions to assure maximum public viewing of the work.

- Mailing list rentals produce UBI except for narrow exceptions allowed to 501(c)(3)s.[36] For business leagues and other non(c)(3) EOs, revenues from the exchange or rental of mailing lists produce UBI. The Disabled American Veterans fought a valiant battle in the tax courts to avoid this tax. Twice—in 1982 and again in July, 1991—they lost in the Tenth Circuit court their attempts to characterize their mailing list sales as royalty income. Refer to the "Royalty" discussion in the *Special Interest Topics* for more information.

- Whether rental charges are at, below, or above cost can be determinative in evaluating relatedness. A full fair market value rental arrangement does not evidence exempt purposes (although the taint can be overcome by other reasons for the rental, such as dissemination of specialized educational information).

- Real estate revenues may also be excluded from UBI under the passive exceptions, but only if the property is unencumbered (see later discussion of debt financed property).[37]

   Providing services (such as billing, technical assistance, administrative support) to other EOs doesn't serve the exempt purposes of the furnishing EO and is unrelated according to the IRS. The fact that sharing services creates efficiencies that allow all the EOs involved to save money doesn't necessarily sway the IRS. Only where the services themselves represent substantive programs better accomplished by selling the services to other EOs has the IRS classified the revenue as related. The services themselves must be exempt in nature. Selling computer time to enable another EO to maintain its accounting records would create UBI, but selling computer time to analyze scientific information might be related. Where an organization is created to serve a consortia of organizations with a common building or pooled investment funds, the IRS has

[36] Section 513(h).
[37] Section 512(b)(3).

generally allowed its exemption where the new organization itself is partly supported by independent donations.

- Certain cooperative service organizations have been specifically exempt by Congress to avoid the IRS position that such rendering of services was a taxable business activity. Section 501(e) grants exempt status to cooperative hospital organizations that are formed to provide on a group basis specified services including data processing, purchasing (including the purchase of insurance on a group basis), warehousing, billing and collection, food, clinical, industrial engineering, laboratory, printing, communications, record center, and personnel including selection, testing, training, and education of personnel services. Note that laundry is not on the list.

Cooperative services organizations established to "hold, commingle, and collectively invest" stocks and securities of educational institutions are also provided a special exempt category under Section 501(f).

Section 513(e) allows a special exclusion from UBI for the income earned by a hospital providing the types of services listed in Section 501(e) to another hospital that has facilities to serve fewer than 100 patients, provided the price for such services is rendered at cost plus a "reasonable amount of return on the capital goods used" in providing the service.

The IRS recently considered "related services" being rendered by a Section 501(c)(6) tourist and convention organization for the local government. Their memo discusses a broad range of services provided to businesses planning conventions in the city (which the EO was organized to benefit) and finds them related activity. Commissions received from hotels in return for referring groups and conventions for reservations, however, were deemed unrelated.[38]

Sale of the organization's name normally is accomplished by a licensing contract permitting use of the EO's intangible property—their name—with the compensation constituting royalty income that is excluded from UBI under concepts discussed later. However, in the IRS's view, such arrangements usually constitute commercial exploitation

[38] IRS T.A.M. 9032005.

of an exempt asset. Since issuing a revenue ruling in 1981, the IRS has been trying to tax EOs on the sale of their names in connection with insurance programs, affinity sales, and other commercial marketing schemes.[39]

To add flavor to the problem, in April 1990, the IRS reversed its position that a "royalty arrangement" licensing an EO's name, logo, and mailing list to an insurance agent (to promote life insurance to its membership), didn't produce UBI for the exempt.[40] Due to the extensive involvement (active, not passive) of the exempt in servicing the membership lists, the Section 513(h)(1)(B)'s narrow exemption of mailing lists, and the agency theory (discussed below), the IRS ruled the supposed "royalty arrangement" produced UBI. The American Bar Association lost a similar battle in 1986, although their case was made more complicated by their arrangement whereby their members made substantial donations of the program profits.[41]

Where the sale of the organization's name or logo is accompanied by any additional requirements on the part of the EO, such as servicing the mailing list as discussed above or endorsing a product or performing any other services for the purchaser, the IRS has made it very clear they consider such arrangements to produce unrelated income. Also suspect would be contracts where the "royalty" amount paid for use of the name is tied to the number of times it is used in solicitations all of which are mailed to the separately purchased mailing list of the EO.

Affinity card revenues are in the same category as far as the IRS is concerned and do not qualify for the "royalty" exception. When first ruling on affinity cards, the IRS allowed royalty exclusion for a fraternal order's card income.[42] By 1988, they reversed the initial position.[43] While use of the EO's name and logo alone can produce royalty income, the credit card arrangements often depend upon an accompanying sale of the organization's mailing list and in some cases, endorsements and promotion by the EO in its publications and member/donor correspondence. The IRS therefore again applies an

---

[39] Rev. Rul. 81-178, 1981-2 C.B. 135.
[40] IRS Priv. Ltr. Rul. 9029047.
[41] *United States v. American Bar Endowment,* 477 U.S. 105 (Sup. Ct. 1986).
[42] IRS Priv. Ltr. Rul. 8747066.
[43] IRS Priv. Ltr. Rul. 8823109.

"agency-type" theory to deem that the EO itself, rather than the intermediary organization, performed valuable services that produced unrelated income. Some organizations try to avoid this problem by bifurcating the royalty and mailing list aspects of the contract. The IRS has commented that "they are probably going to see them as one transaction, in reality, one contract, and apply UBIT."

Sale of advertising in an otherwise exempt publication is almost always considered unrelated business income by the IRS. The basic theory is that the advertisements promote the interests of the individual advertiser and cannot therefore be related to the charitable purposes of the organization.

- The American College of Physicians was unsuccessful in arguing with the IRS that the drug company ads in their health journal published for physicians educated the doctors. The College argued the ads provided the reader with a comprehensive and systematic presentation of goods and services needed in the profession and informed physicians about new drug discoveries, but the court disagreed.[44]

- A college newspaper training program for journalism students enrolled in an advertising course produced related income.[45]

- Institutional or sponsor ads produce UBI if they are presented in a commercial fashion with a business logo, product description or other sales information. Only where sponsors are listed without typical advertising copy can the money given for the listing be considered a donation. Different sizes for different amounts of money may not cause the ad to be classified as commercial.[46]

- Despite classification of ad revenues as UBI, the formula for calculating the taxable UBI yields surprising results, however,

[44] *American College of Physicians vs. U.S.*, 457 U.S. 836 (1986).
[45] Regs. 1.513-1(d)(4)(iv) Example 5.
[46] *Fraternal Order of Police, Illinois State Troopers Lodge No. 41 v. Commissioner*, 833 F.2d 717 (7th Cir. 1987), aff'g 87 T.C. 747 (1986), IRS Priv. Ltr. Rul. 8640007.

enabling some ad sale programs to escape tax. A more thorough discussion of advertising and the formula are covered under *Special Interest Topics.*

Corporate Sponsorships of a wide variety of events—golf tournaments, fun runs, football bowl games, public television, art exhibitions and so on—are a favorite form of corporate support for exempt organizations. The appeal of wide public exposure for sponsoring worthy causes and cultural programs has gained extensive popularity. *The Wall Street Journal* ran a series of articles during 1991 discussing the extent of such support and why it made good business sense.

Under examination and now in a heavily edited Private Letter Ruling 9147007, the IRS says the Cotton Bowl's payments from Mobil Oil Company are taxable, essentially because the Cotton Bowl was rendering services for Mobil. Substantial benefit in the form of advertising was given to Mobil and such revenue was business income, not a contribution. Legislation has been introduced to carve out a special exemption for such revenues, but until then caution is advised. Even if such arrangements create UBI, the EO may be able to argue that the event or activity is irregularly carried on, although as the NCAA found out, the IRS may not agree.

Marcus Owens of the IRS National Office has announced they are developing guidelines for their agents to use in evaluating whether the sponsorship represents a gift or payment for advertising and other services rendered. Among the factors he suggests agents look for are corporate perks, such as preferential seating, attendance, or hotel suites furnished to company executives and any contractual agreement tying payment to attendance or Nielsen rating of the event.

Services to members will be scrutinized carefully by IRS.

- Sale of legal forms by a bar association, billing and credit services for members, and testing fees have all been argued with decisions for and against the organizations. EOs considering this type of income-producing activity should research this question thoroughly.[47]

---

[47] *San Antonio Bar Association v. United States,* 80-2 U.S.T.C. § 9594 (W.D. Tex. 1980).

- Free bus service provided to a particular shopping center versus a downtown area of a city was ruled to produce unrelated income for a chamber of commerce.

The question to watch for is whether services rendered to members constitute private inurement or private benefit for the members versus the general public or the profession (for a business league).

Group insurance programs have been subject of active litigation among trade unions, business leagues and the IRS, with the IRS currently prevailing in classifying revenues produced in an insurance program for members as UBI. The American Bar Endowment lost its battle to classify the dividends assigned to it by members participating in its group insurance plan as donations. Here again, careful planning in view of the most recent rulings and court decisions is in order to avoid UBI.[48]

Real estate development projects can be characterized as related (low income or elderly housing), as a trade or business (subdivision, debt financed rental, hotel), as an investment (unindebted rental), or sometimes as a combination of all three.

Any EO anticipating such a program should study Priv. Ltr. Rul. 8950072 in which the IRS outlines the UBI consequences of four different methods of developing a piece of raw land owned by an exempt. Leasing or selling raw land unquestionably produced no UBI because of the passive income modifications. Completion of the preliminary development work of obtaining permits and approval prior to the property's sale did not convert the sale into a business transaction. But total development of the property prior to the sale converts the property into a business asset and produces UBI.

An *agency theory* may be applied to look through certain arrangements. To avoid UBI classification for potentially unrelated activities listed above, an organization might engage an independent party to conduct the activity in return for a royalty or a rental payment. Inherently "passive" activities for which compensation is paid in the form of rent or royalty are not subject to UBIT, even if the activity is deemed unrelated. The question is, however, whether the

---

[48] *Louisiana Credit Union League v. U.S.*, 693 F.2d 525 (5th Cir. 1982), aff'g 501 F. Supp. 934 (E.D. La. 1980).

IRS can look through the transactions and attribute the activity of the independent party back to the organization as they did in the following example.

The National College Athletic Association (NCAA) hires an unrelated commercial publishing company to produce its tournament programs. NCAA gives the publisher a "free hand" in soliciting the advertisements, designing the copy, and distributing the programs, in return for a percentage of the advertising and direct sales revenues. Because they have little or no involvement in the activity, the NCAA treats the income as a passive and irregularly carried on activity not subject to the unrelated business income tax. There is no argument that selling the program itself produces related income; nor is there any question that the advertising income is unrelated. The tournament lasts only three weeks.

The issue considered by the Tax Court[49] was whether the NCAA has sufficiently disengaged itself under the contract. Did it sell the right to use its name or did it engage in the activity itself? The Tax Court adopted an "agency" theory, stipulating that because the publisher acted as NCAA's agent, the activity was totally attributable to the NCAA. The Tenth Circuit Court agreed with the Tax Court but reversed the decision (because the activity was irregularly carried on and not in competition with business); the agency theory was not disputed. The IRS disagrees with the decision.

Another athletic tournament-sponsoring organization also failed the agency test. The independently hired promoter's efforts during a 15-month ad campaign were attributed to the organization.[50] The agency theory was escaped, however, by an organization who turned over the publication of its monthly journal to the commercial company, retaining one-third of the net revenues from subscriptions and reprints. All advertising income, two thirds of the circulation revenues and all the risk of publication expenses were borne by the company. So, the IRS decided under the circumstances, the company was acting on its own behalf, not as agent for the charity. No advertising revenue was allocated to the charity.[51]

---

[49] *National College Athletic Association v. Commissioner*, 90-2 U.S.T.C. § 50513 (10th Cir. 9/20/90), rev'd. 92 T.C. No. 27 (1989). See also Priv. Ltr. Rul. 9137002.
[50] IRS T.A.M. (T.A.M. 8932004).
[51] IRS T.A.M. (T.A.M. 9023003).

The Exceptions

Despite their literal inclusion in the "unrelated" prong of the UBI rules, certain types of revenue-raising activities are not subject to UBIT presumably because they are not businesslike and do not compete with commercial businesses.[52] Charitable Section 501(c)(3)s qualify for all of the following exceptions. Certain exceptions do not apply to non(c)(3) organizations as noted under the particular exception.

Volunteers

Any business where substantially all the work is performed without compensation is excluded from UBI. "Substantially" means at least 80 to 85 percent of the total work performed, measured normally by the total hours worked. A paid manager or executive, administrative personnel, and all sorts of support staff can operate the business if most of the work is performed by volunteers.

In most cases the number of hours worked, rather than relative value of the work, is used to measure the 85 percent test. This means that the value of volunteer time need not necessarily be quantified for comparison to monetary compensation paid. In the case of a group of volunteer singing doctors, the value of the doctors' time was considered. Because the doctors were the stars of the records producing the income, their time was counted by the court at a premium and allowed to offset administrative personnel whose time was paid.[53]

Expense reimbursements, inkind benefits and prizes are not necessarily treated as compensation unless they are compensatory in nature. Particularly where the expenses enable the volunteers to work longer hours and serve the convenience of the EO, the payments need not be counted in measuring this exception. Where food, lodging, and total sustenance were furnished to sustain members of a religious group, the members working for the group's businesses were not treated as volunteers.[54]

---

[52] Section 513(a).

[53] *Greene County Medical Society Foundation v. U.S.*, 345 F. Supp. 900 (W.D. Mo. 1972).

[54] *Shiloh Youth Revival Centers v. Commissioner*, 88 T.C. 579 (1987).

Donated Goods

The selling of merchandise substantially all of which is received as gifts or contributions is not subject to the UBIT. Thrift and resale shops selling donated goods do not report UBI on donated goods they sell. A shop selling goods on consignment as well as donated goods would have to distinguish between the two types of goods. UBI would be earned for the consigned goods, but might escape tax if the shop is run by volunteers.

Bingo Games

Bingo games not conducted in violation of any state or local law are excluded. Section 513(f) defines bingo as any game of bingo of a type in which usually (1) wagers are placed, (2) winners are determined, and (3) distribution of prizes or other property is made, in the presence of all persons placing wagers in such game.

The regulations expand the definition by explicitly saying, "A bingo game is a game of chance played with cards that are generally printed with five rows of five squares each. Participants place markers over randomly called numbers on the cards in an attempt to form a preselected pattern such as a horizontal, vertical, or diagonal line, or all four corners. The first participant to form the preselected pattern wins the game. Any other game of chance, including but not limited to, keno, dice, cards, and lotteries, is not bingo" (and will create UBI).[55]

Pull-tabs and other forms of "instant bingo" are not bingo in the IRS's opinion and produce unrelated business income despite the fact that such variations of the bingo game are so classified by the state bingo authority. During 1990, they aggressively examined EOs in the Southwest District and assessed tax on any bingo variations not strictly meeting the code and regulation definitions.

Public Entertainment Activities

Public entertainment is defined as traditionally conducted at fairs or expositions promoting agricultural and educational purposes (including but not limited to animals or products and equipment) and does not produce UBI for 501(c)(3), (4), or (5) organizations. Section 513(d)(2)

---

[55] Regs. § 1.513-5.

requires that the event be held in conjunction with an international, national, state, regional, or local fair or be in accordance with provisions of state law that permits such a fair.

Qualified Conventions and Trade Shows

A convention and trade show is one intended to attract persons in an industry generally (without regard to membership in the sponsoring organization) as well as members of the public to the show for the purpose of displaying industry products or to stimulate interest in and demand for industry products or services, or to educate persons engaged in the industry in the development of new products and services or new rules and regulations affecting the industry. A "qualified" show is one conducted by 501(c)(3), (4), (5), or (6) organizations in conjunction with an international, national, state, regional, or local convention, annual meeting, or show. Exhibitors are permitted to sell products or services and the organization can charge for the display space.

Apply Only to 501(c)(3)s and Veteran Posts

Low Cost Articles

Gift premiums costing (not fair market value) the organization no more than $5.72 (during 1991—indexed annually for inflation) and distributed with no obligation to purchase in connection with the solicitations of contributions are not treated as a sale of the gift premium. The gift must be part of a fund-raising campaign.

The recipient of the premium must not request or consent to receive the premium. Literature requesting a donation must accompany the premium and a statement that the recipient may keep the low cost article regardless of whether a charitable donation is made. If the donation is less than $28.59 (during 1991 but indexed annually), the fair market value of the premium reduces the deductible portion of the donor's gift.[56]

---

[56] Rev. Proc. 90-12 (February, 1990).

Mailing Lists

A business involving the exchange or renting of mailing lists between two organizations eligible to receive charitable donations under Section 170(c)(2) or (3) is excluded from UBI classification. In other words, a charitable organization exempt under Section 501(c)(3) and veteran organizations qualify for this special treatment added by Congress in 1986.[57] Sale or exchange of mailings lists by all other types of 501(c) organizations now create UBI. See following *Special Interest Topic* about Mailing Lists for more details.

501(c)(3)s Only Exceptions

Convenience

A cafeteria, bookstore, residence, or similar facility used in the EO's programs and operated for the convenience of patients, visitors, employees, or students is specifically excepted from UBI classification by Section 513(a)(2) for 501(c)(3) organizations only. Presumably, it benefits hospital patients to have family and friends visiting or staying with them in the hospital and the cafeteria facilitates the visits. Museum visitors can spend more time viewing art if they can stop to rest their feet and have a cup of coffee. Parking lots for the exclusive use of participants in an exempt organization's activities also produce related income.

When the cafe, shop, dorm, or parking lot is also open to the general public, the revenue produced by public use is unrelated income. Some commentators suggest the whole facility becomes subject to UBIT, particularly where the facility has an entrance to a public street. At best the income from a facility used by both qualified visitors and the disinterested public off the street is fragmented. The taxable and nontaxable revenues are identified and tabulated and the net taxable portion is calculated under the dual use rules discussed later under **Calculating the Taxable Income**.

[57] Section 513(h).

Where the unrelated income produced is rental income, there is still a possible escape route from application of the UBIT. The technical question then becomes whether the lot rentals are excludable UBI under the **Passive Income Modifications**.

The IRS admits it has issued unclear and conflicting positions on the matter. Their memo states unequivocally that revenue from direct lot operation never produces rent and refers to the regulations.[58] Only where the lot is operated by an independent party under a lease arrangement in which the organization performs no services can the revenue be classified as passive rental income excludable from UBI.

Passive Income Modifications

Income earned from passive investment activities is not included in UBI unless the underlying property is subject to debt. Social clubs, voluntary employee benefit associations, supplemental unemployment plans, and veterans' groups are taxed on such income. Types of passive income excluded from UBI under Section 512(b) include "all dividends, interest, royalties, rents, payments with respect to security loans, and annuities, and all deductions connected with such income." It is important to note from the outset that passive income of a sort not specifically listed is not necessarily modified or excluded from UBI.

Dividends and interest paid on amounts invested in savings accounts, certificates of deposit, money market accounts, bonds, loans, preferred or common stocks, and payments in respect to security loans, and annuities, along with any allocable deductions.

- In 1978, the general exclusion of interest and dividends was expanded to include the words "payments in respect of security loans." Since then there has been uncertainty regarding sophisticated techniques such as "strips," interest rate swaps, and currency hedges. After two private letter rulings were issued in 1991, proposed regulations were announced in September, 1991, to recognize that such investments were

[58] IRS G.C.M. 39825.

"ordinary and routine" and to make it clear that income earned from such transactions in security portfolios would be considered as investment income for Section 512 purposes.[59]

- Such securities acquired with indebtedness are swept back into UBI by Section 514 and an EO must be careful to use new money to acquire each element of investment in its portfolio. A recent Tax Court case provides a good example. A pension fund stuck with five year certificates of deposit in 1979 when the interest rates shot up over five points negotiated a plan to purchase new CDs using its old CDs as collateral thereby escaping an early withdrawal penalty and receiving a higher rate of interest. The court found that despite the fact that the transaction was not abusive, it fell squarely within the literal definition of a debt financed asset purchase. Also the CD switch was not a "payment in respect of a security loan" within the meaning of Section 512(b)(1). Such a loan involves allowing a broker to use the EO's securities in return for a fee, not a loan against which the securities are used as collateral. Thus the Fund's original CD produced "modified" or nontaxable income and the new higher rate CD acquired with the loan proceeds was held to be taxable as unrelated debt financed income.[60]

Gains or losses from sale, exchange or other disposition of property generally is not UBI.

- Gains on lapse or termination of covered and uncovered options, if written as a part of investment activity, are not taxable according to Section 512(b)(5) added to the code in 1976.

- Sales of stock in trade or other inventory-type property or property held for sale to customers in ordinary course of trade or business do produce UBI.

---

[59] Proposed Regs. § 1.509(a)-3, § 1.512(b)-1 and § 53.4940-1.
[60] *Kern County Electrical Pension Fund v. Commissioner*, 94 T.C. No. 41 (June 20, 1991).

Rentals are excluded except:

- Personal property rentals are taxable unless they are rented incidentally (not more than 10% of rent) with real property.

- Net profit (versus gross revenue) interests produce UBI.

- Where substantial services are rendered, such as the rental of a theater complete with staff, the rental will not be considered passive.

Royalties, whether measured by production or by the gross or taxable income from the property, are excluded. Note oil and gas working interest income would not be excluded. (See further discussion under *Special Interest Topics.*)

Controlled subsidiary payments for interest, rents, royalties or annuities, however, are includable in UBI. Control exists when one organization's owners stock possessing at least 80 percent of the total combined voting power of all classes of stock entitled to vote and at least 80 percent of all other classes of stock of another organization (exempt or nonexempt). A nonstock organization measures control by quantifying its interlocking directors. If at least 80 percent of the directors of one organization are members of the second organization or have the right to appoint or control the board of the second, control exists according to the regulations.

That portion of a controlled organization's income which would have been taxed as UBI to the parent EO if the income had been earned by it is includable (whether or not regularly carried on). Thus payments from a subsidiary corporation conducting a related activity would qualify as a modification and not be UBI.

Research income is not taxable under the following circumstances:

- If performed for the United States, its agencies or a state or political subdivision thereof by any EO.

- A college, university, or hospital can exclude all research income from private or governmental contractors.

- An EO performing fundamental research, the results of which are freely available to the general public, can also exclude all research income.

Calculating the Taxable Income

Gross unrelated business income, minus expenses and exemption listed below, is subject to tax. Keep in mind that as long as the percentage of revenues from UBI is modest in relation to the organization's overall revenues, the only problem UBIT presents is the reduction in profit due to the income tax paid. Tax planning of the sort practiced by a good businessperson is in order. Maximizing deductions to calculate the income is important. The Internal Revenue Code of 1986 Income Tax sections govern and the same concepts apply, including:

- *Tax rates.* The income tax is calculated using the normal tables for all taxpayers: Section 1(e) for trusts or Section 11 for corporations. For controlled groups of exempt organizations (also including 80 percent owned for-profit subsidiaries), the corporate tax bracket must be calculated on a consolidated basis under the rules of Section 1561.

- *Alternative minimum tax.* Accelerated depreciation, percentage depletion, and other similar tax benefits are subject to the alternative minimum tax just as for-profit taxpayers.

- *"Ordinary and necessary" criteria.* Deductions claimed against the unrelated income must be "ordinary and necessary" to conducting the activity and meet the other standards of Section 162 for business deductions. Ordinary means common and accepted for the type of business operated; necessary means helpful and appropriate, not indispensable. The activity for which the expenditure is incurred must also be operated with profit motive.[61]

- *Profit motive.* To be deductible, an expenditure must also be paid for the production of income, or in a business operated for the purpose of making a profit. Section 183 specifically prohibits the deduction of "hobby losses," or those activities losing money for more than two years out of every five. The

---

[61] Regs. 1.512(a)-1(a).

IRS will challenge the deduction for UBI purposes of any expenditures not paid for the purposes of producing the profit.[62]

- *Depreciation.* Equipment, buildings, vehicles, furniture, and other properties whose useful life to the business are deductible theoretically over their life. As a simple example, one-third of the total cost of a computer that is expected to be obsolete in three years would be deductible during each year the computer is used in the business under a system called "depreciation." Unfortunately, Congress uses these calculation rates and methods as political and economic tools and the revenue code proscribes rates and methods that are not so simple. Sections 167, 168, and 179 apply and must be studied to properly calculate allowable deductions for depreciation.

- *Inventory.* If the EO keeps an inventory of items for sale, such as books, drugs, or merchandise of any sort, it must use the inventory methods to deduct the cost of such goods. The concept is one of matching the cost of the item sold with its sales proceeds. If the EO buys ten widgets for sale and as of the end of a year only five have been sold, the cost of the five is deductible and the remaining five are "capitalized" as an asset to be deducted when in fact they are sold. Again the system is far more complicated than the simple example and an accountant should be consulted to assure use of proper reporting and tabulation methods. Sections 263A and 471–474 apply.

- *Capital and nondeductibles.* A host of nondeductible items contained in sections 261 to 280H might apply to disallow deductions either by total disallowance or required capitalization of permanent assets. Again all the rules applicable to forprofit businesses apply, such as the luxury automobile limits, travel and entertainment substantiation requirements, and 20 percent disallowance for meals.

- *Dividend deduction.* The dividends received deduction provided by Sections 243–245 for taxable nonexempt corporations are not allowed. As a general rule, a corporation is

---

[62] *Iowa State University of Science and Technology v. U.S.*, 500 F.2d 508 (Ct. Cl. 1974); *Commissioner v. Groetzinger*, 480 U.S. 23 (1987) and Reg. § 1.513-1(4)(d)(iii).

allowed to exclude 70 percent of the dividends it receives on its investments; exempts are not. Note this rule only presents a problem for dividends received from investments that are debt financed. Most dividends received by exempts are excluded from the UBI under the "Modifications" previously discussed.

* Specific Categories of Deductible Costs (New)

As a general rule, there are two categories of expenses allowed as deductions for purposes of calculating UBIT: direct and dual use expenses. No portion of the organization's basic operating expense theoretically is deductible against UBI because of the exploitation rules discussed below. However, where there is an ongoing plan to produce UBI and such revenue is part of the justification affording a particular exempt activity, allocation of overhead is permitted, although technically challenging.

Directly Related

Those expenses attributable solely to the production of unrelated gross income are fully deductible. According to the IRS, a "proximate and primary relationship" between the expense and the activity is the standard for full deduction. Proximate means near, close, or immediate. A "but for" test can be applied by asking the question, "Would the expense be incurred if the unrelated activity was not carried on?" (See note 61.)

Dually Used Facilities or Personnel

A portion of the cost of so called, "dual use," or shared employees and facilities is deductible. An allocation between the two types of activities is made upon "a reasonable basis." The only example given in the IRS regulations allocates 10 percent of an EO president's salary to an unrelated business activity to which he or she devotes 10 percent of his or her time. Where actual time records are maintained to evidence effort devoted to related versus unrelated activities, deduction of the applicable personal costs is assured. The IRS Manual instructs examining agents that any reasonable method resulting in identifying

■ 163 ■

relationship of the expenses to revenue produced is acceptable. There is no particular approved method that must be followed.[63]

Absent time records, an allocation based upon relative gross income produced might be used if the exempt activity reaps income. Take for example the museum bookstore that sells both related and unrelated items. Sales in this case could be used as the allocation base. Where an income producing activity is carried out alongside one not producing revenue, time records must be maintained.

Where a portion of the building is devoted totally to unrelated activity, building costs, including utilities, insurance, depreciation of the cost, interest on mortgage, and maintenance, are allocated based upon total square footage of the building used for the UBI activity. Where UBI space is shared with related space, again a reasonable method is used. For a publication project, the lineage devoted to advertising could be calculated for its relationship to the total publication.

Taxpayers and the IRS have argued about allocation methods and there are differences of opinion. An EO with this question should be sure to determine the current situation. For hospitals, the Medicare cost allocations methods "usually fail to accurately reflect UBI" in the IRS's opinion expressed in General Counsel Memorandum 39843.

Direct vs. Indirect Expenses

A subset of the expense allocation problem is the application of different methods for direct and indirect expenses. Direct expenses are those that increase proportionately with the usage of a facility or the volume of activity and are also called variable. The number of persons attending an event influence the number of ushers or security guards and represent a direct cost, or in other words, the cost is attributable to that specific use that would not have been incurred except for the particular event.

Indirect costs, on the other hand, are incurred without regard to usage or frequency of participation, and are usually called the fixed expenses of the organization, such as building costs. The presumption

---

[63] *Exempt Organization Examination Guidelines Handbook,* Section 720(7) of Internal Revenue Manual 7(10)69.

is that the organization's underlying building costs, for example, do not vary with usage.

Formula Denominator Question

The denominator of the fraction used to calculate costs allocable to UBI is significant in reducing or increasing allowable deductions. The question must be considered in view of the exploitation rules and the point is again whether the EO would conduct the related activity without the unrelated revenue stream. Arguably no fixed costs of an exempt institution should be allocated to UBI, but to date the courts have chosen to allow allocation among both the exempt and nonexempt functions that benefit from building use.

In allocating fixed facility costs, the courts haven't agreed on whether the total number of hours a facility is used versus the total number of hours in the year is the appropriate denominator. To anyone grasping mathematics, it is easy to see each factor yields vastly different results. Watch for new legislation or regulations; more complicated and varied formulas have been proposed.

- The Second Circuit of the federal courts[64] in a college football stadium case allowed:

$$\frac{\text{number of hours or days used for unrelated purposes}}{\text{total number of hours or days in USE}}$$

- The IRS argues that fixed costs were to be allocated by:

$$\frac{\text{number of hours or days used for unrelated purposes}}{\text{total number of hours of days in YEAR}}$$

Gross-to-Gross Method

The gross-to-gross method of cost allocation is applied where costs bear a relationship to the revenue produced from exempt and nonexempt factors. For example, where students and members are charged one fee and nonmembers and nonstudents are charged another (usually higher) fee, an allocation using the total revenue from each

[64] *Rensselaer Polytechnic Institute v. Commissioner*, 732 F.2d 1058 (2d Cir. 1984), aff'g 79 T.C. 967 (1982).

different category would not be reflective of the true cost to produce the revenue. A proration based on the overall number of individuals in each group might better reflect reality and ostensibly be more accurate. This type of formula is often used in calculating allocations for social clubs or publications serving all participants the same price.

Exploitation

When a fundamentally exempt activity, such as publication or bookstore, produces some UBI from advertising or sales of unrelated items, the IRS regulations provide a limitation on the deduction of underlying exempt activity cost against the UBI. This limitation presents a classic "chicken and egg" or "tail wagging the dog" situation. Is the UBI activity an afterthought? Probably the best question is whether the exempt activity would be carried on regardless of the UBI funds. It is curious that the football stadium case cite above allows allocation of expenses despite the obvious assumption that a college must have a sports facility without regard to its ability to rent it during the down time, a seemingly classic "exploitation." Nonetheless, where an EO chooses to consider UBI as produced in connection with an exploited activity, deduction limitations are based upon income.

- Expenses of an exploited activity are allowable as a general rule only to the extent of the gross unrelated income they produce.

- Exempt function expenses related to the activity are first reduced by any related revenues, then the excess expenses are allocated to the unrelated income to the extent of the unrelated income. No loss resulting from an excess of exempt function plus unrelated activity expenses over total revenues can be used to offset other UBI.

- See *Special Interest Topics* for calculation of deductible expenses on an exploited publication.

Charitable Deduction

Up to 10 percent of an exempt corporation's UBI and 100 percent of a charitable trust's UBI is deductible for contributions paid to another charitable organization. Note the deduction is not allowed for internal project expenditures of the organization itself. Excess contributions are eligible for the normal five-year carryover allowed forprofit taxpayers. Social clubs, voluntary employee business associations, unemployment benefit trusts, and group legal service plans can take a 100 percent deduction for direct charitable gifts and "qualified set asides" for charitable purposes.

Administrative Overhead

It bears separate note that a portion of the organization's administrative expenses may be deductible against UBI and substantially reduces the tax burden from unrelated activity. Adequate proof of the allocation methods and escape of the exploitation rule discussed above is important to support an EO's overhead deduction against UBI.

$1,000 Exemption

A specific exemption of $1,000 ($5,000 under Congressional Select Committee Proposals) is allowed.

* Accounting Method Considerations (New)

In-Kind Gifts

Donated goods and services properly recorded under accounting principles promulgated by the Accounting Principles Board (APB 78-10) should be booked and deducted.

Documentation

To correctly calculate the EO's expenses that are allocable to UBI, documentation is critical. Time records, expense identification, departmental approval systems, and similar internal control techniques will allow the organization to compute maximum allowable deductions against UBI. Particularly for staff time allocations and administrative expense items, such as printing and supplies, capturing the information is simple once documentation methods are installed.

Accrual Method

If the EO's gross income from UBI exceeds $5 million annually, the accrual method of accounting must be used. Also if an inventory of goods and products for sale is maintained and is a "material" income producing factor, the accrual method must be utilized.

NOLs

A loss realized in operating an unrelated business in one year may be carried back for three years and forward fifteen years for offset against another year's operating income. Gains and losses for different types of UBI earned within any single EO are netted against profits from the various business activities of the organization, including acquisition indebted investment property. Tax years in which no UBI activity is realized is counted in calculating the number of years for permissible carryovers. Conversely, net operating losses are not reduced by related income.

A social club cannot offset losses on serving nonmembers against income from its other investments, according to the Supreme Court which sided with the IRS in the *Portland Golf Club* case decided in 1990.[65] There has been a conflict of decisions in the U.S. Circuit Courts for several years and clubs claiming such losses must now consider filing amended returns to report tax resulting from the loss disallowance.

It is extremely important for an EO to file Form 990T despite the fact that it incurs a loss. Reporting the loss allows for carryback or carryover of the loss to offset past or future income. Note that an election is available to carry losses forward and forego any carryback in situations where the EO has not previously earned UBI.

Estimated Tax

Income tax liability for UBI is payable in advance during the year as the income is earned similar to forprofit businesses and individuals.

[65] *Portland Golf Club v. Commissioner,* 90-1 U.S.T.C. § 50,332 (Sup. Ct. 1990); *Iowa State University of Science and Technology v. U.S.,* 500 F.2d 508 (Ct. Cl. 1974), and *Commissioner v. Groetzinger,* supra at note 5.

Debt Financed Income

The *modifications* exempting passive investment income from the UBIT, such as dividends and interest, do not apply to the extent the investment is made with borrowed funds. Debt financed property is defined by Section 514 as including property held for the production of income that was acquired with borrowed funds and has a balance of acquisition indebtedness attributable to it during the year. The classic examples are a margin account held against the EO's endowment funds or a mortgage financing a rental building purchase.

* Properties Excluded from Debt Financed Rules (New)

Real or other tangible or intangible property used 85 percent or more (of the time it is actually devoted to such purpose) directly in the EO's exempt or related activities is exempt from these rules. Say a university borrows money and builds an office tower for its projected staff needs over a 20-year period. If less than 85 percent of the building is used by its staff and net profit is earned, the non-university-use portion of the building income is taxable as UBI.

- Property the income of which is included in UBI for some other reason is specifically excluded by the code and need not be counted twice for this reason.

- Future-use property acquired and held for use by the organization within ten years from the date it is acquired and located in the neighborhood in which the EO carries out a project is exempt from this provision.

- A "life estate" does not constitute a debt. Where some other individual or organization is entitled to income from the property for their life or other period of time, a remainder interest in the property is not considered to be indebted.

- Debt placed on property by a donor will be attributed to the organization where the EO assumes and agrees to pay all or part of the debt OR makes any payments on the equity.

Property that is encumbered and subject to existing debt at the time it is received by bequest or devise is not treated as acquisition indebted-property for ten years from its acquisition if there is no assumption or payment on the debt by the exempt.

- Gifted property is similarly excluded if the donee placed the mortgage on the property over five years prior to gift and had owned the property over five years unless there is an assumption or payment by the EO on the mortgage.

- A property used in unrelated activities of an EO, the income of which is excepted from UBI because it is run by volunteers, for the convenience of members, or sale of donated goods, can be indebted and still not be subject to this classification.

- Research property producing income otherwise excluded from the UBIT also is not subject to the acquisition indebtedness taint.

* What Is "Acquisition Indebtedness?" (New)

Acquisition indebtedness is the unpaid amount of any debt incurred to purchase or improve property or any debt "reasonably foreseen" at the time of acquisition which would not have been incurred otherwise.

- Securities purchased on margin are debt financed. Payments for loan of securities already owned are not.

- The formula for calculation of income subject to tax is:

$$\text{income from property} \times \frac{\text{average acquisition indebtedness}}{\text{average adjusted basis}}$$

The average acquisition indebtedness equals the arithmetic average of each month or partial month of the tax year. The average adjusted basis is similarly calculated, and only straight line depreciation is allowed.

* Calculation of Taxable Portion (New)

Only that portion of the net income of debt financed property attributable to the debt is classified as UBI. Each property subject to debt is calculated separately with the resulting net income or loss netted to arrive at the portion includable in UBI. Expenses directly connected with the property are deducted from gross revenues in the same proportion.

The capital gain or loss formula is different in one respect; highest amount of indebtedness during the year preceding sales is used as the numerator.

Planning Ideas

The first rule in reducing UBIT is to keep good records. The accounting system must support the desired allocation of deductions for personnel and facilities with time records, expense usage reports, auto logs, documentation reports, and so on. Aggressive avoidance of the "exploitation rule" must be backed up with proof.

Minutes of meetings of the board of directors or trustees should reflect discussion of relatedness of any project claimed to accomplish an exempt purpose where it could appear the activity is unrelated. For example, contracts and other documents concerning activities the organization wants to prove are related to its exempt purposes should contain appropriate language to reflect the project's exempt purposes.

An organization's original purposes can be expanded and redefined to broaden the scope of activities to justify some proposed activity as related. Such altered or expanded purpose can be reported to the IRS to justify the relatedness of a new activity.

Where dual use facilities can be partly debt financed, partly paid for, the EO could purposefully buy the non-taxable exempt function property with debt and buy the unrelated part of the facility with cash available. Or separate notes could be executed with the taxable and unrelated property's debt being paid off first.

If loss of exemption is a strong possibility because the extent and amount or unrelated business activity planned, a separate for-profit organization can be formed to shield the EO from a possible loss of exemption due to excessive business activity.

Special Interest Topic—Museums

Museum gift shop sales and related income-producing activities are governed by the "fragmentation" and "exploitation" rules discussed earlier under the "substantially related" and "deductions" headings. Since 1973, when it published a ruling concerning greeting cards,[66] the IRS has formally agreed that items printed with reproductions of images in a museum's collection are educational, related to the exempt purposes, and their sale produces UBI. The ruling expressed two different reasons: (1) the cards stimulated and enhanced the public awareness, interest in, and appreciation of art; and (2) a self-advertising theory stating that a "broader segment of the public may be encouraged to visit the museum itself to share in its educational functions and programs as a result of seeing the cards."

Another 1973 ruling[67] explored the fragmentation rule and expanded its look to trinkets and actual copies of objects and distinguished items the IRS felt had educational merit from utilitarian items with souvenir value. Since that time it has been clearly established that a museum shop often contains both related and unrelated items and the museum must keep exacting records to identify the two.

* *Identifying Related and Unrelated Objects (New)*

After the IRS and museums argued for ten years about the relatedness of a wide variety of objects sold, four exhaustive private rulings were issued in 1983 and are still followed (Fall, 1991).[68] The primary concern for a museum is to identify the "relatedness" of each object sold in their shops and segregate any unrelated sales. The connection between the item sold and achievement of the museum's exempt purpose

---

[66] Rev. Rul. 73-104, 1973-1 C.B. 263.
[67] Rev. Rul. 73-105, 1973-1 C.B. 265.
[68] Priv. Ltr. Rul. 8303013, 8326003, 8236008, and 8328009.

is evidenced by the facts and circumstances of each object and the policy of the curatorial department in identifying, labeling and categorizing objects on public view.

IRS rulings direct the *"facts and circumstances"* of each object be examined to prove the objects being sold have educational value and list the following factors to consider in designating an item:

- "Interpretive material" describing artistic, cultural or historical relationship to museum's collection or exhibits.

- Nature, scope, and motivation for the sales activity.

- Are sales solely for production of income or an activity to enhance visitor awareness of art?

- Curatorial supervision in choosing related items.

- Reproductions of objects in the particular museum or other collections including prints, slides, posters, post or greeting cards, are generally exempt.

- Adaptations, including imprinted utilitarian objects such as dishes, ashtrays, clothing, must be accompanied by interpretive materials and must depict objects or identify an exhibition. Objects printed with logos were deemed unrelated.

- Souvenirs and convenience items are generally unrelated unless imprinted with reproductions or promoting a particular event or exhibition. Souvenirs promoting the town in which the museum is located are not considered related to the museum's purposes.

- Toys and other teaching items for children are deemed inherently educational and therefore deemed related in IRS rulings.

Original Works of Art

Original works of art created by living artists and sold by museums are considered unrelated by the IRS. "It is inconsistent with the purpose of exhibiting art for public benefit to deprive public the opportunity of viewing the art by selling it to an individual."

- A cooperative art gallery established to encourage individual "emerging artists" was not allowed to qualify as an exempt organization because, in the IRS's opinion, the interests of the general public were not served by promoting the careers of individual artists. The art sales served no exempt purpose and constituted unrelated business income. Since the organization was supported entirely by unrelated business income from the sales of art of the artists, it was not exempt.[69]

- A community art center located in an isolated area with no commercial galleries obtained exemption and the Tax Court decided its sales of original art were related to exempt purposes. The decision was based upon the fact that no other cultural center existed in the county, the art sales were not the center's sole source of support, and a complex of other activities were conducted.[70]

- An unrelated gallery managed by volunteers and/or selling donated works of art produces unrelated income but the income is not taxable due to exceptions. Note exempt status depends upon whether the gallery is a substantial part of the EO's activities.

Study Tours

Museums and other types of exempt organizations sponsor study tours as promotional, educational, and fund-raising tools. The issue is whether such tours compete with travel agents and commercial tour guides and thus produce UBI. A study tour led by professionals and qualifying for university credit qualifies as related to a museum's educational purposes. Generally the IRS looks carefully and will scrutinize:

- The "bona fide" educational methodology of the tour, including the professional status of leaders and the educational content of the program. The amount of advanced preparation,

---

[69] Priv. Ltr. Rul. 8032028.
[70] *Goldsboro Art League, Inc. v. Commissioner,* 75 T.C. 337 (1980).

such as reading lists, can be a factor. The actual amount of time spent in formal class, mandatory participations in the lectures, or opportunity for university credit are other attributes evidencing the educational nature of a tour.[71]

- Conversely, the amount of recreational time allowed to participants, the resort-taint of the places the tour visits, and holiday scheduling will suggest predominantly personal pleasure purposes and cause the tour to not qualify as educational.[72]

Not only the profit from the tour itself, but the "additional donation" requested as an organizational gift by all participants in a travel tour program, may be classed as unrelated income if the tour is not considered as educational.[73]

Special Interest Topic—Publishing

EO publications present two very different exposures to trouble: the unrelated income tax and potential revocation of exemption. As discussed earlier, the most universal problem is that publication advertising sales create UBIT in most cases. Secondly, the less common, but more dangerous situation, occurs where the underlying exemption is challenged because the publication itself is a business.

Advertising

Revenue received from the sale of advertising in an otherwise exempt publication is considered business income by the IRS, and is taxed unless:

- The publication schedule or ad sale activity is irregularly carried on.

- The advertising is sold by volunteers.

---

[71] Rev. Rul. 70-534, 1970-2 C.B. 113.
[72] Rev. Rul. 77-366, 1977-2 C.B. 192.
[73] IRS T.A.M. 9027003.

- The advertising activity is related to one of the organization's underlying exempt purposes, such as ads sold by college students or trainees.

- The ads do not contain commercial material, appear essentially as a listing without significant distinction among those listed, and represent acknowledgment of contributors or sponsors.

Readership vs. Ad Lineage Costs

Even if ad revenue is classified as UBI, the tax consequence is limited by the portion of the readership and editorial costs allowed as deductions against the ad revenue. The important question is what portion of the expense of producing and distributing the publication can be allocated against the revenue.[74] It is helpful first to study *Calculating Taxable Portion of Advertising Revenue,* a worksheet reflecting the order in which readership and editorial costs versus advertising costs are allocated.

What the formula accomplishes is to prorate deductions in arriving at taxable advertising income. Publication costs are first divided into two categories: direct advertising and readership (details listed in the exhibit). Since readership costs are exempt function costs, under the "exploitation rule" discussed later they theoretically shouldn't be deductible at all against the UBI income. In a limited exception, the regulation allows readership costs, if any, in excess of readership income to be deducted against advertising income. In other words, advertising revenues can be offset with a readership loss.

Arriving at a readership loss, however, means the publication's underlying production costs must be more than its revenues. Where the publication is given free to members, but sold to nonmembers, a portion of the member dues is allocated to readership revenue. The IRS formulas require that an allocation of a hypothetical portion of the dues be made as described in the exhibit.

1. Free copies given to nonmembers are subject to controversy with IRS (check latest decisions).

[74] Regs. § 1.512(a)-1(f)(6).

2. If EO has more than one publication, IRS and courts also disagree on denominator of fraction for calculation of allocable exempt function costs.[75]

Commercial Publication Programs

The overall publication program can be considered a commercial venture, despite its educational content. Distinguishing characteristics according to the IRS are found by examining the EO's management decisions.

The characteristics deemed commercial by the IRS include:

- *Presence of substantial profits.* Accumulations of profits over a number of years evidences a commercial purpose. The mere presence of profits, by itself, will not bar exemption,[76] but other factors will be considered. Among the questions asked would be for what purpose profits are being accumulated? Do the reserves represent a savings account for future expansion plans?

- *Pricing methods.* The method of pricing books or magazines sold yields significant evidence of commercial taint. Pricing at or below an amount calculated to cover costs shows nonprofit motive. Pricing below comparable commercial publications is not required but certainly can evidence an intention to encourage readership and educate, rather than to produce a profit.

- *Other factors.* Other factors can show commerciality:

  — Aggressive commercial practices resembling those undertaken by commercial publishers.[77]

  — Substantial salaries or royalties paid to individuals.

  — Distribution by commercial licensers, such as "est."

[75] *North Carolina Citizens for Business and Industry v. United States,* 89-2 U.S.T.C. § 9507 (Cl. Ct. 1989).
[76] *Scripture Press Foundation v. United States,* 285 F.2d 800 (Ct. Cl. 1961), cert. den., 368 U.S. 985 (1982).
[77] *American Institute for Economic Research v. United States,* 302 F.2d 934 (Ct. Cl. 1962).

Nonprofit Publications,

By contrast, nonprofit and noncommercial publications:[78]

— Rely upon volunteers and/or modest wages.

— Sell some books/magazines that are unprofitable.

— Prepare and choose materials according to educational methods, not commercial appeal.

— Donate part of press run to other EOs or members.

— Balances deficit budgets with contributions.

The Royalty Dilemma

It is the IRS's opinion that Section 512(b)(2), which says royalty income is not unrelated business income, does not apply to certain types of "royalties," including particularly those received in return for the sale of an organization's mailing list and the EO's name or logo.[79] While agreeing mailing lists are intangible property the use of which produces royalty income, the IRS argues that royalties are inherently passive. They say, when the royalty income is produced in an active, commercial manner in competition with tax-paying businesses, it is contrary to the underlying scheme of the UBIT to allow such royalties to escape taxation.

Among the UBIT changes proposed by the House Oversight Committee (discussed following), royalties received for licensing property created by the EO or property involving substantial services and costs on the part of the EO, would be subject to UBIT—a rule the IRS is essentially now applying without statutory authority. After its success in the DAV case discussed below, the IRS may turn its "active" argument to other types of licensing arrangements as it pursues its UBI Compliance Program. The issue is very unsettled and the details of the history may be useful.

---

[78] *Presbyterian and Reformed Publishing Co. v. Commissioner,* 70 T.C. 1070, 1087, 1083 (1982).
[79] G.C.M. 39827 (August 20, 1990) and Priv. Ltr. Rul. 9029047.

Unfortunately the term "royalties" is not defined under the code or regulations concerning unrelated income. In response to objections by large charities who the IRS was subjecting to UBIT on their list revenues, Section 513(h)(1)(B) was added to provide special exception only for organizations eligible to receive charitable contributions, primarily 501(c)(3)s, to exclude from UBI mailing list sales and exchanges with other similar organizations. By reference mailing list sales by all other categories of tax-exempts would be includable in UBI.

In an interesting case, the Sixth Circuit Court[80] in July 1991 reversed the Tax Court and said the Disabled American Veterans (DAV)'s mailing list revenues were taxable unrelated business income. DAV (a 501(c)(4) organization) was arguing in the courts to escape tax deficiencies of over $4 million dollars based upon $279 million of revenue. The IRS partly based their position upon the active business principle contending that the level of active business involvement in servicing the list rental activity prevented the revenue from being classified as passive and, thereby, excludable from the UBIT.

The DAV admitted the revenue was from an unrelated business activity. There was no argument that DAV managed the activity in a business-like manner. Among the stipulations were the fact that DAV had several personnel working full time to keep the list current (not a volunteer operation), placed conditions on the name usage, required advanced approval of the client copy, had a complicated rate structure printed and widely circulated on rate cards, and belonged to DMMA, a trade association composed of organizations using direct mail techniques in their operations.

The DAV argued the revenue was a royalty excepted from UBI. The Tax Court had decided that it was up to Congress to cause "active" royalties to be taxed when the code plainly says all royalties are excluded. They found nothing in the policy of the statute to offer any basis for characterizing royalties earned by a tax-exempt organization differently from royalties earned by a commercial organization. This issue is of particular interest in the scientific and medical fields, where considerable sums are earned from royalties paid for the licensing of patented devices and methods.

---

[80] *Disabled American Veterans v. Commissioner*, 91-2 U.S.T.C. § 50,336 (Sixth Cir. 7/5/91), rev'd 94 T.C. 60 (1990).

The DAV case is complicated by the fact that the Court of Claims had already decided in 1981 that DAV's mailing list sale income was taxable (it specifically declined to decide about exchanges). What the Sixth Circuit decided in overruling the Tax Court was that DAV was collaterally estopped by the 1981 decision from bringing the argument again to court, not that mailing lists sales were necessarily taxable. Thus although the DAV lost on a technicality, the Tax Court decision still stands as to sales and no decision has ever been made about list exchanges.

Look for a new decision on the subject. The Sierra Club filed a suit with the Tax Court in May, 1991, that was yet to be docketed when this book went to press.

Given the present economic climate with Congress responding to revenue raising possibilities, it is reasonable to expect future changes to occur to narrow the royalty exception, particularly as it relates to mailing lists and other types of name or logo sales. The proposals for UBI changes have contained several different versions as it regards royalties since first being proposed in 1987.

House Subcommittee on Oversight Hearing Proposals

In June, 1987, under the leadership of Congressman Jake Pickle of Texas, the House of Representatives Subcommittee on Oversight held hearings on the Unrelated Business Income Tax. The hearings were in response to pressure brought by a wide variety of small business owners complaining that exempt organizations are allowed unfair advantage by the existing UBI tax laws.

Actual legislative proposals have not yet been finalized by the subcommittee and the timing of legislative action is uncertain. The issues of concern and possible changes to the existing rules listed in suggested versions of proposed legislation are outlined below:

- Proposal would tax categories of income deemed to unfairly compete with business:
  - Off-premise (mail order or telephone) sales taxable.
  - Affinity card revenue.
  - Food sales (except for members, patients, students).

— Hotels, condominiums, theme and amusement parks.

— Sales and rental of medical devices.

- Definitions narrowed for the following:

    — Only royalties measured by gross income or expressed as a fixed amount excluded.

    — Deductions from advertising revenue limited to direct costs.

    — General administrative costs and depreciation not deductible against rents from joint-use property.

- Form 990 expanded to report details of revenue sources. Special studies to evaluate "unfair competition" mandated.

- Allocation formula for dual-use facilities costs used in both related and unrelated activities would be revised.

- Exemption raised to $5,000 from $1,000.

- Forprofit subsidiary income is attributed to the nonprofit parent when ownership is 50 percent or more (now must be 80 percent).

- The House committee proposes an "aggregation rule" to combine all subsidiary activities with the exempt parent for purposes of measuring ongoing qualification for exemption. The committee wants some method for measuring the extent of the EO's involvement in the subsidiary's actual operations. Under existing rules there is no cross attribution between controlled subsidiaries of an exempt. Stock owned by one EO subsidiary in another sub is not attributed to the parent EO. The intention is to view a controlled group as an integrated enterprise to assure that the parent exempt's primary purpose remains an exempt. This proposal is not included in the Treasury Department's report.

Surprisingly, as of fall, 1991, none of the proposed changes to the unrelated business income tax provisions have been made and it appears no changes will be proposed until after the IRS completes its study of the UBI with new page 5 of Form 990 in 1992 or 1993.

* Calculation of Taxable Portion of Advertising Revenue (New)

Basic Formula

A − B − (C–D) = Net taxable advertising income or loss

where A = Gross sales of advertising
B = Direct costs of advertising
C–D = Readership costs in excess of readership revenue

Definitions

B = Direct Costs of Advertising:

Occupancy, supplies and other administrative expense $_____

Commissions or salary costs for ad salespeople   _____

Clerical or management salary cost directly allocable   _____

Artwork, photography, color separations, etc.   _____

Portion of printing, typesetting, mailing, and other
direct publication costs allocable in the ratio of total
lineage in the publication to ad lineage   _____

   $_____

C = Readership costs:

Occupancy, supplies and other administrative expense   _____

Editors, writers, and salary for editorial content   _____

Travel, photos, other direct editorial expenses   _____

Portion of printing, typesetting, mailing and other
direct publication costs allocable in ratio of total
lineage in publication to editorial lineage (in general,
all direct publication costs not allocable to advertising
lineage)   _____

   $_____

D = Readership (or circulation) revenues:

If publication sold to all for a fixed price, then
readership revenue equals total subscriptions sales.   _____

or

> If 20 percent of total circulation is from paid nonmember
> subscriptions, then price charged to nonmembers times
> number of issues circulated to members plus nonmember
> revenue equals readership revenues.   _____

or

> If members receiving publication pay a higher
> membership fee, readership revenue equals excess
> dues times number of members receiving publication,
> plus nonmember revenue.   _____

or

> If over 80 percent of issues distributed to members
> free, readership revenue is the membership receipts
> times the ratio of publication costs over the total
> exempt activities cost including the publication costs.   _____

§ 3.8A RELATIONSHIPS (NEW)

Organizational Spin-Offs

Sometimes an exempt organization, its board, or its staff wish to undertake an activity not appropriate for the organization itself, but suitable for another form of EO. There are two classic types of spin-offs the specific aspects of which are presented in other portions of the book. A title-holding company, as discussed in § 1.9, is formed to hold assets for the benefit of the organization. A Section 501(c)(4) organization might be formed by a 501(c)(3) charity to conduct lobbying activities which would be unallowable for the reasons outlined in § 3.9 at page 308.

A new and separate EO might be formed to conduct a program that exposes the organization's assets to unacceptable risk of financial loss. The motivation here is similar to the reasons for forming a title holding company, except that a title-holding company cannot actively operate programs or projects.

A new organization might be formed because it can qualify for funding not available to the existing organization. A common example of this type of spin-off is an auxiliary formed to allow the individuals involved in the fund raising to control the funds that they raise while not controlling the underlying organization. The creation of a charity to benefit a business league or labor union (discussed next in detail) can attract deductible gifts not available to the benefited organization itself.

The new organization must, of course, meet the requirements for the category of exemption under which it is formed. The application for exemption filed to obtain recognition of exemption must describe in detail the relationship and the reasons why the new organization is being created. While interlocking directorates are not prohibited in either situation, prudence usually dictates that a separate and uncontrolling board be established for the new organization. Criteria for attributing activities back to the creating organization have been developed by the IRS to evaluate for-profit subsidiaries and can be referred to below.

As a practical matter, the existing organization's assets are not usually transferred as might be implied by the term spin-off, except in the formation of a title-holding company. In fact, to retain the distinct tax exemption and legal identity, separate and distinguishable operations are imperative. Nevertheless the two organizations often operate side by side and share employees and facilities. Recordkeeping may need to be expanded to assure documentation of the new entity's separate existence. See discussion under "Sharing Facilities, Employees."

Creation of (c)(3) by a (c)(4), (5), or (6) Organization

Business leagues, labor unions, civic clubs, and other exempt organizations other than (c)(3)s are typically organized and operated to further the interests of their members. Conversely, a (c)(3), often called a charitable organization, is created to raise funds in support of programs benefiting the general public as described in Chapter 1, § 1.10. The motivations for non-(c)(3)s to establish a (c)(3) are many. Most often such organizations already conduct charitable programs and wish to raise grant funds from nonmembers to support them. The (c)(3) might also be created as a vehicle to honor respected members upon their death or as the recipient of split-interest trust or life insurance gifts during members' life. A charitable wing might be created to enhance the public image of the profession through the sponsorship of scholarships and educational programs.

Form of Relationship

The relationship between the two organizations can take many forms. Typically the board members will overlap, if not be identical for both, which is acceptable. If public status as a supporting organization is desired, the link must be tight and the purposes and organizational documents must meet the details and specific requirements found in § 3.5A.

Category of Public Charity

Public charity status is perhaps the most important question to answer in structuring this type of relationship. The type of public charity is dictated partly by the anticipated sources of funding. If the majority of the support will be received from the related organization or a small group of members, formation of a supporting organization under Section 509(a)(3) is appropriate. If donations are expected from a wide segment of the membership and general public, the new organization might also qualify for public status under Section 509(a)(1) or (2). Where the proposed organization can qualify as publicly supported under all three of the categories of Section 509, a choice must be made. The 509(a)(1) or (2) categories allow the new organization to operate and be controlled more independently than it could as a supporting organization under 509(a)(3). In making a choice between 509(a)(1) and (a)(2), the difference is primarily mathematical and depends upon the sources of revenue. See § 3.5A for the intricacies of public status.

Donation Collection System

A subset of the public support question arises when the professional society, civic league, or union handles donation solicitations as a part of its annual dues collection process. Typically the separate charitable foundation donations are optional for society members who add whatever amount they choose. The society collects the donations and periodically pays them over to the charity. The question is who is making the gift, the individual member or the society. While there is no statutory authority for the policy, IRS specialists in the Austin District accept treatment of the gifts as individual donations. Particularly for optional gifts, there is evidence of donative intention on the member's part, rather than the society. To so qualify, the donations must be clearly segregated and recorded on the society's financial records as a liability being held by the society as agent for the foundation.

Grants to/from the (c)(3)

The (c)(3) organization raises the funds to carryout the educational, scientific, or other charitable activities on behalf of the organization that creates it. The interesting question which sometimes arises is whether the (c)(3) must disburse the funds itself and directly undertake the charitable projects. Or instead can the (c)(3) grant funds to the (c)(4), (5), or (6) to enable it to undertake the activities? Both scenarios are permissible. If the funds are paid over to the non-(c)(3) organization, the grant should be restricted under a written agreement specifying the qualifying purposes for which the moneys can be spent and, if possible, annual reports should be made back to the funding charity.

Often the society furnishes the charity office space, personnel, and other necessary operating overhead items. Reimbursement of expenses incurred by either organization is permissible as outlined below in the subsection on "Sharing Facilities, Employees." However, the charity has a burden of proving that the expenditures do not benefit the society and its members. Where it is financially possible, payment of the expenses by the society without reimbursement eliminates any possible challenge.

In Priv. Ltr. Rul. 9017003, the IRS decided that a related foundation of a business/professional association (501(c)(6)) was not "truly engaged in appropriate tax-exempt activities" because it operated primarily for the benefit of the association. The foundation's only activity was to provide a nonrent lease to the related membership association.

The IRS concluded leasing is not usually an inherently charitable activity and that the charity in the ruling was only operated to further the interest of the parent organization and therefore not qualified for exemption.

Forming a Partnership with Investors

In the face of declining governmental support for housing and education during the 1970s, EOs began to turn to the private sector for capital funding. In the medical field, the cost of new medical technology and the establishment of health care conglomerates compounded capital needs. Accelerated depreciation rates encouraged such arrangements until 1984[81] and 1986 with the advent of the passive loss limitations. Despite the reduced tax benefits, both to raise capital and to gain their participation and expertise, joint ventures with private individuals and businesses still proliferate.

Exempt as General Partner

While there are a slew of private letter rulings and some important General Counsel Memoranda on the subject, there is very little judicial guidance, except for the well-known *Plumstead Theater Society* case,[82] which means any decision to form a partnership must be considered carefully. The primary IRS policy on the subject has concerned charitable organizations. Originally, the IRS ruled an EO was completely prohibited from serving as a general partner with private limited partners. Since the general partner has an obligation to maximize profits for the benefit of the limited partners, the IRS took the position that the general partner role violates the basic private inurement standards and automatically causes loss of exempt status (the arrangement is "inherently incompatible with being operated exclusively for charitable purposes").[83]

---

[81] Section 168(j)(9), so-called "tax-exempt entity leasing rules" lengthened depreciable lives for certain properties.

[82] *Plumstead Theater Society v. Commissioner*, 675 F.2d 244 (9th Cir. 1982), *affirming* 74 T.C. 1324 (1980).

[83] G.C.M. 36293 (May 30, 1975).

Careful Scrutiny / Facts and Circumstances Test

By 1980, the IRS relaxed the prohibition and agreed that an EO could serve as a general partner *if* (and only if) the venture is one that serves the EO's charitable purposes. Each case is to be carefully scrutinized and the facts and circumstances considered in detail to evaluate purposes served (preferably exempt). Insulating the exempt general partner assets from venture liabilities is also important. Among the facts that provide such insulation are:

1. Contractual limitation of liability.[84]

2. Right of first refusal or option to purchase on dissolution or sale granted to the EO.[85]

3. Limitation or ceiling on returns to limited partners.[86]

4. Presence of other general partners or managers with responsibility to serve the limited partners.[87]

*   5. Amount of organizational control exercised by the exempt partner and attention paid to charitable mission carried on by the partnership.

*   6. Methods for calculating profit sharing, asset purchases or cost reimbursements.

* These two additional factors were used by the IRS in approving the reorganization of a resonance imaging center established by an exempt hospital group's for-corporate subsidiary with its own and funds furnished partly by physician-limited partners. All financial arrangements between the parties were at fair market value and profits and losses are to be allocated in relation to the investment made and risks assumed. Mutually binding termination and buy-out agreements were in place to protect the charitable interests from undue risk of loss.[88]

[84] G.C.M. 39546 (August 27, 1986)
[85] Priv. Ltr. Rul. 8344099.
[86] Priv. Ltr. Rul. 8417054 and 8344099.
[87] G.C.M. 39005 (June 29, 1983).
[88] Private Letter Rulings 9122061, 9122062 and 9122070, dated March 6, 1991.

The first factor is of primary concern in protecting the EO's assets. The organizational test for continued charitable exemption requires that the assets be dedicated to charitable purposes and earnings be similarly used. Consequently, liabilities associated with any joint venture must be identifiable, limited, and not posing a threat to the organization's underlying assets. Such protection can be achieved with insurance coverage, with indemnity agreements specifying the extent of exposure, or the nature of the activities. For example, a student dormitory building project has less inherent risk than a nuclear fission research laboratory and may provide lower exposure to an exempt general partner.

The second and third factors assure that the limited partners do not reap unreasonable compensation or gain at the expense of the EO. Conversely, the EO taking the risk of serving as general partner should be appropriately rewarded with the greater share of the return. Another method of protecting the EO interest is to allow the charity to repurchase the venture asset or to specifically limit the profits. Suitable terms under which a laboratory venture operated can be found in G.C.M. 37852.[89] The following discussion regarding management contracts and compensation levels has more examples of fair compensation.

The last factor mitigates the local law problem. An important objection of the IRS to exempt general partners is the conflict between their responsibility to create gain for the limiteds and serve their exempt constituents. In some cases, the EO requires a dual general partner to actually manage the venture to suitably limit its role.

Trouble-Free Relationships

A joint venture with another EO of the same 501 category to own and operate exempt function assets or sponsor a charitable program poses no threat to either EO's status. A trouble-free example might have three museums buying a Georgia O'Keefe painting, each receiving an undivided one-third interest. The costs are shared equally and each museum exhibits the work one-third of each year. This joint ownership is established to reduce the funds expended by each museum and

---

[89] G.C.M. 37852 (February 15, 1979).

enable them to reduce their storage requirements and thus serves an exempt purpose.

What if the venture borrows money from a private individual to buy the painting? Assume the loan is to be paid back over a four-year period, as fund raising permits. Interest on the debt is paid at the prevailing prime rate. If the loan is unpaid at the end of the four years, the painting can be foreclosed by the lender in return for any principal payments made against the loan adjusted for any increase in value as determined by an independent outside appraiser. Since purchasing and exhibiting art work advances the educational purposes of the museums, since their underlying endowments are not used to purchase the painting (limited liability), and since the museums reap any increase in the value of the art work, this venture involving a private investor should not pose a treat to their exempt status.

Another prototype arrangement occurs where the EO needs to expand. Assume it needs to acquire a building to provide additional space. After meetings with major donors, it is clear the funds cannot be raised entirely through donations. Some of the donors, however, offer to build the facility and lease it back to the organization. If the building serves exempt purposes and the four factors discussed above are present, the relationship of tenant-landlord is permissible.

Unrelated Business Income Aspect

Formation of a partnership does not shelter an EO from classification of an activity's income as unrelated business income because the attributes of income pass directly through to the partners retaining the same character. The partnership itself pays no tax.

Another UBI question is whether the business activities of the partnership (same question for corporate subsidiary) will be attributed to the EO and, if so, will the exempt status of the organization be jeopardized because of the partnership activity? The primary purpose of the EO cannot be to participate in the venture. The IRS has adopted a "more than incidental" test, which in a private ruling it deemed satisfied when an organization projected a ceiling of no more than 15 percent of its computerized database users would be nonexempt users.[90] (See also p. 265.)

---

[90] Priv. Ltr. Rul. 8636079.

Creation of a For-Profit Corporate Subsidiary

A primary motivation for forming a corporation instead of a partnership is to segregate unrelated business activities and to avoid the liability problems inherent in the partnership form of organization. Typically, the subsidiary is formed to conduct a business: to commercially develop a medical school's patents, to operate a restaurant/ski lodge on investment property being held for future expansion, or to establish a computer facility open to the public. More often a corporation is formed when outside investors are not involved and the more flexible profit/loss sharing ratios available to a partnership are not needed.

Maintaining Separate Corporate Identity

Attribution of the subsidiary's activities back to its exempt parent defeats the purpose for its formation. Thus it is important to structure the subsidiary to assure its separate corporate identity. If the EO owns less than 100 percent of the stock (note below for UBIT purposes, under 79 percent is desirable), the outside owners provide the separateness. Where the EO owns all of the stock, proof of independence includes a separate board of directors or officers, and independent management of daily affairs.[91] Actual evidence of separate operation should be maintained, such as board meetings and operating budgets and financial reports. The fact that the parent corporation retains control over significant corporate actions, such as dissolution, does not constitute interference with the subsidiary's day-to-day affairs.[92]

The subsidiary must be established for a valid business purpose to avoid its being considered merely a "guise" to allow the EO to conduct excess business or other impermissible activity. The IRS is concerned that the subsidiary not be merely an arm, agency or integral part of the parent.[93]

    *   In a recent letter ruling, the IRS sanctioned the creation of a subsidiary by a business league to "isolate into one single taxable

---

[91] G.C.M. 39326 (January 17, 1985) and 39598 (January 23, 1987).
[92] Priv. Ltr. Rul. 8909029.
[93] G.C.M. 33912 (August 15, 1968).

entity" all its unrelated activities. The league provided that it would not be involved in the business planning or day-to-day operations of the subsidiary and that all transactions between the two entities would be conducted at arm's-length. There was no mention of interlocking control.

All insurance plans, including the group health and welfare plans, and the Section 401(k) retirement plans were to be transferred to the subsidiary. The Service ruled that the rendering of service by the sub and its payment of dividends to the exempt league would not jeopardize the league's exempt status.[94]

Subsidiary Pays Its Own Income Tax

As a separate taxpayer, the subsidiary pays its own income tax. Dividends are therefore paid to the exempt parent with after tax profits. To avoid circumvention of this rule, payments to a controlled parent (owning 80 percent or more or the stock) in the form of rent, interest, or royalty are taxed to the parent under Section 512(b)(13). In other words, tax on unrelated business income cannot be escaped by paying it back to an exempt parent as a deductible expense. Note the percentage of control is decreased to 50 percent under UBI reform proposals advanced by the Treasury Department (see p. 286).

Sharing Facilities, Employees

Combining EOs of more than one category of 501(c), private foundations, and/or nonexempt organizations into a sharing arrangements for office space, employees, group insurance, project management, or a variety of other operating necessities may be permissible. There is no absolute prohibition as long as the following conditions are met:

1. The activity (rental of office space, hiring of employees, etc.) serves an exempt purpose of the organization.

---

[94] Priv. Ltr. Rul. 9119060, May 20, 1991.

2. The organization reaps cost savings by combining with others in securing the shared item(s) or services.

3. Documentation is maintained to evidence each organization's allocable portion of each expenditure.

   — Time sheets.

   — Space utilization.

   — Asset cost (e.g., we buy the copier, you buy phones).

   — Auto and travel logs.

4. The arrangement does not allow unfair advantage to any of the parties, unless such advantage inures to the 501(c)(3)s involved.

5. The exempt does not assume any risk of loss on behalf of the other organization(s).

6. For PFs only, the organization pays its share directly to the outside vendors? See Chapter 4, Section 4941: Self-Dealing.

The first condition is of primary importance in evaluating a sharing relationship between one EO and another or an EO and a nonexempt organization. The primary motivation for the expenditure of the organization's funds must always be to serve its own exempt purposes, not another's.

The proof is often easy, however. Space in which to operate the EO is necessary. Why not accept the use of space in a major contributor's building? Major equipment, not owned by the organization, may be made available at little or not cost; a lease and/or a deposit may not be required. Often the rent is under market value because it is space not otherwise rentable at the time, although payment of full fair market value is not prohibited.

Another common arrangement is the sharing of employees. If a new charity needs a part time secretary, it may engage the available time of an associated organization's employee. As long as the compensation paid to such workers is fairly allocated among the organization for whom each person performs services, there again is no reason why staff cannot be shared. Evidence of the time actually devoted to each organization must be maintained as a basis for allocating salary and associated costs.

Combining related organization employees into one group for health insurance was specifically sanctioned in Priv. Ltr. Rul. 9025089. In a hospital conglomerate group, the (c)(3) charitable hospital, its (c)(3) supporting, fund-raising arm, and two for-profit subsidiaries (a health equipment rental company and administrative services provider) combined their employees into a self-funded, self-insured major medical plan. The inclusion of the subsidiary employees increased the number of plan participants and resulted in decreased cost of insurance, spreading the risk of loss over more participants. The per-participant cost for all entities was the same. The IRS found providing employee benefits was consistent with the hospital's exempt purposes. It did note that insurance trust was separate from all of the organizations. Presumably this fact was important because the 501(c)(3)s were not assuming any unforeseen risks on behalf of the for-profits.

Active Business Relationships

Partly due to limited access to investment capital and ability to compete for qualified permanent personnel, an EO may wish to engage an outside professional, either an individual or a company, to manager a project, facility, or other activity. The issues involved in consideration of such a relationship with a for-profit company are similar to the partnership/subsidiary issues. There are two primary concerns:

1. Are exempt purposes served by the relationship? Can the EO more effectively promote (insert appropriate exempt purpose, such as the health and well-being of its charitable constituents) by engaging the commercial manager to set up and administrative the new facility (or school or project)?

2. Is the compensation reasonable? Are terms equal to similar commercial arrangements? Is there other evidence of private inurement in the relationship?

Proof that exempt purposes are served could include a broad range of specific factors. The ability to secure, on a part time basis, the medical staff, development personnel, and insurance claims staff necessary to operate a proposed health care facility, at an estimated cost savings equal to one-half of the organization's reserves, allowing the facility to obtain licensing and begin serving the public six months earlier than anticipated, are all good examples of factors indicating that an arrangement serves the organization's underlying exempt purpose. Particularly if the manager is supervised by representatives of the EO, assuring adherence to the EO's standard of care for charitable constituents, there is no constraint against an EO operating efficiently and with a high level of expertise and professionalism. As provided in a recent private letter ruling, "the university lacked the skills to operate a first-rate university press and is concerned about the financial risks inherent in publishing purely academic works." A publishing venture in which the university retained 5 percent of the adjusted gross revenues and proprietary rights in the publications was permissible.[95]

A number of factors can indicate reasonableness of the compensation. An excessive amount, however, cannot be paid to secure such services. To test for reasonableness, another series of questions can be asked:

1. Are the outside managers or professionals totally independent of the organization? Is the compensation being negotiated at "arm's length"? Are there interlocking directorates or family relationship? In other words, can the managers influence the decision to hire themselves?

2. Are the terms equivalent to similar (or more favorable than) commercial arrangements? Is the price equal to the fair market value? Were competitive bids or comparable price studies obtained? Were CPAs, economists, appraisers, or others capable of evaluating the value engaged?

3. Does the relationship prevent earnings accruing to the benefit of the private individuals or provide economic gain to the

---

[95] Priv. Ltr. Rul. 9036025.

manager(s) at the expense of the exempt's charitable, public interests?

4. How is the compensation calculated: a fixed fee, percentage of gross or net income, or some other basis?

5. Does the contract provide for sufficient funds to the EO to compensate for its allocation of resources, the capital it is investing, and the risks it assumes?

6. Is the contract period too long or short?

7. Are services rendered for constituents unable to pay? Will the credit policies of the manager recognize the organization's charitable nature and lack of profit motive in conducting the operation?

The long-standing IRS policy frowns upon net profit agreements. While on one hand, maximizing profits assures efficiency and would provide the funds for the EO as well as the manager, the quality of services might be compromised by the manager's desire to produce profits. Based upon IRS published rulings, net profits-interest contracts must contain a ceiling, cap, or maximum amount the for-profit company or individual is to receive. This policy is intended to avoid the possibility of windfall benefit to the managers.[96]

In any arrangement, it is advisable to require by contract that the compensation terms be alterable, if necessary, to retain tax-exempt status, along with self-serving language that the relationship must be conducted in a fashion that serves the exempt constituents of the engaging organization. Regarding pricing, the IRS has in some circumstances required that charitable services must be provided at the least feasible cost.[97] Again the contract must constrain the manager to operate the project in a fashion that serves the exempt purposes.

In December 1991, General Counsel Memorandum 39862 reviewed three net revenue stream purchase joint ventures and found private inurement that would result in revocation of the hospitals' exempt status.

[96] G.C.M. 38905.
[97] Rev. Rul. 75-198, 1975-1 C.B. 157.

§ 3.9 POLITICAL AND LEGISLATIVE ACTIVITY

p. 287. *Add after second full paragraph:*

The literal definition of political action found in the regulations says an organization has political activity if it "participates or intervenes, directly or indirectly, in any political campaign on behalf of or in opposition to any candidate for public office. The term 'candidate for public office' means an individual who offers himself, or is proposed by others, as a contestant for an elective public office, whether such office be national, state, or local."[98]

What local offices constitute "public office" and when an appointment is in fact an election must be determined under the applicable local election laws and varies from state to state. Organizations have unexpectedly lost exempt status for involvement in school board, water commission, or other local campaigns. The presence of unallowed political activity is determined by application of relevant state election law.

In G.C.M. 39811, the IRS provided an example of an organization losing its exempt status due to involvement in political party precinct elections. An analysis of relevant local election laws indicated to the IRS that the precinct committee position possessed the characteristics of public office. The organization's counsel had advised the positions were administrative, not political. Alongside the exempt's strong and active legislative activities, the organization had classified the expenses as lobbying expense: permissible, but limited.

In another important distinction, the IRS does not view appointed members of the federal judicial system to be elected public officials. Attempts to influence the U.S. Senate confirmation of a nominee to the Supreme Court does not constitute intervention in a political campaign.[99]

* **p. 288.** *Add at bottom of page:*

Voter registration drives do not constitute intervention in a political campaign when conducted in a nonpartisan manner. Drives that

---

[98] Treas. Reg. § 1.501(c)(3)-1(c)(3)(iii).
[99] IRS Notice 88-76, 1988-27 I.R.B. 34.

are targeted at members of a particular party or in support of or against named candidates will be classified as political activity. Partisan language on materials handed out to potential voter registrants will cause the campaign to be classed as political activity.

The IRS retroactively revoked an ostensibly educational organization's exemption due to a variety of political activity. It found the following language incriminating:

> Conservatives in the U.S. Senate and House of Representatives are giving us economic prosperity, reducing government intervention and instilling pride in America and our way of life. All of this will be lost if Conservatives like you and me do not head off the huge voter registration drive by the liberals.

The ruling has a broad analysis of voter education and campaign workshops and is a must read for any organization participating in such activities.[100]

* **p. 292.** *Insert at the end of the second extract:*
Permissible expenditures by political campaign committees may include certain lobbying efforts according the IRS. A candidate's committee funded a direct mail piece promoting a nonbinding statewide referendum on fiscal responsibility. The candidate was named and pictured on the flyer identifying him as the leader of the effort. Even though the candidate had not yet filed to run for governor, the ruling stated the piece was packaged to identify him as a potential candidate for governor and was therefore an appropriate expense for the campaign committee.[101]

* **p. 294.** *Insert after first paragraph:*
In a pair of private letter rulings, the IRS ruled that keeping PAC funds temporarily in a general interest-bearing checking account provided administrative efficiency, rather than constituting an investment of the funds as prohibited by Section 527. For ease of collection, a professional association and a labor union issued billings for normal dues and PAC contributions together to the membership. Moneys were collected continually throughout the year. For the organizations'

---

[100] Priv. Ltr. Rul. 9117001, April, 1991.
[101] Priv. Ltr. Rul. 913008, August 5, 1991.

convenience PAC funds were transferred in one case twice a month and in the other once a month to the PAC. The "negligible" amount of interest that was maintained by the exempts was permissible.[102]

* p. 295. *Insert before What Lobbying Is Not:*

What Is Legislation? (New)

Legislation is specifically defined by the Congress and the IRS to include "action with respect to Acts, bills, resolutions, or similar items by the Congress, any State legislature, any local council, or similar governing body, or by the public in a referendum, initiative, constitutional amendment, or similar item.[103]

"Similar item" according to examples in the regulations includes confirmation of a cabinet level appointee and a Supreme Court nominee.[104] It is important to distinguish the IRS's pronouncement that such appointment proceedings are not elections and the appointees not elected cited at page 287. While intervention in the confirmation process is not prohibited political activity for a 501(c)(3), it does constitute lobbying in the IRS view.

* p. 297. *Add new section at end of page:*

Final Regulations, Finally! (New)

Effective August 31, 1990, the proposed regulations on Section 501(h) are issued in final form. Also finalized were related provisions in regulations under Section 501(c) (conversion of (c)(3) to a (c)(4), 501(h), 504 (revocation of exempt status due to excessive lobbying), 4911 (excise tax on excessive lobbying), 4945 (lobbying by private foundations), and 170, 2055, and 2522 (limitation on charitable donation). It is important to re-emphasize that the regulations only apply to charities electing to limit their lobbying expenditures under Section 501(h), not those charities applying the "substantial parts" test.

---

[102] Priv. Ltr. Rul. 9105001 and 9105002, June 18, 1990.
[103] Section 4911(e)(2) and Reg. § 56.4911-2(d)(1).
[104] Regs. §§ 56.4911-2(b)(ii) (B, Example 4, and § 56.4945-2(d)(iii), Example 5 and 7.

The final regulations make very few changes to the 1988 proposals and the basic materials on pages 294 through 302 remain unchanged except as clarified below. Of particular importance, the definition of grassroots lobbying on page 296 and of "taking action" on page 297 are retained, although the IRS commented that "it is a lenient definition which will permit many 'clear advocacy communications' to be treated as nonlobbying."

Highly Publicized Legislation

Paid advertisements placed in mass media (television, radio, billboards, and general circulation newspapers and magazines) that do not contain one of the four "take action" elements which cause the ad to constitute grassroots lobbying may be grassroots lobbying if:

1. The advertisement is placed within two week period prior to a vote by a legislative body or a committee (not a subcommittee).

2. A "view" on the general subject of the legislation and either (a) refers to the legislation or (b) encourages the public to communicate with legislators on the general subject of the legislation.

The presumption that an advertisement fits the conditions can be rebutted where the organization can show (a) it regularly publishes such communication without regard to the timing of legislation or (b) the timing of the particular advertisement is unrelated to the legislative action. In other words, if the organization can prove it placed the advertisement without any knowledge that the vote would occur within two weeks, it may escape its classification as grassroots lobbying.

Member Communications

The rules for communications with members delineate three possibilities and treat such communications more leniently than those with the general public and provide three possibilities. Members communications are not lobbying if four conditions are met:

1. Communication is directed only at members;

2. Specific legislation in the communique refers to and reflects a view on, and is of direct interest to the organization and its members;

3. Members are not encouraged to engage in direct lobbying; and

4. Grass roots lobbying is not encouraged.

Direct lobbying occurs when requirement three is failed. Grass roots lobbying occurs when four is failed.

Referenda and Ballot Initiatives

The members of the general public constitute the legislature in referenda and therefore the final regulations were changed to provide that attempts to influence a referenda vote is direct lobbying.

Nonpartisan Analysis

An independent and objective exposition on a particular subject that advocates opposition to or a viewpoint on legislation is not considered lobbying if it is nonpartisan analysis study, or research. Sufficiently fair and full exposition of the pertinent facts on the subject, not unsupported opinion, must be communicated to the general public to enable the public to form an independent opinion or conclusion. No direct encouragement to "take action" may be contained in the materials.

Examples

The new regulations[105] contain a number of examples that should be studied by any organization contemplating lobbying. The rules are surprisingly lenient and allow private foundations to publish nonpartisan analyses and comments many have previously thought were not permissible.

---

[105] Treas. Reg. §§ 56.4911-2(b)(4) and 56.4911-2(c)(vii).

Calculation of Exempt Purpose Expenditures

The final regulations make it clear that "exempt purpose expenditures" for the purposes of calculating the percentage limitations *do not include* the expenses of producing unrelated income and *do include* related trade or business expenditures. Costs of managing an endowment or other investments are also not included in exempt purpose expenditures.

p. 299. *Replace second sentence in the second paragraph under Section 501(h) Election:*

The regulations were first proposed in 1980, reproposed in 1986, reproposed again in 1988 after more than 10,000 comments, and made effective August 31, 1990.

p. 301. *Add after item 2:*
For examples and detailed instructions, refer to the IRS regulations.[106]

* **p. 302.** *Add to list of advantages of electing:*

- Degree of certainty provided by specific tests applied to electing organizations versus the subjective and untested standards for nonelecting ones. Section 501(h) allows examining agents to use the definitive rules only for electing organizations, not for nonelecting ones.

- Avoid exposure to examination expected by many practitioners who expect the IRS to place scrutiny upon nonelecting organizations.

- Membership communications exclusion does not classify the "objective reporting on the contents and status of legislation" with members as lobbying.

- Recordkeeping requirements may be less because volunteer time need not be recorded.

[106] Treas. Reg. § 56.4911-3.

* **p. 302.** *Replace the last two advantages of not electing with:*

- Recordkeeping requirements may be less if the organization need not distinguish between direct lobbying and grass roots efforts. With regard to information furnished on Form 990 the information may need to be more detailed.

- Risk of drawing attention to the organization by making the election may (or may not) trigger an audit. (There is disagreement in the field about this issue).

- Directors and officers can be personally liable for penalties for excess lobbying.

- Affiliated organizations' lobbying activity must be consolidated or combined to measure limitations under the election and otherwise are measured on a per entity basis.

- Maximum amount of expenditures allowed is $1 million for any one organization. For an organization with a $50,000,000 annual budget, for example, the maximum of $1 million equals 2 percent of the budget, a deminimus amount in relation to the five percent considered minimally permissible by some experts in the field.

p. 307. *Add a new checklist for Public Interest Law Firms at the bottom of the page:*

Criteria that distinguish a public interest law firm (PILF) from a private law firm (PLF):

- Substantial motivating factor in case selection is not the expectation of receiving fees.

- PILF does not accept a case where the client has sufficient financial resources to allow retention of PLF.

- Less than half of the PILF legal expenses are defrayed by legal fees.

- PILF staff attorney fees are determined without regard to revenue generation.

- PILF takes cases not economically feasible for PLF.

- Fees in excess of litigation costs not accepted.

- Client representation not terminated due to failure or inability to continue payments.

To understand the history of the IRS position on PILFs and the criteria that have developed, read the revenue rulings issued in 1975 on the subject.[107]

§ 3.11 WEATHERING AN IRS EXAMINATION

p. 321. *Add after the third full paragraph:*
See § 3.4A regarding special types of examinations the IRS is conducting under a Congressionally mandated Exempt Organizations Charitable Solicitations Compliance Improvement Program Study.

p. 323. *Add title at top of page:*
Exhibit 3–15 should be entitled, "IRS Examination Request."

p. 325. *Add title at top of page:*
Exhibit 3–16 should be entitled, "IRS Examination Report."

p. 330. *Add new sections at end of § 3.11:*

§ 3.11A WHAT IF THE ORGANIZATION LOSES ITS TAX-EXEMPT STATUS? (NEW)

The National Office of the IRS issued extensive G.C.M. 39813 in April, 1990, to describe the consequences and tax-filing requirements when a public charity receives a retroactive revocation of its exempt status. Remember such revocation occurs after the IRS has found the organization has operated to benefit a limited group of insiders,

---

[107] Rev. Rul. 75-74, 1975-1 C.B. 152; Rev. Rul. 75-75, 1975-1 C.B. 154; and Rev. Rul. 75-76, 1975-1 C.B. 154.

received excessive unrelated business income, engaged in excess lobbying or political activity, or otherwise failed to serve its charitable, or public constituents. The memorandum was reportedly issued to explain the IRS's response to the Tax Court's opinion in *The Synanon Church v. Commissioner.*[108]

Classification of the Organization

For federal income tax purposes, the organization losing its exempt status is treated as a corporation effective as of the date of revocation (except for charitable trusts which will be taxed as trusts). It is some comfort that (for innocent failures as a general rule) contributions received by the EO reclassified as a tax-paying corporation are to be treated as nontaxable gifts under Section 102 during the years the organization considered itself exempt (or arguably Section 118 or 362(c) as capital received from nonshareholders).

Gifts received under false pretenses are to be taxed. Where the organization misrepresented the gifts in its solicitations by stating it was tax exempt and devoting the gifts to exempt purposes when the facts indicate otherwise, the gifts can be deemed taxable income. The tax basis for calculating gain or loss on donated goods and property is carried over from the donors.

Regarding deductions that can be claimed against the retroactively taxed income, the memorandum fortunately prescribes the deduction of expenses related to the production of the business or investment income. To the extent the income is excluded as gifts or contributions to capital, the allocable expenses would not be deductible. Expenditures not otherwise allowable under the normal income tax rules, such as political expenditures or expenses of an activity not entered into for profit motives (a hobby), would not be deductible.

It was also noted that excise taxes could be due and payable by the organization and its officers and directors where the revocation is due to excess lobbying expense or political campaign activities.

---

[108] *The Synanon Church v. Commissioner,* 57 T.C.M. 602 (1989).

Consequences to Individual Contributors

A major concern where an EO loses its status may be who needs to pay tax on the unfairly sheltered income. Should the individuals lose their tax deductions? Should the organization pay tax on the funds? The memo makes it clear that the official who diverts funds to his or her own use (resulting in individual financial gain) realizes personal ordinary income to the extent of the economic benefit so derived. Innocent and unknowledgeable contributors do not lose their deductions until notice of revocation is published in the IRS Revenue Bulletin.

* § 3.11B WHAT IF THE ORGANIZATION DECLARES BANKRUPTCY? (NEW)

Despite the best intentions and dreams of their creators and managers, exempt organizations on occasion do expend funds in excess of their resources. Some organizations are fortunate and lucky enough to have philanthropists or other supporters that are willing and able to cover the operating deficits. Sometimes, however, the EO may become insolvent to the point that it must declare bankruptcy. In such cases, the interests of the forprofit creditors (normally) and the nonprofit constituents of the organization can be in conflict and a number of issues must be considered.

Bankruptcy Code

A thorough consideration of the federal Bankruptcy Code is beyond the scope of this book and any organization facing insolvency and considering bankruptcy should seek an attorney knowledgeable about the field. As a general rule in most respects, the bankruptcy code provides the same rules for not-for-profit and for-profit organizations. The intention of the rules is to protect the insolvent organization, to prevent any particular creditor from taking unfair advantage, and allow an orderly allocation among creditors of the proceeds of the asset liquidation.[109]

[109] Bankruptcy Code Section 303.

Chapter 7

A *Chapter 7* bankruptcy allows the organization, under the supervision of a court-appointed trustee, to sell off its assets, allocate the proceeds of such sales among the creditors, and dissolve its legal existence and cease to operate.

Chapter 11

The other common type of bankruptcy, *Chapter 11*, allows the organization to reorganize and remain in existence after providing for a payment plan for the indebtedness.

Voluntary vs. Involuntary Bankruptcy (New)

A voluntary bankruptcy is filed by the insolvent organization to seek the protection from unfriendly creditors that the rules are designed to provide. Instead an involuntary bankruptcy is filed by three or more creditors together filing the petition for bankruptcy.

Only a "moneyed, business, or commercial operation" qualifies for an involuntary bankruptcy, however, a significant matter on which the Bankruptcy Code provides different treatment for non-profit corporations. "Moneyed" organizations are profit motivated ones operated to create income for their shareholders or members. Most tax-exempt organizations would not continue to qualify for exemption if they could meet such a definition. Thus it is generally the case that an organization qualified for tax exemption under one of the subsections of Section 501(c) cannot be placed in involuntary bankruptcy.

Failure to qualify for the exception from involuntary bankruptcy, on the other hand, can cause the organization to lose its tax exempt status because it would evidence that the assets are not dedicated to exempt purposes as discussed below.

How Is Federal Tax Status Affected by a Bankruptcy?

Section 501 organizations of all categories—(c)(1-25) plus 501(d), (e), & (f)—must be organized and operated for their specifically defined category as discussed in Chapter 1. Charities, social welfare organizations, business leagues, social clubs, and all other types of exempts must dedicate their assets under organizational documents permanently to their specified purposes and then, in fact, operate for such purposes throughout the life of the organization to maintain tax-exempt status.

An insolvent exempt organization considering bankruptcy may have to face a challenge that it did not operate for exempt purposes. Any revocation of exemption would be based upon the facts and circumstances of the case. There is no rule that automatically revokes exempt status upon the declaration of bankruptcy and there are no revenue rulings or other statements of IRS policy on the subject. The questions that must be asked in reviewing a particular situation (all versions of the same theme) would include, among others:

- Were the activities in which the debt was incurred exempt activities?

- Why wasn't adequate revenue provided to pay for the exempt activities? Were revenues diverted to some other nonexempt purpose? Are there unrecorded liabilities attributable to restricted donors whose funds were diverted to other purposes?

- If the debts were incurred in connection with an unrelated business activity, did that business subsume the exempt activities and therefore evidence lack of substantial exempt purposes?

- Were exempt assets diverted to some nonexempt project violating the requirement that assets be dedicated to exempt purposes? Were "jeopardizing investments" purchased? Particularly for a private foundation, this could provide the additional complication of excise taxes discussed in Chapter 4.

- How can assets be allocated to creditors when the organization's charter requires that assets be dedicated permanently to exempt purposes?

- Were members of the governing body of trustees or directors in any way fiscally irresponsible in allowing the deficits to

occur and should any of the deficiencies be paid by such directors to preserve the organizational assets for the exempt constituents?

Revocation of Exempt Status (New)

The Bankruptcy Code's automatic stay against collection, assessment, or recovery of a claim against the bankrupt organization does
not prevent the IRS from revoking exempt status. In abusive situations where the debts were incurred providing benefits to insiders
rather than in serving the exempt public or membership, an attempt
to revoke should be expected. The challenge is also bolstered in
situations where there are no assets left upon dissolution for distribution for exempt purposes as required by any exempt organization's
charter.

The revocation has been ruled to be a preliminary step or pre-
requisite to the collection of tax and not restrained by the filing of
bankruptcy.[110] The anti-injunction provision of Section 7421 prohibits the bankruptcy trustee or others from interfering in the revocation of exempt status where the IRS deems it appropriate. Whether
the IRS can be successful in collecting any taxes assessed is another
question to be answered by a bankruptcy specialist.

When the exempt status is revoked, other tax issues resulting
from forgiveness of indebtedness, deductions for bad debts, and re-
capture of tax attributes, among others, must be carefully considered.
Even if the status is not revoked, such issues would be of consequence
in calculating any tax liability for unrelated business income.

No New Organization (New)

After the exempt organization voluntarily files bankruptcy, a new
organization does not come into being. Under Section 1399, the
existing entity continues and normal filing requirements continue.
As a matter of IRS policy, the exempt status of the organization is
allowed to remain intact unless factors evident in the bankruptcy

---

[110] In RE *Heritage Village Church and Missionary Fellowship, Inc.,* 851 F.2d 104 (4th
Circ., 1988) and *Bob Jones University v. Simon,* 416 U.S. 725 (Sup. Ct. 1974).

indicate that the exempt status of the organization should be revoked as discussed above.

* *Filing Requirements (New)*

The gross annual revenues of the bankrupt organization govern its annual federal filing requirements as outlined in § 3.3 (as updated in the 1991 Supplement) as the bankruptcy proceeds *EXCEPT* in the year of liquidation, dissolution, termination, or substantial contraction. In the contracting and/or final year, a lower threshold, or $5,000 of gross receipts sets the limit for required reporting. In other words, the Form 990 must be filed in almost all cases.

Prior to the actual year of dissolution or termination, the same filing requirements for other purposes—annual information, payroll, and all other types of federal returns—remain the same during the period of bankruptcy. Even though the organization ceases normal operations and receives no contributions, gross revenue for filing purposes includes proceeds from the sale of its assets.

The responsible parties for filing information returns are either the board of directors and the organization's ongoing managers or the trustee in the bankruptcy appointed to replace the directors or organizational trustees.

Information revealing the bankrupt status should be attached to Form 990 in response to the question on page 4, line 76, page 2, line 33 of Form 990EZ, or page 4, question 2 of Form 990PF, "Has the organization engaged in any activities not previously reported to the IRS?" At a minimum the documents filed with the bankruptcy trustee and a synopsis of the expected outcome would be attached to the return. An explanation of the cause of the bankruptcy and its consequence to ongoing operations (if under Chapter 11) or orderly dissolution (under Chapter 7) should also be attached to the return. It is very important at this point to indicate that the exempt purposes of the organization are not compromised by the bankruptcy and that the exempt status should not be revoked or jeopardized as a consequence (where it is possible to so argue).

Section 6043 contains specific requirements for information to be reported in the year of dissolution of an exempt organization that also includes one dissolving due to bankruptcy. Although the answer is full of innuendo from the question of jeopardy to exempt status, the section specifically requires that the following information be reported in Form 990 for the distribution year:

- Fact that the assets are distributed and dates thereof,

- Names and addresses of persons receiving the terminating distributions,

- Kinds of assets distributed, and

- Each asset's fair market value.

When the asset distribution and settlement with creditors takes place over a series of reporting years, the regulations should be carefully considered for determining when a "substantial contraction" occurs to allow properly timed reporting.

*   *Related Organizations (New)*

What if one member of an affiliated group of exempt organizations becomes insolvent and is considering the declaration of bankruptcy? Particularly in a state or nationwide group whose reputation might be damaged by the bad credit rating of a related entity, the question arises of the consequences on the parent organization or another branch of the group bailing out the insolvent entity. All of the questions asked above under "consequences on exempt status" must be considered.

Although there will almost certainly be disagreement on the question, as a general rule, the assets of one member of a group should not be used to bail out the creditors of another branch particularly in situations where each entity is an independent corporate or fiduciary entity. Only where it can be argued that the continued existence of the related entities would be jeopardized, and therefore, the exempt purposes are better served by the preservation of the ailing member, could such a bailout serve the purposes of the remaining members of the exempt group.

The systems for monitoring, planning and controlling related organizations should theoretically prevent such insolvencies. When they occur the systems should be reviewed and the system for monitoring and supervising the group members revised to avoid reoccurrence.

Private Foundations

§ 4.1   HOW AND WHY PFs ARE SPECIAL

p. 337.   *Add after bulleted list:*

See § 3.5A for requirements and definitions of public charities and supporting organizations.

* § 4.2   SUMMARY OF PRIVATE FOUNDATION SANCTIONS

p. 345.   *Correct date in first sentence of Section 4940:*
The Congress first adopted the excise tax in 1969.

p. 349.   *Add to item 5:*
The definition of reasonable compensation relied upon by the IRS National Office is provided in Reg. § 1.165-7(b)(3) as "such amount as would ordinarily be paid for like services by like enterprises under like circumstances."[1]

p. 350.   *Add new examples of self-dealing in middle of page:*

- Disqualified person(s) (DQ) and private foundation (PF) were found to be self-dealing in a scenario where a joint purchase of benefit tickets is made by sharing the ticket cost. The PF

---

[1] T.A.M. 9008001.

pays the deductible or charitable contribution portion of the ticket; the DP pays that part of the ticket price portion allocable to the fair market value of the dinner, entertainment, and other benefits provided to contributors in connection with a charity fund raiser.[2]

Because Section 4941 of the Code provides that "self-dealing" means any direct or indirect transfer to, or use by or for the benefit of, a DP of income or assets of a PF, the IRS decided self-dealing resulted in this case. The DPs reaped benefit to the extent the PF paid expenses the DPs would otherwise have been expected or required to pay. Thus, the partial purchase of ticket by the PF constituted direct economic benefit to the DPs and consequently results in self-dealing.

- Modification of a charitable pledge by reducing the promised payments creates benefit to the DP who promised the funds and therefore results in self-dealing.[3]

- Annual compensation 75 percent higher than the average for a private foundation of comparable size in the Council on Foundations' *1986 Foundation Management Report*, which also represented 35 percent of the foundation's grant expense, was excessive and an act of self-dealing.[4]

* **p. 350.** *Add additional comment in next to last example on the page:*

The regulations not only provide that indemnification of foundation managers against liability for contested excise taxes is not self-dealing, they go on to provide that the payment of insurance premiums to fund the permissible indemnification is also not self-dealing.[5]

* **p. 350.** *Add new comments in last example on the page:*

The IRS issued proposed regulations in December, 1991, to treat "bonafide volunteers who perform services for exempt organizations" as employees eligible for the working condition fringe benefit tax

---

[2] Priv. Ltr. Rul. 9021066.
[3] T.A.M. 8723001.
[4] Supra, note 1.
[5] Treas. Regs. § 53.4941(d)-2(f)(3).

exclusion. Insurance, transportation, meals, and other expenses paid by the PF are thereby now not taxable to volunteer directors, including disqualified persons.[6]

p. 351. *Add new examples of non-self-dealing in middle of page:*

- Furnishing living quarters in a historic district to the substantial contributor who works 25 to 35 hours a week overseeing the complex and managing the foundation financial affairs is not self-dealing, as long as the fair value of the space is treated as compensation and the total compensation is reasonable.[7]

- Formation of a partnership between a private foundation and its three benefactor § 4947(a)(2) split-interest charitable lead trusts did not result in self-dealing.[8]

- Commissions paid to a DP/art dealer are not self-dealing where the terms of the commission are based upon a customary market scale prevailing in the work's normal market (amount is reasonable). Advice was sought by a private foundation created by an artist. After the artist's death, the art work was to be sold by the same dealer who represented the artist while living, to fund the foundation's programs.[9]

The useful aspect of this ruling is an outline of what the IRS calls "comparability factors" the foundation is to use to determine if reasonable compensation is paid. The factors are:

1. Commissions charged by nondisqualified persons for selling the (same) artist's work;

2. Commissions paid by the artist during his lifetime to persons who are now disqualified persons and to others;

3. Commissions that agents charge to sell art of the same school as the artist; and

---

[6] § 1.132–5(m). See Priv. Ltr. Rul. 8708029 and 8503098 and Rev. Rul. 82-223, 1982-2 C.B. 301 for detailed discussion of this issue.
[7] Priv. Ltr. Rul. 8948034.
[8] Priv. Ltr. Rul. 9015070.
[9] Priv. Ltr. Rul. 9011050.

4. Commissions that are received by agents who sell art generally from the foundation's geographic area.

* The contribution of substantially appreciated antique automobiles to a nonoperating private foundation (that according to the facts in the ruling intends to sell them) is not self-dealing according to the IRS.

The "unavoidable use by the contributor collector (DP) to "drive the antique automobiles from time to time and to travel with them on behalf of the foundation to maintain and show them" is also not self-dealing. The foundation in the ruling bears all of the expense of refurbishment, shipment, and travel for the autos.

Because the cars are not capable of producing the types of income specifically listed in Section 4940, such as rentals or dividends, the ruling goes on to say that any gain realized by the foundation upon sale of the cars is not subject to the investment income excise tax nor does it produce UBI. Particularly since the foundation is not an operating one, it would have been useful if the ruling had explained how the cars were related to the foundation's exempt purposes.[10]

* Problems of Sharing Space, People, and Expenses (New)

As a practical matter, many private foundations are operated along side their creators, either a corporation or a family group. Until the foundation achieves a certain volume of assets with the consequential grant activity (and maybe nevertheless), the rental of a separate office and engagement of staff is beyond the PF's reasonable economic capability, particularly when such expenditures take away funds from a grant-making activity.

The question is when can the PF pay for its portion of the expenses in such a sharing situation. The Code specifically prohibits the "furnishing of goods, services or facilities," between (to or from) a PF and a DP.[11] When Congress first imposed these strict rules in 1969, they provided a transitional period until 1980 during which existing and contractual sharing arrangements could be phased out.[12] As time passed and the costlines of the hard-and-fast rule appeared

[10] Priv. Ltr. Rul. 9119009.
[11] § 4941(d)(1)(C).
[12] § 53.4941(d)-4(d).

unreasonable in certain circumstances, the IRS in private letter rulings relaxed what reads like an impenetrable barrier to any arrangements in which a PF and DPs share space, people, or other expenses.

In Priv. Ltr. Rul. 8331082, a PF rented contiguous space with a common reception area, but separate offices from its DP. Separate leases were entered into and the DPs received no benefit in the form of reduced rent because of the PF's rental in the related space. In Technical Information Release 7734022, a PF and DP commonly bought a duplicating machine and hired a shared employee. Time records were kept to determine each entities respective share of the cost of the machine and the allocable time of the employee. Because "nothing was paid directly or indirectly to the DP" and there was "independent use" by the PF that was measurable and specifically paid for to outside parties, no self-dealing resulted from what certainly appears to be a "sharing arrangement" phased out and consequentially prohibited by Section 4941.[13]

Group insurance policies present similar situations. Corporate and other conglomerate groups funding private foundations have been allowed to include their private foundation employees in a common health policy. The foundation directly pays for the premium allocable to its employees and/or reimburses the company. The rationale is found in the "Special Rules" of Section 4941(d)(2)(B) that provides the lending of money by a disqualified person to a private foundation shall not be an act of self-dealing if the loan is without interest or other charge and if the proceeds of the loan are used exclusively for purposes specified in Section 501(c)(3).

See Exhibit 4–3, Expenditure Documentation Policy, for an example of an agreement entered into between a DP and a PF where the PF occupies office space donated by the DP and uses certain equipment but maintains records to document and pay for its "independent use" of the equipment, staff, and other systems in the office.

* Indirect Self-Dealing

Transactions taking place between a DP and an organization controlled by a PF (CO) may be classified as an indirect act of self-dealing.

---

[13] *See also* Priv. Ltr. Rul. 8824010.

The regulations define an indirect transaction by describing circumstances in which a business transaction will not be considered as self-dealing. The regulations provide indirect self-dealing does not occur in the situation described below:

- Pre-existing transactions in place prior to the creation of the controlled relationship caused the self-dealing are allowed.

- Transactions at least as favorable to the CO as an arm's length transaction with an unrelated party and (1) the CO could have engaged in the transaction with someone other than the DP only at a severe economic hardship to the CO or (2) because of the unique nature of the product or services provided by the CO, the DP could not have engaged in the transaction with anyone else.

- Deminimus transactions with a CO engaged in a retail business with the general public, such as office supplies, is not indirect self-dealing if the transactions total amount in a year does not exceed $5,000.[14]

A private foundation was found guilty of indirect self-dealing when space in a building owned by the PF was leased to a company controlled by one of its DPs. The entire building is subleased to an independent management company that subleases the spaces, so that the foundation is not a party to the building subleases. However, the master lease granted the PF as landlord approval over the form and content of any longterm leases entered into by the management company. Thus the PF essentially controlled the management company and for self-dealing persons became a party to the lease with the DP.[15]

p. 360. *Add at bottom of page:*
See comments below regarding grants to foreign charities.

p. 361. *Add to item 2:*

- Charitable projects can be carried out in any location. There is no constraint against a private foundation conducting activities outside the Unites States.

[14] Treas. Reg. § 53.4941(d)-1(b).
[15] Priv. Ltr. Rul. 9047001.

* **p. 361.** *Add new ruling to item 3:*
An academic grant recipient could expend a portion of funds granted on child care, as long as such spending enabled the grantee to continue their research and are not made in accordance with the individual's personal or family needs.[16]

* **p. 362.** *Add after item 9:*
The pledge of $2 million for specific charitable, educational, or religious purposes to be set aside in equal installments over a period of three years qualifies as a "qualifying distribution" where it is shown the purposes are better accomplished by set-asides than by immediate payments according to the Service. It was also noted, however, that the income produced by the moneys set aside must be added to the PF's calculation of minimum distribution requirements.[17]

* **p. 363.** *Add comment after first paragraph:*
The IRS Chief Counsel has issued a memo entitled, "Adjustments-of-Excess Distribution Carryovers From Closed Years" to advance the position that adjustments to years closed by the statute of limitations is permissible. The memo recognizes the fact that in any one year, a nonoperating PF has excessive or deficient distributions and therefore a carryover of excess distributions is an accumulation of all post-1969 years. It is the unusual foundation that pays out the exact minimum distribution amount.

An error in calculating the qualifying distributions or the amount required to be distributed in any one year causes all years to be wrong. Thus the IRS will take the position, as yet unchallenged in court, that the years from 1970 on are open years for purposes of distribution carryovers.[18]

* **p. 366.** *Add new subsection:*

Extension of Time

A foundation that is attempting to sell its excess business holdings within the permissible time period but is unable to do so can request

---

[16] Private Letter Ruling 9116032, April 29, 1991.
[17] Priv. Ltr. Rul. 9117067.
[18] G.C.M. 39808.

an additional five-year extension of the time under Section 4943(c)(7). To obtain permission, the foundation must demonstrate that:

- The gift is an "unusually large gift or bequest of diverse business holdings or holdings with complex corporate structures.

- It has made diligent efforts to dispose of the holdings within the initial five-year period.

- Disposition of the holdings was not possible during the first five years because of the size and complexity or diversity of the holdings, except at a price substantially below fair market value (Congressional hearings noted sale at least 5 percent below FMV is substantial).

- Before the close of the first five years, the foundation submits a disposition plan to the IRS and also seeks approval of its state attorney general (or similar responsible authority).

A plan developed by an independent financial consultant to assist the foundation to sell its holdings in conjunction with the substantial contributor's family members who also owned the same holdings was approved by the IRS.[19]

p. 372. *Add at bottom of page:*

The user fee for making application for approval of an individual grant program is $1,250 ($500 for organizations with annual gross receipts less than $150,000) effective March 31, 1990, as set out in Rev. Proc. 89-13.[20] In considering the viability of seeking plan approval, this fee should be taken into account. IRS procedures for issuing rulings approving scholarship plans were updated in Rev. Proc. 90-4.[21]

* For those organizations wishing to avoid the administrative burden and cost of applying for approval and disbursing scholarships directly, an alternative is to fund a grant program at an independent public charity. As long as the PF has no control over the choice of recipients, the PF is not considered to have made the grants directly to

[19] Priv. Ltr. Rul. 9115061.
[20] Rev. Proc. 89-13, 1989-7 I.R.B., 25.
[21] Rev. Proc. 91-4, 1991-4 I.R.B., 20.

the individuals. The PF can stipulate the parameters of the grant, such as choosing the discipline for study—medicine or law, for example—or recommending qualifications such as grades or civic achievement.

The IRS has ruled that a company foundation established by a business corporation can establish a scholarship fund with a public charity for the purposes of making grants to children and spouses of the company's employees.[22]

p. 379. *Add at bottom of the page:*

Grant to 501(c)(7).   A PF may make a grant to a social club where the grant is suitably dedicated for charitable purposes. A private foundation made a grant to a social fraternity's 501(c)(2) title holding organization to build of a study room in their chapter house. The facility will exclusively contain educational equipment and furniture, along with computers linked to the university's main frame. The university sanctioned the grant in writing by certifying the room benefits the school by supplementing its resources, alleviating overcrowding in its library and study areas, and providing additional computer terminals. The fraternity agreed to return any grant funds not used for construction of the study space. There was no time period stipulated for this guarantee, but the foundation required that it be able to inspect the room annually.[23]

Grant to Foreign Charities.   A PF can make a grant to a foreign charity, but must often take special steps to evaluate the organization's public charity status. Those few organizations with active fund-raising efforts in the United States seek IRS approval (same process as described in Chapter 3) and can readily furnish a determination letter, but many do not have such U.S. recognition.

The regulations contain a relatively lenient guideline.[24] The PF makes a "good faith determination" of qualification as a public charity based upon an affidavit of the grantee organization itself or independent counsel. While it is not stated in the regulation, to find the charity can qualify as a 509a(1), (2), or (3) organization is also to find

[22] Priv. Ltr. Rul. 9050030.
[23] Priv. Ltr. Rul. 9025073.
[24] Treas. Reg. §§ 53.4945-5(a)(5) and 53.4945-5(b)(5).

it could qualify under 501(c)(3). With foreign organizations, the PF often may not be able to obtain sufficient information to be in full faith in considering the organization publicly supported. Therefore, in my experience, an expenditure responsibility agreement is normally executed to avoid any unexpected results. Priv. Ltr. Rul. 8030104 and 8515070 indicate the extent to which some PFs go in assuring that their grants to foreign organizations meet the expenditure responsibility test.

*   Among the reasons a private foundation would involve itself in foreign projects is the Section 170 rule that individual donors may not claim income tax deductions for contributions made directly to foreign charities. On the other hand, where the board of a U.S. charity (private or public) has control and discretion as to the use of the funds raised, the fact the funds are raised for projects outside the United States does not render contributions to the U.S. foundation nondeductible.

In a ruling concerning deductibility of contributions to organizations with foreign activity, the IRS determined deduction was allowed and by reference sanctioned the exempt status for a pair of organizations established to (1) build a basketball stadium in the foreign country and (2) sponsor and operate the games in the foreign country. The interesting aspect was that entity one was designed to qualify for U.S. charitable deductions and two not to qualify. Organization one will raise funds to regrant to organization two and to build and own the stadium in which two will operate. Note the ruling continues the tax law policy regarding charitable organizations that recognizes the exempt nature of the activity regardless of its location.[25]

Strict Enforcement.   The IRS very strictly enforces the expenditure responsibility reporting requirement. Stiff penalties were upheld against a group of three commonly controlled organizations in *Hans S. Mannheimer Charitable Trust.*[26] Their Form 990PF stated the trust did not make grants to organizations other than public ones and no expenditure responsibility agreements were entered into. The foundation argued unsuccessfully that all of its internal documents,

---

[25] Priv. Ltr. Rul. 9129040.
[26] *Hans S. Mannheiner Charitable Trust v. Commissioner,* 93 T.C. 5 (1989).

meeting transcriptions, and actual observations of the activities resulted in the exercise of the required oversight. Despite the actual facts and the foundation's argument that their failure to report was due to oversight, the penalty assessment was upheld.

Meaning of "Outstanding Grants."

Successfully exercising expenditure responsibility involves entering into the proper agreement with the grant recipient, seeing that the grant is spent for the purposes for which it was granted by receiving reports and auditing the manner in which the grant funds are expended, and reporting the grant on Form 909PF for the period the grant is "outstanding." Specific detailed information is required. The regulations say the information must be provided for each grant upon which "any amount or any report is outstanding at any time during the taxable year." As noted in item 3 above, endowment, equipment, or capital improvement grants are deemed by the regulations to be outstanding for the year of the grant and two succeeding years for a total of three. It is critical to note the three-year rule only applies to endowment grants made to another private foundation exempt from taxation.[27]

For program-related investment (PRI) grants, reporting is also required while the investment is outstanding. The regulations Treas. Reg. § 53.4945-5(4) provides that at least once a year during the existence of the program-related investment, a full and complete financial report of the type ordinarily required by commercial investors under similar circumstances and a statement that it has complied with the terms of the investment should be received by the private foundation making the PRI. What it doesn't say is that such information should also be included on Form 990PF for the life of the investment. Nor does it say PRI capital expenditure loans are subject to the three-year endowment rule. Thus it would seem a PRI granted to a taxable entity would be reportable for the entire period of the loan. A 12-year loan would be reported for 12 years.

Unfortunately, the Mott Foundation was reminded that a 12-year loan for low-income housing made to a for-profit corporation should have been reported for the entire 12 years the loan was due

---

[27] Reg. § 53.4945-5(c)(2).

and owing, not the three they thought was appropriate under the regulations applying to endowments. The Sixth Circuit Court stated that in "grants for capital purposes, the reporting obligation of the grantor to the IRS is contingent upon the reporting obligations of the grantee to the grantor pursuant to subparagraph (c)(2)" (the three-year rule). The court failed to note that the regulation section referring to PRI makes no distinction between for-profit and nonprofit grantees. Thus to be safe, any private foundation making PRIs should plan to report the loan status for the life of the loan.[28]

* **§ 4.3   TERMINATION OF PRIVATE FOUNDATION STATUS**

p. 388.   *Replace last paragraph under Transfer Assets to Another PF with:*

IRS Priv. Ltr. Rul. 9033054 and 9033044 make it clear that the division of all assets of a PF to two other PFs to enable the trustees to pursue their divergent charitable interests does not terminate the transferor's PF status or result in a Section 507(c) termination tax. The IRS's conclusion was based upon two facts. The transferor had not given notice of an intent to terminate and there was no evidence that the original PF had violated any of the PF sanctions so as to cause the IRS to terminate it involuntarily under Section 507(a)(2).

The treatment of the old and new organizations in a private foundation split-up was further clarified in a 1991 ruling.[29] According to the IRS, neither the old nor the newly created organization are treated as newly created ones (a seemingly impossible situation). The attributes of the old organization are attributed proportionately to each of the "new-old" PFs.

To understand the importance of the "new-old" label and the need for caution in a split-up, look at the literal language of the Section 507 termination provisions. All of the tax savings received by virtue of the PF's exemption—income tax it never paid and income, estate, or gift tax its contributors saved—must be repaid to the government upon the PF's termination.

[28] *Charles Stewart Mott Foundation v. United States,* No. 90-2132 (6th Cir. 1991).
[29] Priv. Ltr. Rul. 9121036.

Other types of split-up considered by the IRS during the past year include:

- Merger of two private operating foundations to manage a recreational complex.[30]

- Three new organizations—one public to receive half of the assets and two private foundations each to receive one-fourth of the assets—formed from one private foundation.[31]

- A private foundation's legal structure converted to a nonprofit corporation from its original form as a charitable trust.[32]

- One private foundation split into three.[33]

- Combination of three commonly controlled foundations into one[34] or two into one.[35]

---

[30] Priv. Ltr. Rul. 9052025, January 7, 1991.
[31] Priv. Ltr. Rul. 9101020, January 14, 1991.
[32] Priv. Ltr. Rul. 9103035, January 28, 1991.
[33] Priv. Ltr. Rul. 9104016 and Priv. Ltr. Rul. 9104047, February 4, 1991.
[34] Priv. Ltr. Rul. 9132052, August 19, 1991.
[35] Priv. Ltr. Rul. 9115057, April 22, 1991.

C H A P T E R   F I V E

Fiscal Management of a Nonprofit Organization

§ 5.5   FINANCIAL MANAGEMENT CHECKLIST

p. 448.   *Add at end of page:*

CHECKLIST
ENDOWMENT AND RESTRICTED FUNDS

General Information

1. Does the organization have any endowment or restricted funds?   ‾‾‾‾

   a. If so, complete "Endowment Fund Control Report."   ‾‾‾‾

   b. Verify completion of "Endowment Permanent File."   ‾‾‾‾

   c. Inspect "Restricted Grant Control."   ‾‾‾‾

2. Review Permanent File for each fund to familiarize yourself with its terms and restrictions.   ‾‾‾‾

3. If the donor's terms are not clear, has there been a clarification made by a lawyer or descendent or has the board adopted a policy regarding the uncertainty?   ‾‾‾‾

4. Is a fund accounting system used?   ‾‾‾‾

CHECKLIST: ENDOWMENT AND RESTRICTED FUNDS (continued)

5. Regarding endowment funds:

   a. Are the monies separately invested and easily identifiable?   _____

   b. Verify amount of annual income required to be distributed or set aside.   _____

   c. Is there a record of accumulated income, if any?   _____

   d. How is "income" defined? Do endowment terms allow allocation of capital gains to income?   _____

6. Regarding restricted funds:

   a. Can "functional accounting reports," which identify costs allocable to grants, be prepared from the financial records?   _____

   b. Are detailed expense records maintained:

       • Staff time reports.   _____

       • Space usage allocations.   _____

       • Direct and indirect cost coding system in chart of accounts.   _____

       • Encumbrance system controls authorized expenditures under grant.   _____

   c. For government grants (both federal and state), are procedures of OMB Circular A–128 followed?   _____

   d. Is income recognition properly timed?   _____

   e. Are funds held for future periods classified as liabilities?   _____

7. Regarding land, building and equipment (LBE) funds:

   a. Is this fund being reported separately from the unrestricted funds because of donor restriction or accounting practice?   _____

CHECKLIST: ENDOWMENT AND RESTRICTED FUNDS (*continued*)

   b. Does the LBE fund include unexpended donations? If so does their investment placement give regard to the expected timing of the building program? _____

   c. Are transfers to cover depreciation made from the current unrestricted fund? _____

   d. Is an asset inventory system used to control physical loss of assets? _____

Investment Policy

  8. Are yields on investment assets monitored? _____

  9. Do yields furnish a return commensurate with the risk of capital loss? _____

10. Are funds managed by an independent professional manager? See § 3.10 to review private inurement issues. _____

11. Is management fee commensurate with those charged in the area for similar services? _____

12. Consider propriety of having more than one manager. _____

13. Does diversification of investment assets provide inflation protection? _____

Reliance Factor

14. What portion of annual operations are financed with income from endowment funds or restricted grants? _____

15. If income decreased substantially due to market forces, would the organization's programs be jeopardized? _____

16. Are governmental or United Way grants subject to decline in current economic climate? _____

Outside Beneficiaries

17. Review reports of pooled income funds and split-interest trusts:

CHECKLIST: ENDOWMENT AND RESTRICTED FUNDS   (*continued*)

    a. Terms of gift agreement adhered to?   _____

    b. Current income sufficient to make agreed payments to individual beneficiaries?   _____

    c. Distinction between income and principal clear.   _____

    d. Required annual reports prepared.   _____

18. Term endowments or charitable lead trust terms reviewed for termination dates.   _____

19. "Annuity" and "unitrust" computations evaluated by outside independent accountants?   _____

Suitability of Raising Restricted Funds

20. Based upon answers to above questions, should the organization continue to solicit endowment and restricted grants?   _____

    a. Is time involved in recordkeeping excessive?   _____

    b. Could similar levels of support be raised as unrestricted grants?   _____

21. Should existing endowment instruments be reformed to allow allocation of some or all capital gains to income?   _____

    a. Are donors still living?   _____

    b. Would benefit of reallocation deserve cost of court petition?   _____

22. Should instruments for future endowment gifts and other restricted gifts be reformed?   _____

23. Is there adequate communication between the development department, staff, and the board regarding issues raised in this checklist?   _____

Definitions of Terms

Look to the glossary of Financial Terms and Abbreviations, in the Appendix for the meaning of the terms germane to fund accounting.

Discussion of Checklist

The purpose of this checklist is to assure the organization is adhering to the covenants and restrictions, if any, placed upon contributed funds, to evaluate investment policy, and to check for private inurement. Hopefully it will be useful to a broad range of users, but is particularly designed for the audit committee of the board of directors or the chief financial officer of the organization (may be treasurer of board).

Because the organization owes a fiduciary duty to its contributors to use the funds for the purposes for which the funds are given, the checklist is of extreme importance. Knowledge of fund accounting and tenants of nonprofit accounting is not widely disseminated resulting in a fairly high level of noncompliance with grant restrictions.

The checklist can only scratch the surface of the technical aspects of restricted and endowment funds. The issues are not all settled. As discussed below, whether capital gains represent "income" from an endowment depends upon state law and the gift instrument. The reader is urged to require that the principles of fund accounting be followed in any organization with which they are associated and that the advisors be conversant with the subject or at the very least consult the books listed in the Bibliography.

Comments on Character of Capital Gains

Regarding investment yields, the conflict between risks the organization is willing to take and the return on investment needed to pay operating expenses is the same as for individuals or for-profit companies. It is not necessarily conservative or prudent to maintain all funds invested in fixed-money or interest-only bearing securities. To conserve the principal in its original dollar amount, inviolate and permanent into perpetuity, may not necessarily be safeguarding the fund for the donor's intentions.

There is disagreement in the field as to the historic common law of endowments that proscribes that only income be expended. Realized and unrealized gains on the underlying principal, usually called capital gains, have not in the past been treated as income. But the total return concept and the structure of capital markets in the eighties favors capital gains: Dividends are paid at a low rate to allow the corporations to reinvest earnings in expansion and conglomeration.

The Ford Foundation study, *The Law and the Lore of Endowment Funds* states, however, that "we find no authoritative support in the law for the widely held view that the realize gains of endowment funds can never be spent.[1] Prudence would call for the retention of sufficient gains to maintain purchasing power in the face of inflation and to guard against potential losses, but subject to the standards which prudence dictates, the expenditure of gains should lie within the discretion of the institution's directors." The study investigated whether "the directors of an educational institution are circumscribed by the law or are free to adopt the investment policy they regard as soundest for their institution, unhampered by legal impediments, prohibitions or restrictions."

Under a "total return concept" according to the AICPA *Audit and Accounting Guide for "Audit of Certain Nonprofit Organizations,"* the governing board may make a portion of realized, and in some cases, unrealized, net gains available for current use." The Association of College and University Business Officers (NACUBO) and a number of states have adopted this policy.

---

[1] *The Law and the Lore of Endowment Funds,* by William L. Cary and Craig B. Bright, 1969 (study commissioned by the Ford Foundation).

Index

INDEX

INDEX